Getting Started in

Estate
Planning

The Getting Started In Series

Getting Started in
Estate
Planning

Kerry Hannon

John Wiley & Sons, Inc.

New York • Chichester • Weinheim • Brisbane • Singapore • Toronto

Published by John Wiley & Sons, Inc.

Published simultaneously in Canada.

This publication is designed to provide accurate and authoritative information in regard to the subject matter covered. It is sold with the understanding that the publisher is not engaged in rendering professional services. If professional advice or other expert assistance is required, the services of a competent professional person should be sought.

Library of Congress Cataloging-in-Publication Data:

Hannon, Kerry.
    Getting started in estate planning / Kerry Hannon.
       p.   cm. — (Getting started in series)
    Includes index.
    ISBN 0-471-38085-7 (paper : acid-free paper)
    1. Estate planning—United States—Popular works.. I. Title. II. Getting started in.
  KF750.Z9 H33   2000
  346.7305'2—dc21

                                             00-028299

Printed in the United States of America.

10 9 8 7 6 5 4 3 2 1

Contents

Acknowledgments

I never thought that Debra Englander, my editor at John Wiley, and I would still be going strong as a team after three books and countless other journalistic and literary endeavors. This one's for you, Debby. Your patience and support have meant so much to me.

To my husband, Cliff, thank you for continually pushing me to get it done. And a tip of the hat to all my editors, including Joanna Krotz at *Gateway* magazine, Lisa Lee Freeman at *Working Woman*, Jackie Blais at *USA Today*, Matt Schifrin at *Forbes,* Amy Dunkin at *Business Week*, and the editors at iVillage.com, who endured my racing to the wire for deadlines as I tried to cram it all into an intense year. And of course, I would be remiss not to give a nod to my trusty yellow Labrador retriever, Becky, who has kept me company along the way and has never given a thought to estate planning.

Writing is never an easy task and delving into the ponderous subject of estate planning takes some fortitude. I hope my readers will come away from this book with some solid personal finance objectives and a plan to get their future lives organized so that their families and close relatives are not overwhelmed when the inevitable happens. If this book leaves you with one goal only, it should be this . . . write a will.

K. H.

Introduction

Have you done any estate planning? For most people, estate planning is one of those activities they hate to discuss, ponder, or even, heaven forbid, do. It falls into the category "I'll get to it one day." This is personal, private stuff, and at the very heart of it are things none of us really want to confront, like dying.

Consider this: Nearly three out of four people who die each year in the United States have no will or estate plan. That can be a serious problem. Sure, estate planning is a morbid subject. The combination of money and death can be a bitter pill. The common response most people have when asked about their estate plans is, "I don't need one. I'll take it all with me, or I'll spend it all while I'm alive, or I'm not rich enough to have a so-called estate, so why plan for it?"

Trust me. Not having an estate plan is the worst plan. This book is designed to help you stop stalling and get started on your own estate plan, as well as give you the practical tools and knowledge to discuss the need for estate planning with your aging parents. Why? Estate planning isn't ultimately for you. It's for those you leave behind, but it's something we all need to consider—sooner rather than later.

You shrug. Estate planning, that's for the well-to-do, right? After all, the Random House Dictionary defines the word "estate" as "a piece of landed property, especially one of large extent with an elaborate house on it." But by law, an estate is defined as property or possessions—something everyone has. Maybe it's an old Ford Thunderbird, or a diamond brooch, or a yellow Labrador retriever, but it's yours. At its very basic definition, estate planning is your desire to ensure your assets go to the people you want to have them, who can benefit from them, not to your silent heir—the Internal Revenue Service (IRS).

Few of us are as rich as celebrity Oprah Winfrey, but she has a point. "I think it is irritating that once I die, 55 percent of my money goes to the United States government. . . . You know why that's irritating? Because you would have already paid nearly 50 percent. . . . When you leave a house or money to people, then they're taxed 55 percent, so you've got to leave them enough so that once they're taxed, they still have some money." (As reported in the *Wall Street Journal*, July 28, 1999.)

Oprah is right, even though most of us don't have estates as large as hers. Currently, estate tax kicks in for estates valued at $675,000, and the tax starts at a whopping 37 percent rate and moves up smartly to as high as 60% in some cases. The top official rate is 55%. (This $675,000 exclusion will gradually rise to $1 million in 2006.) The top U.S. estate tax rate exceeds that of countries like Germany, Sweden, and Belgium, well known for their hefty taxes.

Money in 401(k) plans or other retirement plans that are tax-deferred is also a tax target of 50 percent, including state tax; and then on top of that there can be an estate tax. At the end of the day, your heirs get maybe one-fourth of the pie, and the government gets three-fourths. Is that what all your hard work and saving was all about? Not a chance.

Estate planning is one of the subjects that editors like to tell their reporters to write more about. Over the years mine have. But when push comes to shove, the very nature of this subject—death and taxes—makes it not exactly cocktail conversation, and almost inevitably the topic is squeezed out by sexier stories. The very mention of estate planning makes people's eyes glaze over—something the mention of the latest Internet stock craze never does.

Nonetheless, as we boomers age, we're all facing it. Our parents are dying without wills and proper estate planning. And we have more money than we ever dreamed of socked away in retirement accounts through our employers such as 401(k) plans and individual retirement accounts (IRAs). It's not unusual to meet someone who has $1 million in retirement money and a $200,000 house. So it's bad news if you die

2

suddenly and without a will. The federal government and state in which you live may gleefully enjoy your spoils, not those folks in your life who could really benefit from your bequests.

At the very least, even if you can't get your head around such arcane terms as credit shelter trusts, the generation-skipping transfer tax, and conservation easements, you can draft a will. It's relatively painless and can be as complex, or simple, as you want it to be. You will need an attorney to handle it for you if you want the document to hold up in court should your heirs disagree with your decisions.

Here are some terms that you will become familiar with as we move through this book:

- ✔ **Assets.** These are your things, your property—in essence, your estate. They include everything from your car to your home, stocks, mutual funds, bonds, collectibles, jewelry, land, a business, and more.

- ✔ **Beneficiary.** This is the person, or persons, that you designate through your will or other contract (such as an insurance policy or retirement plan) who will receive the benefits.

- ✔ **Durable power of attorney.** A durable power of attorney is a written legal document that lets you designate another person to act on your behalf in the event that you are disabled or incapacitated.

- ✔ **Executor.** This is the person named in your will to manage your estate or assets. This person collects the property, pays any debts, and distributes the assets according to your will.

- ✔ **Guardian.** This is the person, or persons, you legally entrust to care for your minor child or children.

- ✔ **Intestacy, intestate.** These terms are applied when you die without a will. Your state will then distribute your assets in fractional amounts to those it determines are your heirs according to state law. One-half might go to your spouse, one-half to your children. The state, in a sense, drafts your will for you—and decides who will administer it.

3

✔ **Probate.** This is the review or testing of a will before a court of law to ensure it is authentic.

✔ **Unlimited marital deduction.** This is a deduction allowing for the unlimited transfer of any or all property from one spouse to another. It is generally free of estate and gift tax.

✔ **Will.** A will is a legal document directing the disposal of your property after your death. You will want to update it if you have any major life changes, such as getting married or having a child. Otherwise, a review every two or three years is advisable.

Having an estate plan in place is critical to family relations. Estate debates are usually about emotions. A plan can help avoid nasty family fractures that can crop up as spouses, brothers, and sisters squabble over money and family treasures, among other things. Family estate battles are legendary and can drag on for years. In the end, they can cause rifts that may never heal.

This book will get you started one step at a time and help take the mystery out of the process. Simply put, estate planning is about control.

✔ The first step is to establish your goals.

✔ You need to define the best way to dispose of your assets at your death.

✔ Ask yourself who you want to receive what, and when.

✔ Who will help with the management of the assets?

✔ If you have minor children, who will take care of them and with what funds?

✔ How can you lower estate taxes, so your heirs get what you worked so hard to build?

✔ If you die unexpectedly, have you left a road map for your survivors to follow?

Putting together an estate plan isn't as daunting a duty as you might imagine, and you can do it in stages. This book will help you get a grasp of the concepts behind estate planning and how you can apply it to your life. It will help you assemble your team of experts to ensure your plan is as foolproof as it can be. It will delve into the emotional side of estates as well as the mechanics, and consider special situations—for instance, gay and lesbian couple considerations, and small business owners.

Planning is important. Your family will thank you for it, and who knows, maybe somewhere beyond the grave you'll know that your wishes were met. A well-organized list of assets and investment accounts with 800-numbers and contacts is paramount. That list is like a bible. Your heirs can go to that file and it will guide them through the process. It's worth the effort to pull it together and keep it current.

Before we get started, here's some boiled-down advice from Joshua S. Rubenstein, a partner at Rosenman & Colin in New York and a fourth-generation estates lawyer. These are his top 10 guidelines for estate planning, as reported in *Bloomberg Personal Finance,* April 1998.

1. Do something. If not, state law will determine who receives your worldly goods.

2. Don't put off making a will.

3. Keep a running list of your assets and liabilities in a location your executor can find.

4. Strike a balance between minimizing taxes and giving up ownership of assets.

5. Choose an executor you trust.

6. Avoid picking a friend or relative as executor whom you'll put in a position that might cause family conflict.

7. Don't give out copies of your will. Knowing its contents will just upset people, and you are bound to make changes over the years.

8. Make your overall wishes known, so that there are no big surprises if you don't divide everything equally.

9. Don't rule from the grave by prohibiting certain types of investments or mandating them.

10. Estate planning is an evolutionary process. Keep tweaking your plan as you go along.

1

Estate Planning Defined

A mericans spend as much time planning their vacations as they do planning their estates, according to a recent Merrill Lynch survey. Most Americans aged 45 and over say they have given much or some thought to providing for their families after their deaths, yet less than a third have a written estate plan. That makes the smooth transfer of assets you've spent your whole life accumulating difficult at best. It also can be a major problem if you have minor children who will be in need of a guardian to help raise them and manage any money you leave to them.

THE ROOT OF ALL EVIL

You shouldn't be shocked to learn that money—especially inherited money—brings out the worst in people. It's all about hurt feelings, and it can get bitter. If you've ever wondered why estate planning is important, you might take a read of Charles Dickens's classic novel *Bleak House*. In a nutshell, here's what happens: A dispute over a will leaves a trail of destruction. A character shoots himself. When the estate is finally settled, the whole fortune has been eaten away by legal fees. In the end, everyone loses.

That book was written nearly 150 years ago, but those same kinds of family battles still take place today and are just as ugly. Many families are able to pass assets from one generation to the next with little conflict or fuss. Others, however, make the process a nightmare and filled with anguish as brothers, sisters, and spouses wrestle to make sense of it all.

Things are usually resolved eventually, but rarely in a pleasant manner. And with all the turmoil, taxes and legal fees do frequently devour much of the estate. Today, the top official tax rate is 55 percent, but some estates are hit with as much as 60 percent. True, few estates are big enough to warrant this wallop, but some 3 percent of all estates do have to file an estate tax return. The best thing you can do for your heirs is to leave your estate affairs in good order. That means spelling out your wishes in a clear, uncomplicated fashion.

DEATH AND TAXES

If you are married, you can avoid estate taxes completely, regardless of your net worth, provided you leave every nickel to your spouse, and your spouse is a U.S. citizen. This is called the *unlimited marital deduction*. It covers bequests made in your will and such things as retire-

unlimited marital deduction a deduction allowing for the unlimited transfer of any or all property from one spouse to another. It is generally free of estate and gift tax.

ment benefits and life insurance policies if your spouse is the named beneficiary.

But after the first spouse dies, unless the survivor remarries, the Internal Revenue Service will be waiting at the door for its share of the spoils. If the truth be known, leaving your entire estate to your spouse might not be the best plan. It can, however, solve your estate-planning woes in the near term.

Regardless of whether you qualify for the marital deduction, almost everyone gets an estate and gift tax credit, also called the Unified Credit. Table 1.1 shows how much you can pass on tax-free.

The estate tax, if any is owed, is paid by the estate, not by the individual who inherits the property. There are several ways to help reduce your estate to make sure you fall below the IRS radar through giving annual gifts of up to $10,000 a year to a number of recipients, which we will delve into in Chapter 5.

OLDER AND WISER AND RICHER

Not surprisingly, older people tend to be better prepared. According to the Merrill Lynch survey, 80 percent of the 895 people surveyed who were 65 and older had a will, 74 percent had organized their financial records, and 68 percent had appointed a trustee or executor. And people

TABLE 1.1 The Unified Credit Exclusion	
Year	Exclusion
2000–2001	$675,000
2002–2003	$700,000
2004	$850,000
2005	$950,000
2006	$1,000,000

with estates valued at $600,000 or more were more likely to have consulted a professional to help them put a plan together.

WHAT DOES ESTATE PLANNING REALLY MEAN?

First, you must know what your estate is. This is the whole ball of wax—in other words, the full value of your property, or one-half of the value of the property you own jointly with your spouse with right of survivorship.

In *community property* states, that equals one-half of the value of your property and assets acquired during you marriage. Gifts or money inherited during your marriage are not considered community property, and their full value is included in your estate.

community property property held jointly by a husband and wife.

Community property states are:

✔ Arizona.
✔ California.
✔ Idaho.
✔ Louisiana.
✔ Nevada.
✔ New Mexico.
✔ Texas.
✔ Washington.
✔ Wisconsin.

Your estate includes everything you own—from stocks, bonds, and mutual funds to individual retirement accounts (IRAs), life insurance policies, 401(k) plans, a home, a dog, a cat, clothing, a car. You name it. We all have estates, and they aren't necessarily huge stone homes nestled in the rolling countryside.

Other aspects of estate planning are:

✔ Having a will—or written document stating clearly how you want your belongings distributed—that is current, and making sure your heirs know where to locate it.

✔ Hiring an estate planning attorney who knows the rules of the state you live in to make sure your will is a legal document in your state. That will go a long way toward ensuring that your will says precisely what you want it to and sidesteps *probate* or at least minimizes the process.

✔ Having a list of your assets that states where they are and how they are titled. Jointly held assets like a home, for example, generally pass to survivors or beneficiaries outside the will and without going through probate.

✔ Naming beneficiaries, or those people you want to inherit your assets.

✔ Writing out any funeral wishes you have, as morbid as it might seem at the time. You may want to be cremated, for instance, or not buried in a family plot on Long Island.

✔ Staving off family arguments by being clear with your heirs about how you want your assets distributed and why.

probate the review or testing of a will before a court of law to ensure it is authentic.

The bottom line: Having organized financial records and communicating your plan are the most important aspects of estate planning.

ASSETS VERSUS LIABILITIES

There are two broad categories when it comes to estates.

First, what you have are your so-called *assets*:

✔ Personal property.

✔ Real estate holdings such as your home.

✔ Stocks and bonds.

✔ Mutual funds.

✔ Retirement accounts, IRAs, Keogh plans, and so on.

✔ Checking and savings accounts.

✔ Proceeds of life insurance policies.

✔ Collectibles and antiques.

✔ Furniture.

✔ Cars.

assets the things that make up your estate. They include everything from your car to your home, stocks, bonds, mutual funds, jewelry, land, and so on.

Second, what you owe are your *liabilities*. These include:

✔ Credit card debts.

✔ Mortgages.

✔ Bank loans.

✔ Car loans.

✔ Education loans.

✔ Taxes.

liabilities your debts.

WHO ARE YOU GOING TO CALL?

Getting a team of professionals to help you put a plan together and keep it current over the years as your life changes is important. Here are some of the people who can help you design your plan:

✔ A lawyer who specializes in estate planning.

✔ Your accountant.

✔ Your stockbroker.

✔ Your financial adviser or planner.

✔ Your insurance agent.

THE SANTA CLAUS MENTALITY

Perhaps the easiest way to describe estate planning would be to envision yourself magnanimously doling out presents to your heirs to help enrich their lives. You might want your spouse to inherit everything, so he or she is able to continue living without you in a comfortable fashion. You might want your daughter or son to have enough wealth to be able to pursue an education. You might want to make sure your pets are cared for after your death. You might want to give to a favorite institution, say your alma mater, or a medical center, to help foster intellectual pursuits or medical research. It's a way of giving back after you have gone.

REALISTIC ESTATE PLANNING

Few of us want even to think about dying, let alone make the tough decisions about who will get what and when and how. Each individual or

13

couple needs to set some objectives and goals and then outline a specific estate plan that will achieve those desires. As you will learn in future chapters, estate planning can be complicated, but doing nothing is the worst course to take. It's your money and your responsibility to design a plan that will meet your needs, your spouse's needs, and your potential heirs' or beneficiaries' needs.

THINK IT THROUGH

Before you begin your estate plan, you must complete a thorough examination of what you possess and what debts you carry. But an estate plan involves far more than that. You also need to take the time to consider what you can do to make a difference after you are gone. What do you value? Maybe it's animals and you want to leave some of your assets to the local humane society. Maybe it's the arts, and you want to leave something to Juilliard or an art museum. Whatever it is, it's up to you to make the choices. Otherwise, as we will discuss later, your state will divvy up the pie for you and it may have nothing to do with how you would have spent your money.

YOUR GOALS AND YOUR SPOUSE'S OR PARTNER'S WISHES

Two of the biggest stumbling blocks for couples when it comes to estate planning are deciding how to divide the assets up in a fair fashion and picking an executor. One person, for instance, might feel strongly about naming a sibling to take on the task of handling the estate, or you may disagree on leaving funds to a certain charity. With most topics, and especially money issues, feelings get in the way of actions. It might be wise to try to focus on dividing your assets in half; then each person can make out a separate will. In life, couples have a hard time agreeing on how to tackle money issues. When it comes to death, the difficulties are tenfold.

14

ESTATE PLANNING FACTORS

To create the best estate plan, you must consider a number of factors. We've discussed the emotional aspect of it and personal objectives. But in effect, the biggest factors will be how large your estate actually is today and what it is likely to be in the future. Since none of us really know when we are going to die, the plan has to be a fluid one that can be updated along the way as your estate grows or your family dynamics change. You might get married, divorced, have a child or several children. You could lose your spouse and be left with an inheritance of your own—and on it goes. An estate plan is ever-changing and a work in progress. Just because you sit down this week and scroll one out doesn't mean you can forget about it in the days ahead.

However, here are some factors to consider when creating your estate plan:

✔ Your age and your partner's age.

✔ Your life expectancy and your partner's.

✔ Whether you will inherit money or assets one day.

✔ Your income and your partner's income.

✔ Your current assets and future assets.

✔ Your children and their ages.

✔ Your extended family.

✔ Children from previous marriages.

✔ Other dependents.

GETTING ORGANIZED

Having your records and important information neatly tracked and updated regularly makes a big difference when it comes to estate planning. Figure 1.1 is a tool, prepared by the Big Five accounting firm Deloitte &

GENERAL INFORMATION

Last updated: _____

Copies given to:_____

1. Information about Yourself

Name: _____

Address:_____

Telephone:_____

Occupation:_____

Citizenship:_____

Social Security number:_____

Date of birth:_____

2. Information about Your Family

Mother's name/address/phone (day/eve): _____

Father's name/address/phone (day/eve): _____

Brother/sister's name/address/phone (day/eve):_____

Brother/sister's name/address/phone (day/eve):_____

Son/daughter's name/address/phone (day/eve):_____

Son/daughter's name/address/phone (day/eve):_____

Other relative's name/address/phone (day/eve):_____

Other relative's name/address/phone (day/eve):_____

Former/separated spouse's name/address/phone: _____

Date and location of divorce/separation: _____

Location of divorce/separation documents:_____

3. Other Important Contacts

Employer's name/address/phone:_____

Key work contact: name/phone: _____

Family doctor's name/address/phone: _____

FIGURE 1.1 The Estate Planning Record Keeper
Source: Deloitte & Touche.

YOUR INSURANCE POLICIES

1. Life Insurance

Type of policy: _____

Expiration date: _____

Company's name/address/phone:_____

Policy number: _____

Face value:_____

Cash value: _____

Beneficiary(ies): _____

Agent's name/address/phone: _____

Location of policy documents: _____

2. Health Insurance

Type of policy: _____

Expiration date: _____

Company's name/address/phone:_____

Policy number: _____

Agent's name/address/phone: _____

Location of policy documents: _____

3. Disability Insurance

Type of policy: _____

Expiration date: _____

Company's name/address/phone:_____

Policy number: _____

Agent's name/address/phone: _____

Location of policy documents: _____

Continued

FIGURE 1.1 *Continued*

4. Long-Term Care Insurance

Type of policy: _____

Expiration date: _____

Company's name/address/phone:_____

Policy number:_____

Agent's name/address/phone: _____

Location of policy documents: _____

5. Medigap Insurance

Type of policy: _____

Expiration date: _____

Company's name/address/phone:_____

Policy number:_____

Agent's name/address/phone: _____

Location of policy documents: _____

6. Excess Personal Liability (Umbrella) Insurance

Type of policy: _____

Expiration date: _____

Company's name/address/phone:_____

Policy number:_____

Agent's name/address/phone: _____

Location of policy documents: _____

7. Homeowners or Rental Insurance

Type of policy: _____

Expiration date: _____

Company's name/address/phone:_____

Policy number:_____

Agent's name/address/phone: _____

Location of policy documents: _____

FIGURE 1.1 *Continued*

8. Automobile Insurance

Type of policy: _____

Expiration date: _____

Company's name/address/phone:_____

Policy number:_____

Agent's name/address/phone: _____

Location of policy documents: _____

9. Boat Insurance

Type of policy: _____

Expiration date: _____

Company's name/address/phone:_____

Policy number:_____

Agent's name/address/phone: _____

Location of policy documents: _____

YOUR ASSETS

1. Cash

Value:_____

Location:_____

2. Savings Account

Account number:_____

Financial institution's name/address/phone:_____

Location of passbook or statements: _____

3. Checking Account

Account number:_____

Financial institution's name/address/phone:_____

Location of passbook or statements: _____

Continued

FIGURE 1.1 *Continued*

4. Term Account (Certificate of Deposit, Etc.)

Identifying number and maturity date:_____

Financial institution's name/address/phone:_____

Location of documents: _____

5. Other (Gold, Silver, Traveler's or Cashier's Checks, Etc.)

Description:_____

Value: _____

Location:_____

6. Pension and Profit-Sharing Plan

Company and account number:_____

Employer's name/address/phone:_____

Beneficiary(ies): _____

Location of documents:_____

7. Keogh Plan and/or Individual Retirement Account (IRA)

Financial institution's name/address/phone:_____

Account number:_____

Beneficiary(ies): _____

Location of documents:_____

8. Securities

Broker's name/address/phone:_____

Account number:_____

9. Stocks

Company, number of shares, certificate number:_____

_____

_____

Location of documents: _____

FIGURE 1.1 *Continued*

10. Bonds

Issuer, face value, certificate number, maturity:_____

_____

_____

Location of documents:_____

11. Mutual Funds

Company, number of shares, account number:_____

_____

_____

Location of documents:_____

12. Other Financial Instruments

Description, location:_____

Description, location:_____

Description, location:_____

Description, location:_____

13. Business Interests

Description (include ownership share if appropriate): _____

Type of organization (partnership, corporation, etc.): _____

Name/address/phone of other partners, owners: _____

Location of financial records, etc.:_____

14. Notes Receivable (People/Organizations Owing You Money)

Description:_____

Debtor's name/address/phone:_____

Amount of debt:_____

Terms:_____

Location of lending documents:_____

Continued

FIGURE 1.1 *Continued*

15. Annuity(ies)

Account number:_____

Company:_____

Payments' scheduled start date: _____

Payments' scheduled duration:_____

Payments' scheduled amount: _____

Beneficiary(ies): _____

Agent's name/address/phone: _____

16. Real Estate

Location of property:_____

Title owned by: _____

Name/address where taxes due:_____

17. Automobile

Make, type, year, vehicle identification number: _____

Location of title: _____

18. Boat

Make, type, year, registration number: _____

Location of title: _____

19. Other Valuable Personal Property

Description:_____

Location:_____

Estimated value:_____

Location of any associated documents:_____

FIGURE 1.1 *Continued*

YOUR DEBTS

1. Credit Cards

Company, account number, name on card: _____

Company, account number, name on card: _____

Company, account number, name on card: _____

Company, account number, name on card: _____

Company, account number, name on card: _____

Company, account number, name on card: _____

Company, account number, name on card: _____

Company, account number, name on card: _____

2. Real Estate Loan

Description of property: _____

First mortgage held by: _____

Amount of first mortgage: _____

Location of first mortgage documents: _____

Second mortgage held by: _____

Amount of second mortgage: _____

Location of second mortgage documents: _____

3. Automobile Loan

Creditor's name/address/phone: _____

Cosigner's name/address/phone (if any): _____

Amount of debt: _____

Terms: _____

Location of lending documents: _____

Continued

FIGURE 1.1 *Continued*

4. Boat Loan

Creditor's name/address/phone: _____

Cosigner's name/address/phone (if any): _____

Amount of debt: _____

Terms: _____

Location of lending documents: _____

5. Student Loan

Creditor's name/address/phone: _____

Cosigner's name/address/phone (if any): _____

Amount of debt: _____

Terms: _____

Location of lending documents: _____

6. Other Debt

Description: _____

Creditor's name/address/phone: _____

Cosigner's name/address/phone (if any): _____

Amount of debt: _____

Terms: _____

Location of lending documents: _____

7. Memberships and/or Other Regular Obligations

Description: _____

Amount due and frequency: _____

Location of documents: _____

Organization/creditor's name/address/phone: _____

FIGURE 1.1 *Continued*

DOCUMENTS

1. Safe-Deposit Box

Box registered in the name of: _____

Bank's name/address/phone: _____

Location of key: _____

Box contents: _____

2. Tax Returns

Location of returns: _____

Accountant's name/address/phone: _____

3. Will

Location of original: _____

Location of copy(ies): _____

Attorney's name/address/phone: _____

Executor's name/address/phone: _____

Children's guardian's name/address/phone: _____

4. Trust Agreement

Location of original: _____

Location of copy(ies): _____

Trust officer's name/address/phone: _____

5. Living Will

Location of original: _____

Location of copy(ies): _____

6. Durable Power of Attorney

Location of original: _____

Location of copy(ies): _____

Continued

FIGURE 1.1 *Continued*

7. Miscellaneous Documents

Birth certificate (location): _____

Adoption documents (location): _____

Baptismal certificate (location): _____

School transcripts (location): _____

Military service records (location): _____

Marriage certificate (location): _____

Passport (number and location): _____

Residence deed (location): _____

Cemetery deed (location): _____

OTHER IMPORTANT INFORMATION

_____

_____

_____

_____

_____

_____

_____

_____

_____

_____

_____

_____

FIGURE 1.1 *Continued*

Touche, that can help you get your plan jump-started. In other chapters we will explore in more depth the workings of some of these categories, such as trusts. And of course many may not apply to you at all. But for now, just fill in as much as you can to give yourself a sense of where you are and to help provide the most detailed information you can to the attorney or other financial adviser who will help you put your plan together.

ESTATE PLANNING OBJECTIVES

In this chapter, we explained the basics of estate planning and why it is important. To sum it up, here are the three major advantages of having an estate plan:

  1. *Eliminate taxes.* Don't underestimate the size of your estate. You might not think it is possible that your estate could exceed that $675,000 limit, but the fact is your actual estate can be far larger than you imagine since it includes everything from your home to your 401(k) plan, investments, and other personal property. An estate larger than $750,000 could be hit with a tax of $37,000, and it elevates from there to more than $2 million on a $5 million estate. It can be a stark reality for your heirs.
  2. *Spare the family.* Have a will that states plainly your desires and eliminates family fighting.
  3. *Give on your terms.* Careful planning can make sure the money you have worked for, saved, and invested for all these years actually gets to the people and organizations you want to benefit and prosper with your help. Should you die without a will, your state court can decide who will inherit your assets and even name a guardian for your dependent children.

  By having a plan, you can smooth out the process for your heirs and make what will inevitably be an emotional time for them as stress-free as it can be. Moreover, the U.S. Treasury is not going to be your primary heir. Makes sense, right?

Chapter

Wills

Getting your estate plan together is about as much fun as going to the dentist, but you have to grin and bear it. Once you have a plan in place, it won't be as painful to keep it current.

The cornerstone of any estate plan is your will. In some ways, if you do nothing more than draw up a will you will save your family, and even business partners, potential battles, infighting, legal hassles, and cash to boot.

MAJOR REASONS FOR HAVING A WILL

- ✔ A will lets you provide for your spouse, dependent children, and other relatives and friends after you die.
- ✔ It makes sure any minor children are cared for and financially okay should you and your spouse die.
- ✔ It lets you legally pass your property on to the people you want to have it.
- ✔ It means a smaller chunk of your estate will go toward legal fees and other expenses and more to your beneficiaries.

✔ It cuts estate taxes.

✔ It speeds up the distribution of your estate.

✔ It makes sure any business you may own stays on track.

✔ It lets you deal with funeral costs and other details.

✔ It helps you arrange for your financial world and business obligations to be taken care of if you are incapacitated or seriously ill.

A *will*—a document that states how you want your assets or property divided among your heirs—has no legal effect until you die or are incapacitated. If it is a "living will" that spells out your instructions it must be signed by yourself, dated, and witnessed by two or more credible individuals. It does not have to be notarized to be legal.

will a legal document directing the disposal of your property after your death.

Here's what a will should include:

✔ Your name.

✔ The date you wrote it.

✔ Your bequests.

✔ The names of your beneficiaries.

✔ Trust information.

✔ Your executor's name.

✔ Your guardian or guardians' names.

✔ Your trustee or trustees' name.

✔ Your signature.

If you die without a will, you are considered to have died *intestate*. Everything you possess will be divvied up in portions to certain heirs, as the laws of your state determine descent and distribution. Each state has a different way of doling out your wealth. In Virginia, for example, all of your estate would go directly to your spouse. In Illinois, half would go to your spouse and half to would go to your children. A local court will pick an *administrator* to manage your estate.

> **intestate** term applied when you die without a will.

The administrator is required to post a bond as security and basically act as an executor would with similar duties. Keep in mind that the administrator will be paid from your estate. And the process can be excruciatingly long at a tenuous time when your family may need your assets to live on.

> **administrator** a person picked by the local court to handle your estate when you die without a will.

WRITING A WILL

Now is a good time to write or update your will. This is your personal plan of what you want to have done with your goods. The basic goal is to decide how you want your property to be distributed when you die. Grim it may be, but reality.

Even anyone under age 50 who owns real estate worth less than $675,000 in 2000 (rising to $1 million in 2006) should have at least a basic will. If you are older or have a larger estate, you may need some extra planning help to make sure your property is passed on smoothly. A will lets others that you have handpicked act on your behalf when you die.

Here are the basic elements of a simple will:

✔ You leave your property to those you want to receive it, or to organizations like a university or a charity.

✔ You appoint someone as a guardian to take care of your minor children in case of your death.

✔ You name someone to handle any property or money you leave to minor children.

✔ You pick a person to act as your executor to be sure what you have stated in your will is acted upon in the way you wanted it to be handled.

SIZING UP YOUR SITUATION

Your failure to write a will can throw your family into turmoil. Sounds obvious, right? It's easy to avoid thinking about something as basic as writing a will, but that means someone else will have to sort it all out in the end, and that can get ugly. These are tough choices to make and ones most of us would prefer not to deal with until sometime in the future. We think we're too young to need a will, or we have so few material goods to pass on. Not true.

Just take a moment to consider what you actually have as possessions and in retirement income from 401(k) plans and the like. Even if you already have a will, it may be out-of-date, given the major tax law changes in recent years, the roaring stock market, and life events like marriage, divorce, a change of state residence, or family deaths. If you're altering your will, be sure to have copies of your old will destroyed once the new one is inked.

QUESTIONS ABOUT WILLS

The three biggest questions to ask about wills are:

1. What information do I need to put a will together?
2. Where should I keep my will?
3. What about funeral plans and wishes?

What Information Do I Need?

This information is going to be both personal and financial, and getting it together can be a stumbling block for many couples. Individuals will find it easier to come to some of these delicate decisions, but the choices are never simple and can bruise feelings of relatives and friends in the end. But here is what you need before you draw up your will. Keep in mind that although you can do it yourself it's a good idea to have an attorney write or at least review your will to make sure all the information is correct and legal. We'll discuss finding a will/estate attorney later on, as well as web sites and books to guide you on your own.

✔ Have a list of all the names, birth dates, addresses, and Social Security numbers of any *beneficiaries* you plan to name—persons or institutions that will receive benefits or a financial payout under your will or other contract such as an insurance policy.

> **beneficiary** person or institution designated through your will that will receive the benefits of your estate at your death.

✔ Compile a complete listing of all your assets, liabilities, life insurance policies, retirement plan savings, and what you own outright. Make sure you have a record of who the beneficiary is on any of those documents. Have a copy of the deed of any property you own and a record of how it is titled.

✔ Have a record of any inheritances you are expecting in the future.

✔ Know who you want to name as the *executor* of your will, and list the person's address, phone number, and Social Security number. The executor does not have to be your spouse. Name someone you feel will carry out your wishes in a capable manner and is going to be comfortable with that role. The individual will handle your estate, pay off any debts you have, and make sure everything gets into the right hands.

executor person named in your will to manage your estate.

✔ If you have *minor children* (under the age of 16 or 18, depending on your state), you should know who you want to name as their *guardian* to be legally responsible for them. You might choose two, one to raise the children and one to manage any financial assets you leave to them.

minor children children under the age of 16 or 18, depending on the state's laws.

guardian person legally entrusted to care for minor child(ren).

✔ As part of your will, you can designate an individual to take over for you, represent you, and take care of your financial and personal business should you become disabled or incapacitated. Have the person's correct name, phone numbers, address and Social Security number in hand. This is called *durable power of attorney*.

If you are disabled, the person you select under a durable power of attorney can act on your behalf to sign checks, invest, file insurance claims, access your safe-deposit box, file your tax return, and more. The authorization becomes effective only on the date that your medical physician signs a form certifying that you are unable to perform those duties yourself.

 durable power of attorney a written legal document that lets you designate another person to act on your behalf in the event you are disabled or incapacitated.

✔ Finally, should you need life support due to a health-care catastrophe, have a clear idea of what your wishes are in regard to disconnecting that apparatus. This is called *durable power of attorney for health care*. It, too, is a legal document attached to your will that hands over the authority to act for you regarding health-care decisions.

 durable power of attorney for health care a written legal document that lets you designate another person to act on your behalf regarding health-care decisions.

Where Should I Keep My Will?

If you have your will drawn up by an attorney, as most people do, he or she may agree to keep it in a vault at the law office. A safe-deposit box is another option, but may not be a terrific solution since, depending on where you live, state laws may freeze any removal of documents. It's a good idea to be sure the person you name as executor has a copy of your will as well. Here are some simple steps that will serve you well: Staple the pages together so nothing gets lost. Put the will in a sealed envelope clearly labeled that it is your will. Make sure it's stored in a fireproof box. You might also give copies of your will to the major beneficiaries. But there is no legal reason to show your will to anyone if you choose not to.

What about Funeral Plans and Wishes?

These particulars generally aren't part of a will, but you might have a separate document that explains what you want and be sure your executor or close family members know where those instructions are stored.

UNUSUAL BEQUESTS

What about Rover?

As ludicrous as it may sound to non–pet lovers, if you die without any survivors except your loyal yellow Lab, wouldn't you want to name a guardian for your pooch to make sure she's taken care of after you are gone? Maybe that's being overly sentimental, but for many Americans ensuring a pet's future well-being can be a real dilemma.

True, you can't leave money or property to pets because they aren't people, even if you secretly think they're on that plateau. But you can leave pets to friends or family members in your will. And in some states you can actually name a pet as a beneficiary of a *trust*, but you'll need to have a lawyer help you write it into your will. These are the states that allow for pet beneficiaries of trusts:

35

- ✔ Alaska.
- ✔ Arizona.
- ✔ California.
- ✔ Missouri.
- ✔ Montana.
- ✔ New Mexico.
- ✔ New York.
- ✔ North Carolina.
- ✔ Tennessee.

In this type of trust, you pick a trustee to care for your pet using funds from the trust. In a sense, this is on the honor system, so choose someone you know will follow your wishes. We'll discuss more about trusts in Chapter 4.

> **trust** a legal document created during your lifetime that allows you to pass assets on to another person or persons through a legal entity. The assets are then managed for you or someone else.

What You Can't Pass On in a Will

Excluded from your will are the following bequests:

- ✔ Retirement plans such as 401(k) plans that already have specific beneficiaries unless you make the change with your plan as well.
- ✔ Life insurance you already have named a beneficiary for, again unless it is also changed on that contract.

✔ Property or land you hold in joint tenancy.

✔ Any real estate or property held in trust.

OTHER TYPES OF WILLS

Handwritten Wills

If your *handwritten will* is not witnessed by at least two people it will be valid in only a few states. After you die, it's easy for heirs to challenge the fact that you actually wrote it if no one witnessed it.

handwritten will must be witnessed by at least two people to be valid in most states.

Oral Wills

Oral wills hold even less weight when it comes to challenges, and only a few states accept them. Should you decide to video your last will and testament, you'll be out of luck as well because no states have authorized them.

oral will most states do not accept oral wills.

Living Wills

Most states have statutes now that let you choose if you wish to stop life-sustaining procedures. A *living will* is a document that allows you to lay out simply the type of medical treatment you would want if you can't make those decisions because you have been critically injured.

You might be in a coma. Would you want medical personnel to do everything possible to keep you alive, or would you want the least-intrusive actions? This decision has a lot to do with your heartfelt beliefs about human life and religion. But with a living will, you can have your say.

living will legal document that allows you to lay out the type of medical treatment you would want if you have been critically injured and can no longer make the decision.

The requirements: A living will must be in writing, signed by you and witnessed by at least two people, as with a regular will, and you must be at least 18 years old. You can change it in writing or revoke it at any time. It normally comes into play only in life-and-death situations. The person to whom you have given durable power of attorney for health care will ensure you get the treatment you want.

REVIEWING YOUR WILL

It's important to go over your will every few years. Here are the major reasons to do so more frequently:

✔ *Your marital status changes.* When Britain's Princess Diana died in a car accident in 1997, England's Inland Revenue Service became her biggest heir. Forty percent, or $14.3 million, of Diana's $35.6 million estate was expected to go to taxes. Why? Her will was written in 1993 and hadn't been updated after her divorce settlement from Prince Charles. (Her lawyers did get court permission to alter her will after her death).

✔ *You move to a new state.* Your will is still valid, but there can be a hitch if you move to a community property state and vice versa. Community property states are Arizona, California, Idaho, Louisiana, Nevada, New Mexico, Texas, Washington, and Wisconsin. In those states each spouse has rights to half of the income and property they own together, so you can leave by will only your own share.)

Other reasons to update your will:

✔ The executor you named can no longer handle the duties.
✔ You become a parent.
✔ You marry or remarry.
✔ Your spouse dies.
✔ One of your beneficiaries dies.
✔ You decide to change beneficiaries.
✔ Your wealth changes significantly.
✔ The person you have designated to be your children's guardian is unable to act as one.
✔ You buy or sell property.
✔ You start a small business or sell one.

Chapter

Putting Your
Team Together

As we discussed in the previous chapter, it is important to have a will even if you skip any other estate planning techniques. It really is the key document you can prepare for your children and heirs. And of course you can draft one on paper all by yourself and have two friends watch you sign it. But although it is not required by law, it's a good idea to have your homemade will notarized, signed, and dated, and then stored in a safe place. A notary public should charge you under $10.

There are plenty of $25 to $50 computer software programs on the market like WillMaker that will guide you through the will and estate planning process. In the end, though, it's a good idea to have a lawyer pore over the fine print. That said, a do-it-yourself will is not usually the best route to take, even if some do hold up in court when they are contested.

HIRING AN ESTATE ATTORNEY

It's best to hire an estate planning attorney who knows the ins and outs of your state's laws to handle your will for you. This is especially true if there are any major changes in tax law. Moreover, estate law is complex and if you don't adhere to the strict wording of state laws, your will can easily be declared invalid and your heirs have to wrestle with dealing with an intestate estate—no doubt not what you had in mind.

Of course, there's no harm in pulling your will together with software or online help, then making an appointment with a lawyer. That homework can save serious time in billable hours.

When do you really need an attorney? There are dozens of scenarios. A will can be fairly easy to put together and cheap to have a lawyer okay for you. But there are plenty of other times when it's critical that you hire a highly experienced lawyer to help you through the maze of estate planning—for instance, if you are interested in setting up a trust (which we'll learn more about in the next chapter), or if you have real estate holdings in more than one state. Spend the time to make your will and wishes legally binding.

To find a good lawyer, ask for referrals from friends or business associates. This is often the best way to find someone suitable. Your accountant or financial adviser should also be able to pass along names of a few reputable attorneys in your area.

If not, contact the American College of Trusts and Estate Counsel (310-398-1888; www.actec.org), the American Academy of Estate Planning Attorneys (800-846-1555; www.aaepa.com), the National Network of Estate Planning Attorneys (800-638-8681; www.netplanning.com), or the American Bar Association (312-988-5000; www.abanet.org) for referrals.

You can also refer to the *Martindale-Hubbell Law Directory*, which you can find in most libraries and on the World Wide Web at www.martindale.com. It has a complete listing of lawyers around the country and rates them based on evaluations by their peers in your community. The top rating is AV for top-notch legal acumen and ethical standards. The directory provides data on how long the lawyer has been practicing, where the attorney studied, and areas of specialty.

Visit more than one estate attorney and find out what they charge. Don't be intimidated or too bashful to ask. Most have hourly rates.

Get at least two names of clients as referrals to contact if possible.

Because of privacy issues this can be a little tricky, but well worth asking. You should suss out what percentage of the practice is devoted to wills and estate planning and how long the attorney has been working in that area.

Ask if there is a questionnaire you can fill out before you come to your appointment. That paperwork can help speed the process along. Most estate attorneys will provide you with a list of what you need to bring with you and a series of questions you should have answered before you arrive.

Moreover, you must have faith in the professional you choose. Not only will you be disclosing personal and very private details of your life, but hopefully this attorney will be able to steer your estate plan for years to come. Having a competent lawyer will make the process as smooth and uncomplicated as possible, but communication is the name of the game. Choosing the right professional takes time and, yes, legwork.

Exposing your financial life to a stranger takes trust and confidence. Find the time to pick the right lawyer for the job. This is a business decision, not a personal one, although it may feel like a personal one.

And don't ever feel intimidated by the process. Ask questions if you're confused. You're paying for it. A good working relationship is paramount. The key to a successful partnership is going to be your own involvement and understanding of the decisions you are making that will affect you and your family for years to come.

SELECTING A FINANCIAL ADVISER

Putting together an estate plan takes time and patience. It's not a bad idea to seek out professional help, in addition to a lawyer, to get your plan in motion. There are droves of people who call themselves *financial advisers* to pick from. These include financial consultants, financial planners, life insurance agents, money managers, and stockbrokers, among many others.

financial adviser professional who can help you get your estate plan in shape.

A financial planner will typically charge you anywhere from $500 to $1,500 for a basic estate plan. It might be just a road map to get you started in the right direction, but it will be well worth it. The planner's first job is to figure out what assets you have at the present time from the materials you provide, such as your past tax returns and statement of net worth.

Your estate plan will run the gamut from providing for dependent children to paring taxes on any assets that you will leave to your heirs. Investments, too, will be part of the considerations, as will life insurance. Your planner should be able to give you advice on your specific insurance needs and get your estate plan rolling.

If all goes well, you will have an ongoing relationship that will help you review and change your estate plan as your circumstances change. Finding a good financial planner can be tough. For the most part, the industry is still unregulated, which means it is hard to figure out who is a legitimate adviser.

In general, you are better off with a fee-only planner. There are more than 4,000 of these individuals currently practicing. They charge an up-front fee for their advice, or a basic fee for a planning session. You'll want to ask for referrals from friends or other professionals you work with, such as your attorney or accountant.

The bottom line is that you want to feel at ease with the planner and comfortable that he or she has your best interests at heart. It pays to spend some time interviewing at least three potential planners.

Seek out advisers or planners who have a *Certified Financial Planner (CFP)* accreditation. A CFP is a professional who has completed a rigorous series of courses and exams in planning and undergoes 15 hours of continuing education each year.

> **Certified Financial Planner (CFP)** a finance professional who has completed a series of courses and exams.

Where to Get Help

The Certified Financial Planner Board of Standards offers "What You Should Know about Financial Planning," free. 888-237-6275.

Get referrals from:

✔ American Institute of Certified Public Accountants' Personal Financial Specialists. CPAs with particular experience in personal finance who have passed an exam sponsored by the AICPA. 888-999-9256; www.cpapfs.org.

✔ Institute of Certified Financial Planners. Planners who pass a one-hour exam administered by the CFP Board of Standards. 800-282-7526; www.icfp.org.

✔ The Financial Planning Association. A trade group for financial planners and advisers. 888-806-7526; www.fpanet.org.

✔ National Association of Personal Financial Advisors. A trade group for advisers who charge a fee for service, rather than work on commission. 888-333-6659; www.napfa.org.

QUESTIONS TO ASK A POTENTIAL LAWYER AND FINANCIAL ADVISER

✔ How long have you been a lawyer or adviser?

✔ How many years have you worked for this firm?

✔ What are some details about the firm's history and the areas you specialize in?

✔ How do you get paid?

✔ How do your contracts work? Are they written or oral?

✔ Are there any restrictions on terminating your services?

✔ Do you take part in any continuing education programs?

✔ What percentage of your clients come to you for estate planning?

✔ How big are your clients' estates on average?

✔ What is your area of strength from an estate planning perspective?

✔ Would you give me three references?

✔ What can I expect from you in the way of services?

✔ How often will we need to meet?

✔ Based on what I have told you, how much time do you think it will take you to draw up a will and plan for me?

QUESTIONS A LAWYER OR FINANCIAL ADVISER SHOULD ASK YOU

✔ How old are you?

✔ Do you have any dependents?

✔ Are you married?

✔ What are your assets?

✔ What are your liabilities?

✔ What is your total income?

✔ What is the current value of your home?

✔ What are your goals and objectives for your will?

✔ What are your goals and objectives for your estate plan?

✔ Do you have life insurance?

✔ Do you already have a will in place?

✔ Will you inherit money one day?

✔ Do you expect to remarry in the next year?

✔ Do you plan to become a parent in the next year or so?

WHEN YOU SHOULD CONSIDER A LAWYER

In some situations, there really is no way to avoid hiring a specialist to draft your will and assist you with estate planning. Here are some situations to consider:

✔ It is likely that someone will contest your will.

✔ You've remarried and there are children from an earlier marriage by either of you.

✔ Your own estate exceeds the $675,000 federal tax exemption limit for this year, which will rise to $1 million in 2006.

✔ The combined estate of your spouse and yourself is more than double those individual amounts.

✔ You have a disabled child or family member who will need special care and specifically earmarked funds.

✔ You want to set certain limits on how your estate is passed along, whether it be in a certain time frame, say a payout at age 30, 40, and so on, or by beneficiary.

✔ You want to control how your heirs live after you are gone. For instance, they can receive their shares only if they are fully employed.

CUTTING YOUR LEGAL BILLS

A lawyer can usually help you design a straightforward will for under $100, but the fee can range from $50 to $300. Trickier plans can cost anywhere from $1,000 to $5,000. There are several ways you can trim your legal bills if you are willing to do the groundwork before you arrive for your appointment.

✔ Know what the net worth of your estate is or as close to it as you can get and have the documents to back up your figure. That means a list of assets and liabilities.

✔ Know who you want to name as executor and have the person's vital information, such as correct name, phone number, and Social Security number, on hand.

✔ Choose a guardian or guardians for your child and have their information with you as well.

✔ Have a diagram of who your estate is going to go to and when you want them to receive their shares.

Hiring a lawyer is a big step and choosing the right one will take some patience. In some ways, though, picking the other three people to have on your team might be even more difficult from a personal standpoint.

SELECTING AN EXECUTOR

You really need to think long and hard about your choice of executor. This is the person you will trust to handle all your financial affairs. Your executor should be someone who is comfortable with handling finances and able to take the time to handle yours ultimately.

Being an executor is a time-consuming process. So picking your favorite child to do so might not be your best move if this son or daughter isn't up to speed on money and financial dealings, or won't have the time to deal with the issue.

This is why. The executor of your will and estate must determine the value of all your assets. The executor isn't necessarily handling those assets that are held jointly, such as life insurance policies or pension plans, and property that should pass straight to your named beneficiaries, but will often need really to appraise what the current value of the rest of your estate is at the time of your death.

That might mean hiring a professional appraiser or accountant.

That professional will be paid, of course; and that fee will come from your estate—right off the top. In addition, the executor, even a close family friend, usually is paid for work done. That can run as high as 5 percent of your estate.

What Are the Executor's Responsibilities?

The executor's duties are:

✔ To pay off your remaining debts or liabilities from the estate.

✔ To make sure your tax return is filed for the year of your death.

✔ To make sure your heirs get what you have left to them.

✔ To give probate court a careful record of all the money that has been taken from your estate to pay debts and so forth.

Who Should be Your Executor?

Your choice for executor really depends on the size of your estate. If it is $1 million or less, and you have a relatively simple will with just a few beneficiaries and not a lot of complex investments to untangle, go with a close friend or your spouse or offspring. Otherwise, you might want to consider naming two executors. The first should be someone who can make wise financial decisions and deal with tax issues and the like, maybe your financial adviser or banker. The second should be that close friend, spouse, son, or daughter who can make sure your wishes are met.

When you name an executor, it's your responsibility to inform him or her of your decision and make sure the individual is willing to take on that role. Don't be surprised, or hurt, if you get turned down. Lots of people shy away from this type of financial unraveling.

Once you both agree, go over all the details of your will together so the executor knows where you are coming from and is aware of who will need to be contacted to execute your will, such as your lawyer. Give the executor a copy of your will if you feel at ease doing so. Otherwise, leave instructions of where to find a copy of it.

CHOOSING A GUARDIAN

While picking an executor can be trying and emotional, deciding who you want to name as guardian for your minor children can be a real wringer. Your best choice will probably be a sibling or close friend of the family who is youthful enough for the task. The guardian should also be someone who shares your views on parenting and will raise your children in the manner you would have yourself. You will need to talk to whoever that is ahead of time to make sure you are on the same wavelength and the person is willing to accept that role should something happen to you or to you and your spouse.

It is possible that person might be the perfect choice to raise your children, but not be particularly astute financially. In that case, naming a second guardian is a good idea. The second guardian would be in charge of managing your property and managing your children's finances. Again, discuss it ahead of time. And be sure the two people you choose are aware of your goals.

NAMING A TRUSTEE

Whether you will need to name a *trustee* will depend on the size of your estate and how complex it's going to be to distribute and manage. This is the person who will manage any of your property that is owned by your trust. We will discuss trusts in more detail in the next chapter. Your trustee will be in charge of distributing any income from the trust. You can pick a specific person or an institution, like a bank or a trust company.

Acting as a trustee can be a trying task. The hardest situation for a trustee to manage is when there are several beneficiaries being doled

trustee the person who will manage any property that is owned by a trust.

49

out unequal shares. Infighting can easily erupt after you are gone by those who feel slighted or feel that the distribution was unfair in some way. It's common for heirs to charge trustees with mismanagement, neglect, and misuse of funds.

You don't need a large estate to warrant naming a trustee to handle this thicket. More and more middle-income families are opting for this route to keep things moving along professionally. Today's trustees no longer just work to keep the money intact until it is time for payouts. They must actively manage the funds as well to keep pace with the bull market.

Then, too, people are living longer and need their inheritances to last longer as well. They need to provide income and protect against inflation. They need to keep the assets growing, and they need to minimize capital gains taxes.

It's a demanding financial and psychological job. Often, beneficiaries take umbrage at trust officers who seem smug and keep an iron fist on the funds, doling out money only when absolutely necessary. They see these trustees as power grabbers who just want to bring in fees for their banks or financial institutions and are not really looking after the beneficiaries' interests in the way you certainly would have. It is about control, and it can get ugly.

Bottom line: You need a real expert in most cases if there is a trust involved and a long payout period through the generations that follow you. A pro can be found at a trust company. It usually is part of a bank or investment bank, but can be a separate trust company altogether. As with an attorney, you will want to interview at least three companies to research the one that will be right for your circumstances. You might also consider naming as cotrustee a friend or family member who has the expertise to keep an eye on how the trust is being managed and the ability to make changes in its management if need be.

The Questions You Need to Ask a Trust Company

✔ What are your fees? (Generally, figure 1 percent to 1.5 percent of the assets under management, which is why trustees tend to want to hang on to the funds rather than distribute any of the principal to your beneficiaries.)

✔ What is your investment philosophy?

✔ Are you conservative or aggressive in investing?

✔ What is the typical size of a trust you manage?

✔ How often do you meet or correspond with the trust beneficiaries?

✔ How long have you been in business?

✔ Who will be assigned to my trust?

✔ What is that person's experience?

✔ What is your area of strength from a financial perspective?

✔ What can we expect in terms of service?

✔ Can I have three references of trust clients?

✔ How do your contracts work?

✔ What was your best investment last year?

✔ What was your worst investment?

✔ Are there any restrictions on terminating your services?

In the next chapter, we will delve into the intricacies of trusts and what you may want to consider today and in the future as you build your estate plan.

Chapter 4

Putting
Together a Trust

T hink you need to be rich to set up trusts for your kids? Think
again. Trusts are a great way to pass your money on to your children and slash income and estate taxes as well. Thanks to the ro-
bust economy of late and the soaring stock market, more of us are poised
to leave an inheritance far larger than we ever dreamed we would.

But leaving a windfall to an heir can be troubling. You worry that he
or she will be unable to handle it in the manner you would want. One solution is to pass the stock shares or other assets to a trust that will invest
and manage those assets. Trusts don't have to carry too many restrictions,
but they certainly can if you want to write in your own rules.

For instance, you might want to say that your heirs can't touch
the assets until they've retired or some such time frame. You might allow them to withdraw funds if they plan to set up their own businesses
or buy homes. These restrictions can get prickly, but the notion of
keeping tabs on heirs is catching on.

According to the *Wall Street Journal*, when Atlanta Braves pitcher
Tom Glavine, who pulls in an annual salary of $8 million, decided to
set up a trust for his children, the 33-year-old wanted to make sure his

kids worked. In the trust he established, they must have earned income. He will match whatever they earn, up to $100,000 annually. His young daughter wants to be a veterinarian, so he wrote in a provision that will give her $200,000 to set up a veterinary practice as long as she has done well in school. She was only four years old at the time he drafted the will. Then, too, as a way to encourage her to be a stay-at-home mom if she has children, he's considering giving her as much as $10,000 a month to raise her children.

Trusts can be as flexible or rigid as you deem. There can be no deviation allowed from what you have set down as the criteria for withdrawals. Conversely, you can allow for special requests that a trustee must consider—maybe to pay for college or for medical bills. It's usually a good idea to make the trust flexible, so that you aren't controlling your beneficiaries from the grave, so to speak.

WHAT IS A TRUST?

A trust is a legal document that is created during your lifetime that allows you to pass assets on to another person or persons through a legal entity. It holds assets that are then managed for you or someone else. You may have to give up ownership of the assets, depending on the type of trust you choose. A trust is administered by another individual, a trustee from an institution, or yourself.

Trusts can give you major advantages regardless of the size of your estate. You can use them to buy or sell assets or transfer them to someone else. In many instances, they can make the estate settling process much smoother. A trust can let you transfer a sizable amount of your assets with little interference from the Internal Revenue Service, state courts, or other family members.

Probate, the review of your will before a state court to determine if it is valid, can take anywhere from several months to several years to complete, at substantial cost to your estate. It can be startling for people to realize that all property distributed via a will must go through this process. If there's a trust in place, that procedure can be limited. (We will discuss more about probate in Chapter 6, "Settling an Estate.")

SETTING UP A TRUST

You'll want to name a professional trustee, such as a bank or a trust company officer, to manage the funds for a fee (typically 1 percent to 1.5 percent of your trust's assets), but it will be well worth it. That fee is to cover accounting and other investment services.

You might possibly name a second trustee who is a close friend or relative to keep an eye on the trust, as we discussed in Chapter 3. It is paramount to pick a trustee you can rely on and who has the expertise to manage the trust.

Setting up a trust can be costly. Depending on how complicated it is and where you live, the cost can run anywhere from $1,000 to $12,000.

Trusts usually pay out interest to heirs each year, sometimes quarterly, and dole out portions of the principal only on preset dates, maybe one-third when your heir reaches 25, another third at 40, and a final third at age 65.

Other Tips for Setting Up a Trust

✔ Have your lawyer add a spendthrift clause to shield the trust from your heir's creditors getting access to the funds. This can protect the inheritance from legal claims that can stem from events such as a divorce or bankruptcy.

✔ If the beneficiary of your trust is also the trustee, limit the use of the principal to education, medical bills, and maintenance to avoid having the trust's assets become part of the beneficiary's estate.

TYPES OF TRUSTS

Here are several types of trust arrangements you might consider.

Living Trust

A *living trust* is active while you are alive and isn't considered to be a part of your will. It's been touted since the 1960s as the best way to keep your estate free of probate court. Any assets you have in a living trust are not subject to probate. With a living trust, you transfer ownership of your assets to a trust. You are able to keep any of the income from that trust, be the trustee, and change it or end it whenever you choose. In other words it is flexible during your lifetime. But once you die, the trust becomes irrevocable (see "Irrevocable Trust" and "Revocable Trust" later in the chapter).

> **living trust** a trust that is active while you are alive and isn't considered to be a part of your will.

Advantages of Having a Living Trust

✔ Your assets in the trust go straight to your heirs without going through probate. That means your heirs get their inheritances quicker and without the cost of probate.

✔ The provisions of the trust are not subject to probate, so unhappy heirs have more difficulty contesting the trust's provisions.

✔ If you own a business, you can place it in the trust and name a trustee. That means if you die your successor can take over management of the firm at once.

✔ Gay couples may opt for this type of trust to avoid family infighting and will challenges. Your partner can be named as cotrustee or successor trustee and have control of the assets straightaway if you are incapacitated or die.

Drawbacks of a Living Trust

✔ A living trust is not for everyone. It just might not be necessary or worth the cost or hassle. It all depends on how much you actually have in the way of assets that will pass through probate. Insurance payouts, retirement accounts, and any property you own jointly are not subject to probate.

✔ A living trust is subject to estate taxes. Since this type of trust is revocable, the assets are part of your taxable estate.

✔ It will take time to retitle all of your assets that are going into the trust, from stocks and mutual funds to real estate and bank accounts. And that can eat up lawyer fees in a blink of an eye.

✔ When your estate is in probate, creditors have only a limited time period to make claims. With a living trust, they can make claims at any time.

What's a Pour-Over Will? Should you opt for a living trust, it might be a good idea to have your lawyer draw up a *pour-over will*. This type of document lets you leave certain property to specific individuals and name a child's guardian. Any belongings you forget to include in your living trust or pour-over will are going to be subject to probate.

pour-over will in a living trust, this document lets you leave certain property to specific individuals and name a child's guardian.

Testamentary Trust

A *testamentary trust* is created in your will and is activated only upon your death. This is the most common type of trust.

testamentary trust a trust created in your will and activated only upon your death.

Irrevocable Trust

An *irrevocable trust* can't be changed materially after it has been legally put in writing, but you also have no control over the assets held in the trust. None of your assets or property held in an irrevocable trust are included in your estate in regard to estate tax. This can be a real boon for your heirs in terms of tax savings. If you choose to go this route, be sure to put any appreciating assets in this type of trust, so they can avoid estate tax.

irrevocable trust a trust that cannot be changed materially after it has been legally put in writing.

Revocable Trust

A *revocable trust* can be changed over time. You can even end it during your lifetime. You won't get any estate tax benefits here because any property in this kind of trust is considered by law to be part of your taxable estate. The good news is that a revocable trust is shielded from probate court, so it will remain private.

revocable trust a trust that can be changed over time.

Trusts are often viewed as exotic estate-planning tools used only by the very wealthy, according to David Kay, a Certified Financial Planner based in Dayton, Ohio. In reality, however, trusts are versatile planning tools that can benefit even modest estates, he says.

To summarize, here are the goals of a trust:

✔ Reduce estate taxes.
✔ Manage asset distribution.

✔ Give to charities.

✔ Enlist a professional to manage and invest assets.

✔ Manage funds that are left to your children until they are old enough to manage the money on their own.

✔ Avoid probate.

Other Types of Trusts to Consider

Bypass or Credit Shelter Trust. This trust is probably the most common type. A *bypass or credit shelter trust* allows you and your spouse to leave $1.35 million to your heirs totally exempt from estate tax. This figure will escalate until 2006. The way it works is that your assets aren't transferred to your heirs until both of you have died. Most often, people set these up as living trusts and each spouse has a separate one in his or her name. If your husband dies, up to $675,000 of his assets are then placed in the trust and you begin to draw income each year. Then, too, if you need money to cover medical costs for your spouse or for your own medical bills, the trustee you have named for the trust can authorize those payouts.

bypass or credit shelter trust a trust that allows you and your spouse to leave $1.35 million to your heirs totally exempt from estate tax.

Charitable Remainder Trust. These trusts have come under increased scrutiny during the past year, but in essence, a *charitable remainder trust* is used to make a hefty charitable contribution to your alma mater or some other charity and save being hit with a large capital gains tax bill. It lets you gift an asset, typically one that has surged in value, while you are alive. You get the tax deduction at the time, and you and your heirs can draw out income from that trust for life. In most cases, there is a cutoff point—say, when the second spouse dies. Then the charity takes over complete ownership of the asset you have gifted.

> **charitable remainder trust** a trust used to make a
> charitable contribution and avoid a large capital gains
> tax bill.

A remainder trust can be part of a living will or a testamentary one where you write the gift into your will itself. If it is part of your will, it will be subject to estate tax, but a chunk of the property value will be considered deductible. In general, to set up this type of trust you will need property or assets worth $50,000 or more. And you can change the charity you are gifting it to in the future.

Irrevocable Life Insurance Trust. An *irrevocable life insurance trust* is one that makes sure any payout from an insurance policy is exempt from estate taxes. Obviously, proceeds from a life insurance policy often make up a sizable portion of one's estate. What happens is that the proceeds are directed into a trust and not into your estate, which lowers any potential estate tax. Your spouse will usually receive income from that life insurance trust and be able to draw off the principal if need be. Your heirs will inherit it after your spouse dies. The one hitch to this plan is that if you die within three years of setting this trust up, all the life insurance benefits revert back into your taxable estate. Have your lawyer write a clause stating that should that happen, all the proceeds from your policy go straight to your spouse and will be tax-free until he or she dies. Also, if it's a cash-value life insurance policy, you will not be allowed to borrow against it as you ordinarily can with a cash-value policy.

> **irrevocable life insurance trust** a trust that makes
> sure payouts from an insurance policy are exempt from
> estate taxes.

Cash-Value Insurance. *Cash-value life insurance* blends a death benefit with a tax-deferred investment fund. That means a portion of your annual premium goes to pay out the death benefit, and another portion is invested for you at a set interest rate of 5 percent or so. As you build up the investment portion, you can borrow against that cash value or withdraw it altogether.

cash-value life insurance type of life insurance which blends a death benefit with a tax-deferred investment fund.

Charitable Remainder Annuity Trust. The *charitable remainder annuity trust* is much like the charitable remainder trust discussed earlier, but the charity is required to pay you a certain sum annually, maybe 8 to 10 percent of the principal.

charitable remainder annuity trust remainder trust in which the charity is required to pay you a certain sum annually.

Charitable Lease Trust. A *charitable lease trust* pays a charity a set amount of income over a certain time period. Then the principal passes to your named beneficiaries.

charitable lease trust a trust that pays a charity a set amount over a certain time period, after which the principal passes to the beneficiaries.

Qualified Personal Residence Trust. With a *qualified personal residence trust*, you place your home in an irrevocable trust. You hang on to the right to live in the home for a set number of years, say 10 to 20 years. (It can also be a vacation home.) At the end of the trust's term, the ownership passes to your beneficiaries. The estate tax value is figured from the date your house was placed in the trust. But should you die before the end of the trust's term, your home is included in your estate at its current market value.

qualified personal residence trust a trust where you place your home in an irrevocable trust. At the end of a specified time period the ownership passes to the named beneficiaries.

Qualified Terminable Interest Property (QTIP) Trust. A *qualified terminable interest property (QTIP) trust* ensures that your assets are passed on to your handpicked heirs without allowing your spouse who survives you to make changes. What you do is place any assets in excess of the *lifetime gift and estate exclusion* ($675,000 in 2000, but scheduled to increase to $1 million in 2006) in a trust. Your surviving spouse can receive income during his or her lifetime and won't have to pay estate taxes on the funds or property after you die. Then when your spouse dies, the principal is passed on to the heirs you chose.

qualified terminable interest property (QTIP) trust this trust ensures that assets are passed on to named heirs without the surviving spouse making changes.

Generation-Skipping Trust. A *generation-skipping trust* lets married couples sock away up to $2 million for their grandchildren and other generations. If you are not married, that sum is $1 million. This trust grows tax-free. Otherwise—without a trust—there is a 55 percent generation-skipping transfer tax on money left to grandchildren (over the $1 million exemption).

lifetime gift and estate exclusion you have a $675,000 exclusion from estate tax on your property in 2000 rising to $1 million in 2006.

Crummey Trust. You can put $10,000 a year into a *Crummey Trust* tax-free, just as you can give that amount away tax-free to an individual annually. Your heirs or beneficiaries are allowed to pull out dough within a certain period after you have established the trust. (We'll learn more about taxes and estates in Chapter 5.) The motive behind this type of trust is to keep your heirs, whether they are adults or minors, from sucking all the funds out at once. The trustees notify them when you make a contribution and typically they're free to withdraw the funds after a one- to three-month time frame if they choose. The key is to make sure your heirs get a written notice each year that they have the power to withdraw the funds.

generation-skipping trust allows married couples to save up to $2 million for their grandchildren and other generations, tax-free. For single people, the cut-off is $1 million. These savings are free of the 55% generation-skipping tax normally paid on gifts to grandchildren.

Land Trust. As property values around the country have escalated in the past decade, more and more property owners are opting to transfer their property to a kind of trust that is known as a conservation easement or *land trust*. The acreage can be as tiny as a single acre or encompass thousands of acres. It preserves open space and provides property owners with significant estate tax savings. Property is protected from future development when it is given to a land trust.

Crummey Trust allows you to give $10,000 a year tax-free but limits access to the funds for beneficiaries.

You have to show that the easement provides a public benefit such as preserving a habitat. You give up your rights to build on the property in a deed to a nonprofit charitable organization—in other words, the land trust. The value is then deducted from the market value of the land for estate tax purposes.

land trust allows you to transfer land into a trust that will protect the land from future development.

This is also considered a charitable donation that you can deduct from your income taxes. There is a limit set by the IRS on what you can deduct. Typically that's no more than 30 percent of your adjusted gross income in any one year, but you can carry the excess over for another five years. You can even put an easement into place after you've died by writing instructions into your will.

There are additional tax breaks up to as much as 40 percent of the land under easement that can be taken off the value of the land, with a cap of $500,000 in 2002. One caveat: The land must be near a city, national park, or wilderness area.

Clearly, setting up a trust can be complex, but it's worth considering depending on the size of your estate. In the next chapter we'll learn more about the nuances of estate taxes.

Estate
Planning and Taxes

Death and taxes. In a way, that's what this is all about, right? Probably the biggest motivator for anyone to draw up an estate plan is to stop good old Uncle Sam from getting his mitts on what you have worked your life to amass. And truly, taxes may be more of a factor than you even imagine.

It has been reported that:

✔ When Joe Robbie, founder and owner of the Miami Dolphins and Joe Robbie Stadium, died in 1990 his family was forced to sell its share of the team to pay estate taxes estimated at $47 million.

✔ William Paley founded CBS, but when he died in 1990 his estate had to sell its entire block of CBS stock to pay estate taxes.

The lion's share of estate plans are written to deal with one undeniable fact: Federal and state governments might impose a tax when you give property to another person upon your death. As we discussed earlier, your property consists of the current market value of your possessions ranging from cash to stocks, mutual funds, and other investments, including jewelry, automobiles, real estate, and more. In essence, whittling down an estate's exposure to taxes is frequently the ultimate goal of an estate plan.

TYPES OF TAXABLE PROPERTY

There are three kinds of *taxable property*:

1. Real property—a house, commercial real estate, raw land.
2. Tangible property—automobiles, paintings or other art work, jewelry.
3. Intangible property—securities such as stocks, bonds, and mutual funds; bank or brokerage accounts.

> **taxable property** this includes real property (a house, commercial real estate, or raw land), tangible property (autos, art, jewels), and intangible property (securities such as stocks, bonds, and mutual funds, and bank or brokerage accounts).

STEPPED-UP BASIS

The basis of inherited property is considered to be its value on the date of the owner's death. However, there is no tax due on the property appreciation during the owner's lifetime. Your heirs will then use the higher basis value to determine the gain when the property is eventually sold.

A good accountant should be able to help you design your road map to sidestep some of the more egregious tax implications. But remember, as Oprah lamented, the federal estate tax can run up to 60 percent on large estates. The marginal estate tax on a transfer of $10,000 is 18 percent. The rate on a transfer of $3 million is 55 percent.

SLASHING YOUR TAX BITE

For a married couple, the main deduction that will lessen any gift tax or estate transfer tax is the *marital deduction*. This deduction has no limits and lets one spouse transfer any or all property to the surviving spouse tax-free. Generally, your spouse must also be a U.S. citizen to take advantage of this deduction. That means that taxes are deferred until the surviving spouse dies.

marital deduction allows for the unlimited transfer of property from one spouse to another, generally free of estate or gift tax.

The other major tax break on estates is called the *Unified Credit*. Since 1987 every taxpayer has been allowed this credit, which results in an exemption from gift and estate taxes. The credit was set at $600,000 originally. However, under the 1997 Tax Act, that exclusion is being increased from $600,000 to $1 million over a 10-year period. The Unified Credit is sometimes referred to as an *applicable exclusion*.

Unified Credit also referred to as an applicable exclusion, this credit allows taxpayers an exemption from gift and estate taxes.

Why did Congress change the Unified Credit limits? Investments in securities, a rise in real estate values in many parts of the country, inflation, and other economic factors have meant that more and more U.S. taxpayers are being hit with hefty estate taxes, particularly second-to-die spouses who are liable for the whole tax burden on their estates. Constituents have complained bitterly to their representatives.

> **applicable exclusion** this is commonly called the Unified Credit to exclude from estate and gift tax up to $675,000 in 2000 and increasing to $1 million in 2006.

Nonetheless, Treasury officials say that very few people are directly hurt by federal estate taxes; they estimate that only 1.8 percent of Americans who die each year leave estates large enough to be taxed. This year estate tax revenues should be around $27 billion, up from $23 billion in 1999.

Table 1.1 shows how the estate-relief exclusion should play out going forward. But remember that if the Congress runs into budget snarls, it's always possible that legislators will eliminate those phase-in limits.

True, this increased credit will help millions of families avoid an estate tax, but that doesn't mean you should quit planning. Even with a slow rise in the inflation rate, a continued hardy stock market, and burgeoning self-directed retirement accounts such as 401(k) plans, that credit can be topped faster than you might fathom 20 years or so from now.

STATE DEATH TAXES

You have to plan for state death taxes in almost every state in the country. Regardless of where you live, though, your real property will be taxed only in the state where it is located. Your intangible property will be taxed in the state where you live at the time of your death. You will need to establish what is known as *domicile* to avoid being taxed in more than one state, though. For example, if you own homes in Florida and Maine, your estate could be subject to tax in each state if it is not spelled out clearly which is the primary state of residence. That usually means you need to live there for more than six months a year. However, across the country, many states have begun to change the laws on gift and estate taxes to keep residents from fleeing to low-tax states as they grow older.

> **domicile** a person's fixed, permanent, and principal residence for legal purposes.

To Establish Domicile

✔ Make sure you are registered to vote in the primary state.

✔ Check to see if the state requires a certificate of domicile.

✔ Get a driver's license in the state.

✔ Have your major bills and checks sent to your address there.

✔ Have most of your bank accounts in that state.

✔ File tax returns for that state.

State tax can often exceed federal tax. Under federal law, you are credited dollar for dollar what you pay in state death tax which can be as high as 16 percent. You'll want to refer to federal estate tax Form 706 for more information. There are two different types of taxes due, depending on where you live.

Inheritance Tax

This is owed on the portion each beneficiary receives, not the entire estate. Community property states usually opt for an *inheritance tax* on half of the community property when a spouse dies. You'll want to contact the state office for inheritance tax, typically listed under state agencies in the local phone book.

> **inheritance tax** tax owed on the portion each beneficiary receives, not the entire estate.

Estate Tax

This is what is due on the entire estate. This *estate tax* is levied instead of the inheritance tax in some states. Some states require both.

> **estate tax** tax due on the entire estate.

Life Insurance and State Death Tax

If the policy is paid out to the estate of the insured or your executor or creditor, it is taxed as property in many states. Some states do exempt life insurance payouts regardless of who the beneficiary is, but it varies from state to state.

ANNUAL GIFT TAX EXCLUSION

Taking advantage of the *annual gift tax exclusion* is probably the most basic move you can make when it comes to estate planning. You can give tax-free gifts of up to $10,000 per person to as many people as you want each calendar year. That amount is now indexed yearly for inflation. The gift can go to a child or anyone else. Donors don't pay tax on the amount, and your donee won't pay any tax on it, either. A married couple can each give $10,000 to each recipient for a nice $20,000 gift.

> **annual gift tax exclusion** allows you to give tax-free gifts of up to $10,000 per person each calendar year.

You must make the gift by December 31st each year. This gift is typically one of cash or securities. It's a yearly exclusion that does not interfere with your unified credit. Anything beyond that amount is considered a taxable gift, but that tax does not have to be paid until you as the donor exceed your lifetime unified credit. Then the rate of tax paid can range from 37 percent to 60 percent.

GIFT PLANNING AND TUITION BREAKS

Doling out for qualified tuition expenses for a child or grandchild has long been a popular tool. Done correctly, no gift tax is owed provided the tuition is paid straight to the institution itself. Moreover, these gifts do not interfere with your annual indexed $10,000 gift tax exclusion or your once-in-a-lifetime unified credit ($675,000 in 2000 and rising).

However, the 1997 tax law changes introduced several additional ways that can help reduce your taxable estate and take advantage of some income tax deductions straightaway.

Lifetime Learning Credit

Under the *Lifetime Learning credit*, you can deduct up to 20 percent of the first $5,000 that you spend on tuition and related expenses. The amount is set to double in 2002. But there are four caveats:

lifetime learning credit allows you to deduct up to 20 percent of the first $5,000 that you spend on tuition and related expenses.

1. The student must be yourself, your spouse, or a dependent child.
2. The tuition and expenses paid are deductible only if the student is enrolled at least half-time.

3. The tuition must be paid to a degree or certified program. This type of program generally has a full-time faculty and a consistent enrolled student body size.

4. Your *adjusted gross income (AGI)* must be under $80,000 for the full credit on a joint tax return and $40,000 on an individual return. At that level, the credit begins to phase out. Earn an AGI of $100,000 or more on a joint return and $50,000 on an individual return, and you don't qualify at all.

adjusted gross income (AGI) this is your taxable income minus any deductions for IRAs, Keogh plans, alimony payments and other deductions.

HOPE Scholarship Credit

You can now claim a tax credit of up to $1,500 each tax year for a student's tuition and other educational costs. These limits are to increase with the inflation rate after next year.

HOPE credit allows you to claim a tax credit of up to $1,500 each tax year for a student's tuition and other educational costs.

To qualify for a *HOPE credit*:

1. The expenses must be incurred during the first two years of postsecondary education. And the school must be able to take part in the U.S. Department of Education's student aid program.

2. You are ineligible for a Lifetime Learning credit if you opt for the HOPE credit, and vice versa.

3. Your adjusted gross income (AGI) must be under $80,000 for the full credit on a joint tax return and $40,000 on an individ-

ual return. After that, the credit begins to phase out. You don't qualify at all if you earn an AGI of $100,000 or more on a joint return and $50,000 on an individual return.

Education Individual Retirement Accounts

An *education individual retirement account (IRA)* lets you set aside up to $500 each year to put in the account. Unlike a traditional IRA, you can't deduct the funds from your current tax return. But the account will grow tax-free. You can make tax-free distributions to pay for certain educational expenses like college or graduate school tuition, room and board, and books. Otherwise, if you pull the funds out, you will be slapped with a 10 percent penalty and pay income tax on the funds as well.

education individual retirement account (IRA) lets you set aside up to $500 each year to pay for certain educational expenses.

1. To qualify for the full amount, your AGI can't be over $150,000 on a joint return. It's phased out completely at $160,000. For single filers, the sum is phased out between $95,000 and $110,000.

2. If you pay into a qualified state tuition program, you can't set aside money in an education IRA for the same person in the same year.

3. Again, you can't have it all. You must select one of the three tax benefits.

MEDICAL EXPENSES AND TAXES

It's also possible to pay out an unlimited amount for a family member's medical bills without taking away from your $10,000 gift exclusion. Doing so can help a family member in need who doesn't have the means to pay off medical bills or maybe even the ability to get treatment if he or she is lacking insurance or proper funds. For those of you who want to reduce the size of an estate, and make sure your money goes to something worthy and not the state or federal coffers, it is worth looking into. You must, however, pay the tab directly to the medical institution as you do with educational gifts.

GENERATION-SKIPPING TRANSFER TAX (GSTT)

The *generation-skipping transfer tax* is a flat 55 percent, but the good news is that each donor has a $1 million exemption that is indexed annually for inflation, then rounded to the closest multiple of $10,000. This exclusion is the sum you can gift to your grandchildren either directly or through a trust without being taxed on that amount.

generation-skipping transfer tax (GSTT) there is a 55 percent tax applied to transfers to grandchildren or following generations.

CONCLUSION

When it comes to estate planning and taxes, things can get darn complicated and convoluted. In the meantime, Congress is forever fiddling with the tax code in this area. While some of the basic tools are fairly easy to grasp, such as the marital deduction and annual gift tax exclusion, much of it is tough for the layman to handle alone.

Look for good professional advice to help you tackle this central need of estate planning. The larger your estate, the more in need of sound, up-to-date advice you'll be. And remember, don't underestimate the potential size of your estate in future years. We'll learn more about estate taxes as they apply to small or closely held business succession in Chapter 8.

Chapter 6

Settling an Estate

W hile getting started with estate planning is the focus of this book, you can't write a book about the topic and not address the issue of how to settle an estate. You want the process to be as painless as possible for all involved.

If you have ever been called on to be the executor of an estate, you'll know what I mean when I say it can be really panic-inducing and stomach-churning to boot. The main reason you are reading this book—to learn how to get started with an estate plan—is that you want to be sure when you go the folks you leave behind will not have a hard time of it. You want them to be able to enjoy what you have left for them as quickly and with as little hassle as possible.

What you will learn in this chapter are estate planning basics that will help you understand why your plan is so important and what things you need to have in place to avoid any problems. When you figure that about $143 billion is expected to shift hands in 2000—up from $84 billion five years earlier—and that by 2040 baby boomers are expected to inherit more than $10 trillion from their parents, according to a Cornell University study, you get the picture. There are going to be millions of convoluted estates that many of us are going to be faced with unraveling.

Here's how it all starts. The phone rings after midnight. It startles you, and the message is not what you want to hear. A loved one has died—a parent, a sibling, or a dear friend. The person may have been ill and in some ways it is a relief that the pain is ended. Or it could be a complete shock. But the bottom line is that there is now an estate that must be handled. Don't be put off by the work that lies ahead. Depending on the estate, the process can be complex or relatively straightforward.

Settling an estate in essence means ensuring the smooth, legal transfer of assets after someone's death according to the decedent's wishes. It entails handling tax issues and other legal requirements both for federal and state purposes. It's the way of gathering assets, detailing all account inventories, paying any debts owed, handling the administrative paperwork, and finally passing on what property remains to the proper heirs and beneficiaries with the proper titles.

settling an estate ensuring the legal transfer of assets after someone's death, according to their wishes.

Settling an estate requires figuring out taxes due, poring through paperwork to locate all the assets, finding and reading the will, and much more. If you have been named executor, or person appointed in the will to manage the estate, this can be a very time-consuming experience. Chances are you are a member of the family or a close friend, but you could be a professional, such as an attorney, who was trusted to make things easy for the survivors. For you, this can be a day-to-day management job.

THE INITIAL TASKS

You may worry that if you don't get cracking on day one that the estate may somehow be penalized with extra taxes and penalties. But in reality, the only big deadline to meet is to file an estate tax return for any estate with assets over $675,000. And you have nine months after the date of the death to do so.

Legal and Financial Documents

Locate the key legal and financial papers. If you are lucky, they will be all together in a safe place that you were informed of. Unfortunately, that rarely happens, and you'll have to do some sleuthing. Here's the information that you will need to have on hand. The documents should be originals or certified copies.

First is the will. Locate it and read it. Make sure it is signed and the signature is legitimate. If you can't find it, look through papers for the name of an attorney who could have drafted it. You might be able to track down a canceled check or number in an address book. The attorney typically keeps an original copy of the will in his or her office safe. If it is stored in a safe-deposit box, you will need to have your name on the box in order to retrieve it without some legal wrangling.

Other documents to locate:

✔ Power of attorney.

✔ Documents for trusts the person has set up.

✔ Tax returns from the past five years.

✔ Most recent W-2 forms from the person's employer and 1099 forms.

✔ Records of retirement accounts—401(k)s, IRAs, pensions, profit sharing.

✔ All insurance policies, including homeowners, auto, health, life, and disability.

✔ Current statements for bank and brokerage accounts.

✔ Mutual fund holding statements.

✔ The deed to any property owned, such as a home, or lease agreement.

✔ Any business partnership agreements and company records.

✔ Birth certificates for the deceased.

✔ Marriage certificate.

✔ Divorce papers, if applicable.

✔ Adoption papers for any beneficiaries, if applicable.

✔ Social Security card or number.

✔ List of credit cards and names under which they are listed.

✔ Title to automobile, or lease and loan information.

✔ Motor vehicle and/or boat registration documents.

✔ Most recent mortgage statements and other loan papers.

✔ Receipts for major purchases.

✔ Warranties.

✔ Prenuptial or postnuptial agreements.

✔ Inventory of a safe-deposit box if one exists.

✔ Inventory of the estate's assets.

✔ Death certificate.

Advisory Team

Make appointments to meet with the key team of advisers:

✔ *Attorney.* The lawyer most likely can handle the lion's share of settling the estate.

✔ *Accountant.* This pro can prepare the estate tax and income tax returns and help keep the tax burden to a minimum.

✔ *Financial adviser and/or broker.* They can help track down financial assets held by the estate and plan future moves for beneficiaries—who might include yourself.

✔ *Insurance agent.* The agent can provide the originals of any policies.

Government Offices

- ✔ State office for inheritance tax.
- ✔ Social Security Administration (800-772-1213).
- ✔ The U.S. Department of Veterans Affairs (if it applies).
- ✔ The state motor vehicle department.

Other Contacts

- ✔ Mortgage bank or company and other lenders.
- ✔ Credit card companies.
- ✔ Banks and brokerage firms.
- ✔ Utility companies.
- ✔ Clubs and associations.

You may be able to get help from other friends and family members to handle all these calls, but plan to go it alone. The load of settling your parent's, spouse's, sibling's, or friend's estate may be entirely up to you, so brace yourself. You're in charge and will need to follow the terms of the will and adhere to state law.

THE PROBATE PROCESS

Next, file the will with a probate court and make sure the court certifies by a written document that you are the representative of the estate. Probate is the process that distributes property according to the terms of a will.

What Does Probate Mean?

The word "probate" does sound a bit off-putting. It's derived from the Latin word "probare," meaning "to approve." Before property can be distributed to the beneficiaries and heirs, a special court—called a probate court—must review the will to make sure it's authentic. If someone dies without a will, the court will appoint an administrator to review and distribute assets as the court's administrator sees fit.

The probate merry-go-round begins when you file the deceased's original will at the court that has local jurisdiction over probate concerns. Here's the goal of the process:

First, to certify the domicile, or home, of the deceased to make sure that state and court have proper jurisdiction over the will.

Second, to prove that the will was in fact the last will signed.

Third, to give the executor the authority to act for the estate.

As the executor, you will be peppered with questions about the materials you have gathered—from Social Security numbers to the names of financial advisers. The court may need to contact certain lawyers associated with the estate or advisers and will need telephone numbers for them.

What Will It Cost?

The cost of probate varies, depending on the assets in the estate and how complicated the issues are.

When Elvis Presley died, for instance, in August 1977, his gross estate was figured at $10,165,434. After his 13-page will, signed March 3, 1977, was admitted to probate in August of that year and run through the process, the settlement costs shrunk his estate to a mere $2,790,799. Talk about *shrinkage*. Elvis is an extreme example, but worth noting.

shrinkage the sum of assets or property that will be whittled away due to the costs of the estate's settlement.

Most likely there will be attorney fees. A lawyer is usually not required for a will to be probated, but unless you are up to speed on the issues, you should consult one. This is usually the biggest chunk—say, 2 percent to 3 percent of the total value of the estate—so make sure you ask up front what he or she may charge.

These are some of the other fees you can expect:

✔ Probate court filing fees.

✔ Executor fees.

✔ Accounting fees.

✔ Appraisal fees.

How Long Will It Take?

People recoil in horror about probate, fearing that it is a lengthy and expensive process. How long the process takes will vary as well, again depending on how organized the estate plan was and the size of the estate. It can take months and sometimes years after the death. When the court is happy that no one is challenging the will—or that there is no will—property can be distributed. That's when the court determines that the estate is settled.

How Public Is Probate?

The probate process does require a full listing of all the deceased's assets and liabilities, and that listing is generally open to the public to read. If you have a revocable trust, as mentioned earlier (Chapter 4), you can retain your rights to privacy.

What Assets Must Go through Probate Court?

Assets may be considered probate or nonprobate. Nonprobate assets do not need to pass through probate court and pass directly to survivors and beneficiaries. In most states, if the estate consists solely of nonprobate assets and there are no children under 18 involved, you can skip probate court entirely.

Here are nonprobate assets:

- ✔ Life insurance payouts.
- ✔ Property held in a living trust set up during the deceased's lifetime.
- ✔ Retirement plan benefits from a 401(k), IRA, or traditional pension when there are named beneficiaries. (If the estate is the beneficiary or the beneficiary has died and a new one not selected, the estate will go through the probate process.)
- ✔ Property held in *joint tenancy with right of survivorship*. (At the death of a co-owner, the other becomes the sole property owner.)
- ✔ Savings bonds that are payable to a named beneficiary or co-owned with a survivor.
- ✔ Any earnings or leftover vacation or sick pay owed by one's employer and not yet paid can skip probate in most states.
- ✔ Automatic death transfer accounts that are usually offered by mutual fund companies.

joint tenancy with right of survivorship type of title placed on property that is co-owned. At the death of a co-owner, the other will become the sole property owner.

What this means is that if the estate consists of a house that is jointly held or co-owned, a life insurance policy, and a 401(k) plan, none of the assets would require probate.

Probate can take time. There are some actions you as executor can take to keep the process moving along as rapidly as possible.

✔ Keep tidy records.

✔ Get permission from the court to spend the estate's funds to pay expenses.

✔ Keep the court updated on what property you have located or received and what expenses you have had to spend from the estate for legal fees and the like.

✔ Meet with the deceased's bank manager. If the individual had an account in his or her name alone (e.g., Jay Jones), it should be changed to an account called "The Estate of Jay Jones, Deceased." Your name should be listed as the executor. You'll need to have a Social Security number to secure an estate tax identification number, which you can then use as the bank account number. Deposit all income from the estate's assets under the new number, and pay all estate administration expenses (such as the funeral cost) from this account. The key is that if checks come in payable to the deceased, you as the executor can endorse them and deposit them in the estate's account. Any joint accounts should be transferred into the account name of the survivor.

✔ If the deceased's bank is not convenient, you should select a bank that is near you and the attorney. Select one that has low fees and minimum balances. This is a temporary account, after all, and there is no reason to have the assets chewed up by unnecessary bank charges.

✔ Contact stockbrokers and ask them to change any joint accounts into the survivor's name, depending on what trusts you have established. You'll need to show a death certificate and affidavit of domicile (the stockbroker has a blank affadavit form on file that you complete at that time, or your executor does), and a letter of request with the Social Security number of the survivor.

✔ Change any accounts held in the deceased's name solely to the estate's account.

✔ Request a value on the assets in the accounts—both joint and individual—at the time of the death. The estate taxes will be based on that valuation.

✔ If there are minor children named as beneficiaries, set up individual bank accounts for them.

✔ Contact creditors and inform them of the death. Do not feel that you need to pay them right away. Creditors have three or four months in which to file claims. Once a formal claim has been made, you can pay the creditor. Don't make a payment until you legally must, though. You may find you have additional taxes or even lawsuits that will sap the estate's assets.

✔ Have appraisals done of any estate property if you don't already have one in hand.

✔ Monitor the filing of all tax returns—income, estate, and inheritance.

✔ Get court approval to distribute any assets.

✔ Distribute the estate's assets.

✔ Prepare a detailed accounting to the court and be fully accountable for it.

ESTATE DEBTS AND TAXES

Keep track of legal and accounting expenses related to settling the estate. They may be tax-deductible. Debts that are incurred in just the deceased's name are the estate's responsibilities alone.

Here are the tax returns you will probably need to file to settle the estate:

✔ *Form 706, U.S. Estate Tax Return.* This is filed only for gross estates over $675,000 in 2000 and increasing to $1 million in 2006. This return is to be filed within nine months of the date of death. You may be able to file for an extension.

You will need to include a certified copy of the death certificate, a copy of the will (typically certified by the probate court), property appraisals, life insurance statements listed on IRS Form 712, and state treasury department statements that all death and inheritance taxes have been paid.

✔ *Form 1040, U.S. Individual Income Tax Return.* This form is filed for earnings and investment income that the deceased accumulated during the year up to the date of death. The return for that year must be filed with the Internal Revenue Service by April 15 of the following year. "Deceased" must be inserted after the name, along with the date of death.

If it's your spouse who died, you may file a joint tax return for the year in which he or she died and pay under a joint filer's tax rate. On the line where you sign the return, you must indicate in writing that you are filing as a surviving spouse. The following year, you may file as a single taxpayer. Or, if you have a dependent child, you may file as a qualifying widow or widower for two years, and after that as head of household.

✔ *Form 1041, Income Tax Return for Estates and Trusts.* This is to report income generated from someone's assets after the person has died.

DISTRIBUTING THE ESTATE

After you have paid all the claims and taxes on the estate and any debts are wiped clean, you are ready to distribute what's left. Once this is completed according to the instructions in the will or probate court, you must file a precise accounting with the court of the entire administration and paperwork you have handled. At that point, the court considers the estate settled.

ESTATE PLANNING MOVES AFTER DEATH

Often relatives and beneficiaries feel that the estate needs to be distributed in a more fair fashion. You might even want to protect certain estate assets from creditors or lower taxes. There are a few ways to handle those changes even after someone has died and has a legitimate will.

- ✔ *Homestead exemption.* Some states allow a house and land to be designated as a homestead. When the head passes on, the *homestead exemption* enables the surviving spouse and children to be exempt from estate taxes and claims by creditors on the property itself.

- ✔ *Spouse's election against the will.* *Election against the will by the surviving spouse* lets the surviving spouse receive at least the amount of property determined by state statute if he or she has been left less than that amount in the will.

- ✔ *Family settlement agreement.* As informal as it can be, this allows all the heirs to redistribute the estate in a fashion they all agree upon.

- ✔ *Alternative value date.* This method lets you figure the value of an estate six months after the date of death for federal estate tax purposes, unless the property has already been sold or passed along (if it has been, it must be valued at the date of death). The *alternative value date* method can be a big help if assets have depreciated after the date of death.

homestead exemption when house and land have been designated as a homestead, the surviving spouse and children are exempt from state taxes and claims by creditors on the property itself.

election against the will by the surviving spouse
lets the surviving spouse receive at least the amount of
property determined by state statute.

✔ *Installment payments of estate tax under Section 6166.* This
section of the Internal Revenue Code allows for estate tax payments to be paid in installments if the deceased had an interest
in a closely held business that was considered part of the estate. The total value of the business must equal more than 35
percent of the adjusted gross assets to qualify.

alternative value date lets you figure the value of an
estate six months after the date of death for federal
estate tax purposes, unless the property has already
been sold or passed along.

EXECUTOR'S ESSENTIAL CHECKLIST

1. Obtain death certificate and make at least a dozen copies.
2. Make funeral arrangements if necessary.
3. Help with burial arrangements and obituary.
4. Get funeral receipts.
5. Discuss handling of mail and make arrangements.
6. Notify bank and other financial institutions.
7. Locate and read will.
8. Meet with an attorney.
9. Estimate assets and liabilities.

10. Go to the Registry of Wills office and probate will.

11. Call life insurance agent and request claim forms.

12. Survivors should redraft their wills.

13. Arrange for property appraisals.

14. File both federal and state tax returns.

15. Pay bills.

16. Make claims for retirement benefits for survivors.

17. Open a bank account for the estate.

18. File asset inventory and valuation with court.

CONCLUSION

With a dollop of luck and some sensible planning, you may sail through the process of settling an estate. You may be able to avoid probate altogether. But even if you don't, you have four months from the time you're named executor to file that asset inventory and valuation with the court. You have a year at the earliest to file an exact accounting of the estate's assets. Until the estate settles, you'll have to file that accounting every 12 months.

Before you agree to be the executor, make sure you have a solid idea of the inventory of the estate and are not going to be compromised by personal and family conflicts in your ability to carry out the job. You're placing yourself in a trusted position, so think hard before you sign on.

Chapter

7

IRAs and
Estate Planning

W hat's estate planning all about? By now you know it's about distributing your assets when you're gone and making sure as much of your estate as possible gets to your heirs and beneficiaries and not the tax collector.

So what's your biggest asset? You'll probably say your house. But for many Americans that is simply not the case these days. We have large chunks of our assets in *individual retirement accounts (IRAs)*. Will your IRA outlive you? Probably.

> **individual retirement account (IRA)** a tax-deferred pension plan that allows you to invest in an account that is tax-free until you withdraw the money at retirement.

Confusion regarding IRA inheritance is rampant. There are myriad complications and qualifications that can impact how the money is eventually distributed. As your IRA grows, it needs to be coordinated with good estate planning. After all, what good is building a million-plus IRA if the government takes more than 70 percent of that after you die?

The typical IRA is an account that has been designed to encourage people to save. It is a tax-deferred pension plan that allows you to invest $2,000 annually ($4,000 if married filing jointly) in an account that is tax-free until you withdraw the money at retirement. There is a penalty for removing the funds before age $59\frac{1}{2}$, and you must start withdrawing the money by age $70\frac{1}{2}$.

Assets in IRAs have ballooned as people have changed jobs or retired and rolled over employer-sponsored pension plans such as 401(k) plans into these accounts. About one-third of American households own at least one IRA. More and more of them now contain sums in the six digits plus.

That isn't a bad nest egg for your retirement, and often these money pots are more than enough to get you through your golden years. As a result, if you are fortunate to have enough for your own retirement security, you might want to find a way to use estate-planning techniques to make sure that what you don't need doesn't get gobbled up by taxes and to ensure all that loot you've accumulated goes to your child or grandchild. Some studies have shown that taxes on a hefty retirement account can exceed 90 percent.

So tax-deferred savings plans are perfect when left to a surviving spouse. That said, if they are left to one of your adult children, your heir will be required to pay income tax on the IRA. If the IRA is worth $1 million and they are in the top 39.6 percent tax bracket that tax bill would soar to $396,000.

In truth, even if you have a modest account and you die unexpectedly, your survivors could find that more of your savings will go to the tax collector than to their accounts. The point: You can't take it with you, but you can cushion the tax blow.

EXAMINE YOUR BENEFICIARY OPTIONS

Who inherits the IRA? If you die before you run through those savings, the money might not go to your chosen heir. Why? Money in an IRA goes to the individual who is listed on the account's beneficiary form. Every IRA account requires you to name a beneficiary. Most people select their spouse or a close relative. You file the form when you open the account. And as the years go by, it's easy to forget who you even listed on the form. The person may not even be alive. You may be divorced from the individual. You may have a child you would rather name as beneficiary. You may have a new spouse. You may not even remember ever selecting someone, and indeed you might not have.

It doesn't matter who you name in your will to inherit the assets. What rules is the person who is listed as your beneficiary on that form, because a beneficiary designation for an IRA takes precedence over a will. That means that when you die, your retirement account assets are paid to your named beneficiaries, period. So while you might remember to rewrite your will with changes in your family circumstances, the odds are good that you have completely zoned out on renaming your IRA beneficiaries.

It really isn't hard to take care of this. You call the fund company or financial institution that you have your IRA invested with and ask it to send the paperwork. You make your changes and mail the form back. Nowadays, many companies will let you do this online and then mail you a confirmation for your file.

If your estate is fairly modest and your spouse needs the entire IRA to live on, then name your spouse as beneficiary. Otherwise, consider naming your children or grandchildren as beneficiaries. You can also split your IRA to name your spouse beneficiary on $600,000 and your children as beneficiary on $400,000 with a $1 million IRA. As a general rule, the larger your estate, the less likely it is that your spouse should be named as beneficiary on the entire sum.

Here are questions to ask yourself:

✔ How old is my spouse? The older your spouse, the less of the IRA she or he will need to inherit.

✔ Will my spouse have his or her own IRA or pension plan to live on?

✔ Will my spouse need to tap the IRA for medical care?

✔ Will my spouse inherit money from a parent or relative that will ensure financial security?

✔ Will my spouse remarry and rename the beneficiaries?

✔ Do I have a child or relative with special needs who could benefit from my IRA assets after I'm gone?

✔ Will I lose my estate tax exemption by passing it all directly to my spouse?

If your account isn't substantial, you can handle all this yourself. It's a no-brainer. But if you're one of those lucky Americans with a fat nest egg, you will probably need professional advice to help you figure out how to divide your assets. That's the basic issue.

IRA WAR STORIES

Ed Slott, a Rockville Centre, New York, certified public accountant who specializes in IRAs and publishes a newsletter, "Ed Slott's IRA Advisor," offers this tale:

The husband died young at age 62. At death he had a $300,000 IRA with a broker. He left over $500,000 of life insurance to his wife. She was 56. The wife was named as the primary beneficiary on the IRA. The four children were named on the IRA beneficiary designation form as contingent beneficiaries. The deceased husband/father was meticulous and had all the beneficiary forms filled out properly, something almost no one does. The children ranged in age from 24 to 35 years old. Immediately after death, the broker set up a spousal IRA rollover account for the wife, moved the husband's $300,000 IRA to that account, and told the wife she could treat it as her own IRA. All other assets passed estate tax–free to the wife, including the home. The wife also had substantial assets of her own.

The Result

A valuable tax exemption was completely lost. Everything the husband owned passed to the wife estate tax–free, but this was not the best tax plan in the long run. The husband (who died in 1997) did not use his $600,000 estate tax exemption because all of his property went to his wife, who really didn't need it.

The IRA is now growing tax-deferred, not tax-free, in the wife's name and will one day be taxed on the wife's estate.

If the wife lives her normal life expectancy, she will live another 30 years. She won't have to withdraw from the IRA until $70^1/_2$. At even a modest rate of return, that IRA should be worth close to $2 million at her death. When added to approximately $2.5 million of other assets, it will be subject to a 55 percent estate tax. The children will wind up with about $1 million. The value of the lost estate tax exemption will be $235,000. If the children had been left the $300,000 IRA to withdraw over their life expectancy of an average of 50 years, the IRA would have been worth over $5 million, estate tax–free.

The Lesson

The wife should have disclaimed her right to the IRA. For the disclaimer to be effective, you must do that within nine months of the date of death. If she had disclaimed it, the husband's $600,000 estate tax exemption could have kicked in and the children would have gained access to the IRA and could have used it or kept it growing tax-deferred over their lives.

Mistakes like this are common. It's a minefield. And the rules keep changing. But letting an IRA live on should be a goal of a good estate plan.

NAMING YOUR BENEFICIARY

Anyone can be a beneficiary. Your spouse may not need the money or may have his or her own IRAs, or maybe there are other assets in the estate that your spouse would be better off inheriting rather than the IRAs. Anyone who inherits an IRA will pay the income tax as the person draws down.

In general, if you fail to name a beneficiary, your estate is the beneficiary. That means that the entire IRA is subject to income taxes when you die. If your spouse, however, is the executor of your estate, the IRS may allow the money to be rolled into a spousal IRA. Ultimately, the IRA is eventually going to be subject to income tax because the distributions are considered to be income, unless it's a *Roth IRA*. If your spouse is under $59^1/_2$, withdrawals are generally considered to be taxable as income, but if withdrawals come from a deceased spouse's IRA, they will not be subject to the 10 percent penalty that is normally charged for early withdrawals.

Roth IRA individual retirement account in which your contributions are not deductible, but are tax-free when withdrawn at retirement.

If a surviving spouse rolls the IRA into one that is in his or her own name and tries to make withdrawals before age $59^1/_2$, there will be a 10 percent penalty assessed. So it does usually make sense to keep the funds in the deceased spouse's IRA and withdraw as need be, depending on the size of the widow or widower's assets.

Beneficiaries who are not spouses cannot roll inherited IRAs into IRA accounts in their own names. As soon as you do that, the entire amount becomes taxable, according to CPA Ed Slott.

The Roth IRA is an individual retirement account in which your contributions are not deductible, but when you withdraw in retirement they are tax-free. You can make nondeductible contributions up to $2,000 to a Roth IRA; earnings and withdrawals are never taxed if the account has been open five years and you meet other conditions. The contribution is phased out for single filers with adjusted gross income (AGI) of $95,000 to $110,000, and $150,000 to $160,000 for couples.

ESTATE PLANNING ADVANTAGES OF A ROTH IRA

Unlike a traditional IRA that makes retirees withdraw money starting at age $70^1/_2$, the Roth has no required distribution, and you can even continue to contribute if you meet the income criteria. The accounts can compound explosively for an heir. You can name a child or a grandchild as your Roth beneficiary, and the heir can withdraw the balance tax-free over one's life expectancy, starting December 31 the year following your death, or can cash out completely within five years.

A traditional IRA left to anyone but a spouse has the same distribution rules. In contrast, though, the money is taxed as income to the beneficiary.

The proceeds of both traditional and Roth IRAs are subject to estate tax. As I mentioned earlier, today $675,000 of inherited property is exempt from federal estate taxes. Above that, the tax can climb to 55 percent of assets over $3 million. That exemption will rise to $1 million by 2006.

Someone nearing retirement or already retired might want to consider converting a traditional IRA to a Roth if adjusted gross income is $100,000 or less. The stumbling block is that you must pay income tax on any earnings or tax-free contributions in your existing IRA. And if you are converting a large sum, that can hurt.

Because you report the proceeds from the existing IRA as taxable income, that can push you into a higher tax bracket for that year or prevent you from taking advantage of other tax breaks. Nevertheless, for young investors, the decades of tax-free growth and ultimate tax-free distributions from a Roth should more than make up for paying some taxes now.

You can run the numbers with software like T. Rowe Price's $9.95 IRA Analyzer (call 800-333-0740) or calculators on web sites offered by mutual fund companies such as Fidelity Investment (www.fidelity.com),

Vanguard (www.vanguard.com), Strong Funds (www.strongfunds.com), or brokers such as Charles Schwab (www.schwab.com). If you don't have a personal computer, call the fund company 800-number and ask for a worksheet.

BENEFICIARY OPTIONS

So who gets the assets when you die? Many mutual fund companies are making it easier for you to customize your beneficiary designations. For example, Vanguard (800-523-7708) has five beneficiary designations offered for its IRA and 403(b) accounts, which can be valuable estate-planning tools. (A 403(b) is a plan similar to a 401(k) plan that is set up for public employees and nonprofit organization workers.)

1. ***Per stirpes.*** This option divides your assets equally among your children. If one of your children dies before you, that child's share is divided equally among his or her own children.

2. ***Per capita.*** This method divides your IRA assets equally among your children and the descendants of any child who dies before you. So if one of your three daughters dies before you, each of her children will receive a share equal to that of your other two daughters.

3. ***"All My Children."*** This divides your account proceeds equally among your surviving children only. The children of a deceased child will not receive any of your IRA.

4. ***Designation with disclaimer.*** You can select a primary beneficiary, an alternative beneficiary, and a secondary beneficiary. The alternative receives funds from your IRA if the primary beneficiary disclaims or renounces any claim to all or a portion of the assets. The secondary beneficiary receives the assets only if the primary beneficiary dies before the account owners. So your spouse could disclaim all or some of the assets and allow them to pass to the alternative beneficiary.

5. *Designation with a 30-day contingency.* With this designation, you select a primary beneficiary who is to receive your assets provided he or she survives you by at least 30 days. A secondary beneficiary receives the assets only if the primary beneficiary does not survive you by at least 30 days.

Check with the financial institution that holds your IRA to see if it has special designations to help you organize your beneficiary options.

WHAT IF THE BENEFICIARY IS A MINOR?

A minor is typically considered to be someone under the age of 18, but the age can be as low as 16 in some states. This can get tricky. If you die and your three children are named as beneficiaries, they can open three new IRA accounts, but they should be titled "Harry Hackel Sr. IRA, deceased July 1, 2000, for the benefit of Harry Hackel Jr." and so on. The children's Social Security numbers must also be listed on the new accounts.

You can also name a trust as the beneficiary for a minor child. If so, you will want to amend you beneficiary form to state that the money be transferred under the *Uniform Gifts to Minors Act (UGMA)* or *Uniform Transfers to Minors Act (UTMA)*, with a custodian selected by the executor of your will. You should deal with a trust or estate attorney who is familiar with IRA distribution rules. This is still a relatively new field, and it's unlikely you'll get enough information from software or books to handle all the nuances on your own. IRA trusts are clearly not for everyone. But if you are leaving your IRA to a minor who will need help managing the IRA funds, *custodial accounts* are worth looking into.

Both UTMA and UGMA accounts can consist of cash, mutual funds, shares of stock, and bonds. The UTMA account lets you transfer property, life insurance, and pension funds to a minor child. Opening an account is fairly straightforward. Your bank or financial institution—say, a mutual fund company—will send you a form to fill out. An adult must be named as custodian. You might choose your spouse or a close relative.

Uniform Gifts to Minors Act (UGMA) this act allows certain types of property to be gifted to minors without creating a trust. Legally the child is the sole owner of the property although the adult is the custodian.

The custodian then has the power to invest the funds and withdraw the money as he or she sees fit for the sake of the child. Any income earned by the account is taxed at the child's rate. When the child reaches the age of majority—usually 18—he or she receives the funds from the account. Be aware, though, that if you are both the donor and the custodian for the account and you die before your child is of age, that money might be considered as part of your taxable estate.

Uniform Transfers to Minors Act (UTMA) same theory as UGMA, but allows any kind of property to be transferred—personal, tangible and intangible.

If you don't have the UTMA clause on your beneficiary claim, in some states the court must approve any investment changes that a guardian might want to make to the account. Make sure that you have a copy of the form from the financial institution that has been marked received and dated and that your executor has a copy as well.

If you have or anticipate a very large IRA, get expert help. Working out the distributions and tax consequences to your heirs' best advantage is key.

MORE IRA PITFALLS

Failure to Deduct Estate Taxes

A beneficiary of an IRA may neglect to deduct any estate taxes on the IRA from his or her own income tax bill. If the money is subject to a federal estate tax and the person chooses to take the money and run, your beneficiary is able to deduct that tax from his or her own federal income tax.

Forgetting to File a Distribution Method

Any beneficiary who is not your spouse should file a distribution method with the IRA custodian and the IRS by December 31 of the year after the death. If you as the deceased IRA owner hadn't reached the required beginning date (RBD) for taking your distributions (April 1 of the year after you turn $70^1/_2$, your nonspouse beneficiary has a choice of draining the IRA within five years or taking distributions over his or her life expectancy.

If the IRA owner dies after his or her RBD and the beneficiary is a nonspouse, then distributions must begin by December 31 of the year following the year of the IRA owner's death. There is no five-year rule available when the IRA owner dies after his or her RBD.

If nothing is filed for a distribution method, the five-year rule is in place. But the election has to be in writing. You can speed up distributions if you need to, but make that clear in writing from the start if you opt for the life expectancy method.

NAMING A CHARITY AS BENEFICIARY

Since taxes at death on substantial IRAs can eat up more than 70 percent of their value, leaving your beneficiaries with a fraction of the balance, it might make sense to leave a part of your IRA to a charity. The main advantage is that no estate tax or income tax will be due. But as always, the rules are complex. Often, IRA owners will split the IRA into separate accounts. A $1 million IRA could be divided so a spouse gets 70 percent and a favorite charity gets 30 percent.

Charitable contributions of IRA assets offer significant opportunities for tax savings as part of an overall estate plan. But again the main issue is figuring out the required minimum distributions and stretching them out to your heirs' benefits.

IN SUM

Learning to integrate your IRA into your estate plan today is paramount. Multimillion-dollar IRAs are increasingly common, so spend time understanding the importance of naming beneficiaries and making the transfers of funds as seamless as possible with as much going to your loved ones or charities as possible.

Chapter

Estate Planning for Family Businesses

state taxes have been a horror for family-owned businesses for years. But changes of the 1997 tax act were designed to help these closely held businesses stay afloat. The goal was to help keep many small businesses in the family and avoid liquidation to pay onerous estate taxes.

While passing a business from one generation to the next is something we all want, if you don't plan accordingly, your heir's new partner is Uncle Sam. And in fact, the value of your business could be the lion's share of your estate. If you don't plan ahead for a potential estate-tax hit, your family could lose the business, or have to sell it for far less than it's worth just to pay the tax.

To qualify as a *family business*, the business must be owned at least 50 percent by one family, 70 percent by two families, or 90 percent by three families. When you die, your family must not own less than 30 percent of the business. Members of your family are your ancestors and lineal descendants of you or your spouse, or the spouse of any lineal descendant.

family business legal designation of a business that must be owned at least 50 percent by one family, 70 percent by two families, or 90 percent by three families.

THE LATEST TAX LAWS

Family-owned businesses can now shelter up to $1.3 million in assets from estate taxes. The prior law limited that amount to $750,000. But the executor must elect for "qualified family-owned business interests." Moreover, the assets must make up more than 50 percent of the decedent's estate. Then the value of those business interests can be excluded from the gross estate up to that $1.3 million, which exceeds the estate tax exemption. (A married couple can exclude $2.6 million.) In 2000, the estate tax exemption is $675,000. So, in 2000, a maximum exemption of $625,000 ($1.3 million minus $675,000) of small business interests can be excluded from the taxable estate. The exclusion for family businesses is fixed, so as the standard estate tax exclusion or unified credit rises, the benefit for family businesses falls (see Table 8.1).

TABLE 8.1 Family Business Exclusion of $1.3 Million Minus the Unified Credit Exclusion	
Year	Exclusion
2000	$625,000
2001	$625,000
2002	$600,000
2003	$600,000
2004	$450,000
2005	$350,000
2006	$300,000

Still following me? There's more.

To qualify for the exclusion, the business must be owned for five of the eight years prior to the decedent's death by the decedent or his or her family. Then, the heirs are required to participate in the business and are taxed on any interests sold within a 10-year period following the death. So if your son agrees to run your business, but leaves after five years, your widow will be left with a hefty tax bill that might be worth more than the business is all together.

You can leave the business to your spouse to take advantage of the marital deduction. But if he or she passes it on to the next generation, there will be a tax.

In essence, it might be easier just to purchase a *second-to-die life insurance* policy. The goal of these life insurance policies is to make sure there is enough cash available to pay estate taxes. The premiums are calculated on two life expectancies rather than one, so they tend to be cheaper than a single life policy.

second-to-die life insurance a life insurance policy that makes sure there is enough cash available to pay estate taxes.

One of the best places to find a policy is with a discount broker who sells low-load insurance without going through an agent. The commission can be as much as 50 percent cheaper.

✔ Check out insurance firms like USAA Life (800-531-8000) or Ameritas (800-552-3553), which sell policies directly to you without going through an agent.
✔ To get the best-priced policy, you might ask a quote service company to send you the five best-priced policies that suit your needs. Most don't charge for the service, and you can buy the policy from that company.

Where to Find Quotes Online

www.accuquote.com

www.consumerquote.com

www.instantquote.com

www.insuremarket.com

www.masterquote.com

www.quickquote.com

www.quotesmith.com

www.selectquote.com

Where to Call

Insurance Quote Services Inc., 800-972-1104

SelectQuote, 800-343-1985

TermQuote, 800-444-8376

Quotesmith Corp., 800-556-9393

INSURANCE TIPS

✔ Buying via a Web-based service may mean a lower premium if you know what you want. If you need hand-holding, an agent is worth an initial meeting to get you up to speed on what your needs might be.

✔ Before buying, be sure the insurer is financially sound. Look for ratings of AAA, AA, or A++. Each rating service has a different system. Check with A. M. Best (908-439-2200, www. ambest.com); Duff & Phelps (312-368-3157, www.dcrco.com); Moody's Investors Service (212-553-0377, www. moodys.com); Standard & Poor's (212-438-2000, www.standardandpoors.com/ratings); or Weiss Group (800-289-9222, www.weissratings. com).

Clearly, there are some flaws to the new tax legislation, but claiming the special exclusion is worth exploring.

VALUING THE ESTATE

Get a handle on what your business is worth. That will give you a base to begin your plan. Figuring out how much a closely held business is really worth for estate purposes can be a process. You'll probably need a business appraiser to help. To have a business appraised, you might be able to find someone trustworthy through your attorney or accountant. If not, you can call the American Society of Appraisers at 800-272-8258. The Herndon, Virginia–based association can provide a list of accredited appraisers in your area.

In a firm with several partners, there is usually a prior pact, known as a crisscross agreement, stating that if a partner dies, the other partners might opt to buy the heirs out. Partnerships might also have agreed legally when the firm was formed to valuate the business on something concrete, like the prior year's profits. A judge, however, might insist on the present-day value.

The history of the business and its financial performance as well as the performance of other businesses in the same industry will be taken into account. Revenue and sales growth are reviewed. The company will typically be compared to the financial statistics available on public companies that operate in the same arena. Balance sheets, of course, will be scrutinized. Having financial statements prepared with accountant reports will help your heirs sort through this process. Tax returns for a family or closely held business are the primary documents needed for the review.

There will be an appraisal of all real estate holdings, equipment, and other assets. The balance sheet information will need to be at least three years of records, but often five. Then the fair market value of all those goods, inventory, equipment, and so forth will be taken into account.

FAMILY LIMITED PARTNERSHIPS

These are one of the hottest estate-planning tools today. The IRS isn't so thrilled about that, so changes could be afoot. But here is how they work. They have been popular with small-business owners for ages as a way to protect assets from creditors and former spouses.

Typically, a small business owner passes the assets over to a limited partnership. He or she holds on to the major ownership stake and is listed as the general partner who is in charge of the decision making. Other stakes in the partnership are parceled out to other family members. Gifts of these shares can be doled out gradually to take advantage of the $10,000 a year gift-tax rules.

These can be expensive to set up and administer, since you will need some pretty sharp accounting and appraisal records to verify what the company is worth and so forth.

Say you want to place $1 million in a partnership and give each of your four children a limited share. Since they have no control over their stock, their shares are discounted by anywhere from 25 percent to as much as 60 percent for estate tax and gift tax purposes. That allows your heirs to inherit more after estate taxes are paid than if you had given them the business outright.

No doubt this is a tremendous tax shelter, but the IRS is starting to crack down, so you should follow a few guidelines:

1. Make sure you have a partnership agreement that is drafted by an attorney that explains that you are setting this up to protect your assets from creditors. Be sure that it is clear that avoiding taxes is not your singular goal. Call the American College of Trust and Estate Counsel (310-398-1888) or the American Bar Association (312-988-5000) for referrals in your area.

2. Set up a separate bank account for the partnership and keep detailed records.

3. File IRS Form 1065 to make all the appropriate distributions to limited partners.

4. Get an appraisal done. This might cost as much as $15,000, but it will give you the ammunition to contest any complaints the IRS might have regarding the partnership.

5. Keep good records of all account statements, receipts, and correspondence with family partners, accountants, and lawyers.

DELAYING THE BLOW

If your estate does wind up owing taxes on your family business, the financial stress can be devastating. In general, federal estate tax is due nine months from the date of your death. However, in certain circumstances, the tax can be paid in 2 to 10 installments and deferred for up to five years after the original due date. The estate will be liable for a 2 percent interest rate on the first $1 million of taxable value of a closely held business. (The rate had been 4 percent before the 1997 tax act.)

There is also special estate tax relief if the interest in your business makes up more than 35 percent of your taxable estate. In many cases, the estate tax can be paid over 14 years, with only the interest due in the initial four-year period.

There are many options available to help you cushion the estate taxes due on a family or closely held business. Again, an expert in the field is worth consulting to really dissect the best plan for your company and family.

SUCCESSION PLANNING

This is an entire book in itself, but suffice it to say that any owner of a closely held or family business should take the time in the estate planning process to plan for a successor.

This is a difficult task for many business owners; but should something happen to you, you risk throwing the entire business into turmoil and possible bankruptcy and costing your family emotional and financial stress beyond belief. Don't wait until you are sick or getting ready to retire to make these plans. You won't be losing control, but rather taking control.

Many family businesses die with the founder. Properly planned, that doesn't have to happen and your family can continue to prosper from your lifework. Your successor doesn't have to be a family member at all—just so a plan is in place to keep the business afloat when you are gone. This will not be simple. You'll need to consider family dynamics—who is really qualified and interested in the business. You want to be fair to children in the business and those not in the business as well.

CONCLUSION

You should be concerned about whether your business can afford to pay the estate taxes if something happens to you. Getting started with planning and discussing the issue with your family members and associates is something that shouldn't wait. There are dozens of potential issues and problems to confront, and the more time you have to straighten it out, the healthier your estate will be for it. And hopefully your business will continue to thrive for another generation or more.

Estate Planning
and Special Situations

So much of estate planning is about leaving your worldly goods to your children or your spouse. But what if you don't have any kids or are now on your own due to a divorce or a death of a spouse? It doesn't mean that estate planning is any less important.

It's not uncommon for couples without children not to bother writing wills. And in some states that might be fine, but everyone should have an estate plan pulled together. It doesn't have to be fancy or complicated. But no matter what life stage you are at, you are responsible for making sure your assets are dispersed according to your wishes when you die and your heirs won't get stuck paying tax on what you leave behind.

Moreover, in some states if you die without a will, your spouse can wind up the loser. In Colorado, if you die childless and without a will but your parents are still living, your spouse gets the first $200,000. Afterward, it's a 75/25 split between your spouse and your parents. That's the law.

WIDOWS AND WIDOWERS

If you become widowed and have dependents, you should review your life insurance policy. You need to ask yourself how long your children will need your financial support. How much life insurance you need will depend on how many children you have and their ages. One guideline suggested by financial planners is about 8 to 10 times your annual salary.

Term life insurance is the simplest and most affordable life insurance to buy if you plan to insure yourself for at least 20 years. You pay an annual premium based on your age, your health, the cost of the agent's commission, and how much the insurer thinks it can earn by investing your premiums until you die.

Recently, term insurance buyers have been enjoying some of the lowest rates in history thanks to increased competition and the ability to buy policies over the Internet or telephone without going through an agent.

A 45-year-old man in good health who wants a 20-year, $1 million term policy with level premiums (you pay the same amount each year), can pay a premium as low as $964 a year. Term policies provide insurance for a set period—5, 10, even 50 years—without the savings and investment features you'll find in whole or universal life coverage. You can, however, drop coverage without penalty. If you aren't up for shopping on the Net or by phone and really want a person to talk to, you can visit an agent or broker and pay a commission to buy.

Insurance quote services and mutual fund companies like Fidelity can help you evaluate your options and needs with online calculators. Ultimately what you pay will depend on a mandatory physical exam and lifestyle factors. If you are a scuba diver, for instance, don't dream of a low rate.

See Chapter 8 for places to check up on an insurer's financial stability and shop for the policy that is best for you.

CHANGING BENEFICIARIES

If you are widowed, don't forget to change beneficiaries on any retirement, life insurance, or brokerage accounts. If you are naming a minor, you may want to consider naming a trust as beneficiary in your child's name.

Other things to do:

✔ Take stock of your property and assets.

✔ Update your will.

✔ Name a guardian for any minor children.

✔ Designate someone to have a durable power of attorney to act for you if you are incapacitated or out of the country.

✔ Sit down with a financial planner or accountant to assess your estate today and where it might be in 5, 10, and 20 years hence.

NO KIDS, THEN WHAT?

Okay, so you don't have the two perfect kids and the dog to worry about leaving your life's savings to. Childless couples including gay and lesbian partners addressing estate planning issues with no dependents have some thinking to do.

Married couples with kids usually leave everything to their spouses and kids and are done with it. If you are married and have no children, single with no children or in an alternative partnership you might choose to leave it all to your partner, or favorite brother Jack, nephew Mike, or niece Caitlin. You might opt to divide it among several members of your extended family. But be clear in your will about your intentions and make sure it has been drawn up airtight by an estate attorney to avoid any challenges.

OTHER TECHNIQUES

Here are some other estate planning techniques to consider:

✔ *Tuition payments.* You can fund anyone's education expenses without paying tax as long as you pay the funds directly to the university or school. The money must be used to pay for tuition and books, not room and board. It is a great way to give money to someone that has a specific purpose.

✔ *Annual gifts.* You can gift your favorite relative or friend $10,000 per year free of gift taxes.

✔ *College savings.* You can open a $10,000 tax-free college savings account in some states like New Hampshire and New York for anyone. The money grows tax-deferred until it is issued to pay for tuition, books, and perhaps room and board. The earnings are taxed at the student's tax bracket.

✔ *Grantor Retained Income Trusts* (**GRIT**) A *grantor retained income trust* allows you to transfer assets to your heirs while you are still alive. You can't give away to lineal relatives like your children. But non-relatives or nephews, nieces, and cousins are eligible.

✔ *Starting a foundation.* This might be a stretch for most of us, but what if you think you may wind up leaving an estate of $10 million or so in assets and you have no one to give it to when you die? You might consider leaving the balance of your estate to a private foundation. It's estate tax–free and can be designed to benefit your favorite charities. You can design it so your nieces or nephews can draw some salary from the foundation and be responsible for distributing its funds.

grantor retained income trust (GRIT) a trust that allows you to transfer assets to your heirs while you are still alive.

It can be expensive to launch and there are maintenance fees. Moreover, it can be an unnecessary responsibility for your sister's kid that you named as trustee. Nonetheless, if you have a substantial estate, it might make sense that the organizations you want to benefit from your good works enjoy your spoils and not the IRS.

DIVORCEES

Basically, heed the advice for widows and widowers.

- ✔ Change beneficiaries.
- ✔ Update insurance policies.
- ✔ Do a net worth statement.
- ✔ Get your financial papers in order.
- ✔ Update your will.
- ✔ Name a guardian for minor children.
- ✔ Consider a durable power of attorney.

CONCLUSION

For estate-planning purposes, these life stages can be among the most troubling and confusing when it comes to financial planning. It's easy to just forget about it and go on with your life. But when you are on your own, in a gay or lesbian partnership, or without kids, you have lots of choices of how you can give back to society and the people you love with what you have achieved in your lifetime.

Talking to Your Parents

Your parents are in their seventies and you have never discussed estate planning with them. Sound familiar? Estate planning is a darkly personal matter and one that many people feel uneasy delving into. Most of us haven't a clue about what our parents have done in terms of estate planning.

But should you lose a parent, you also lose the chance to help make the transition in a coherent fashion, at least, money-wise. The best way to bring this up is simply to ask your parents if they have done any estate planning. Skip the money stuff at first and just see what they have done, where their wills and important financial papers are, and if there is anything you can do to help.

Sussing out who is getting what down to the bone china is not called for. This is just an initial discussion to make sure everyone knows what your parents have in mind. Death, as we mentioned many times before, is something no one really wants to address, particularly with their children. But what they have planned could affect what you have planned and your strategies.

Find out if they have wills and where they have stored copies. Is there an executor named? Explain that you are not trying to be a doom-sayer, but you would hate to have family conflict when one of them goes just because no one understood what the plan was.

With up to $12 trillion in wealth expected to be transferred inter-generationally between now and 2040, this is a major issue.

Money and gifts after someone dies are the equation of love for most of us, but if you are surprised at the end of the day, things can get ugly between those left behind—be it your sister or your mother. Litigation and family infighting are the last things you want.

If your parents die without a will, things can really get out of whack between siblings. Even if there is a will, a phrase suggesting that the contents of the house be divided equally between the siblings can start a family feud that never ends. My parents are both still healthy at 80 and 70, respectively, but, believe me, I always ask them about what household items they have set aside for me. It sounds morbid, but we are Irish after all and they get it. I'll do anything to try to avoid being angry at one of my siblings for something Mom and Dad neglected to do or decided to do without informing us.

Then, too, you need to know who the executor of the will is. For instance, in my family, it's my older brother. Once I learned that, I have tried my darnedest to stay on good terms with him. Just kidding, but it's important to understand who will bear the brunt of the estate deal-ings and work to avoid any friction from the start.

HOW TO GET PREPARED

1. If your parents are still alive, get all your siblings together for a family powwow to go over with your parents what to do when they die. This will be a tough discussion, and it really doesn't have to be too spe-cific in the initial meeting; but get the ball rolling so there are no mis-understandings.

2. If your parents die without clear instructions, you might sug-gest a family get-together where you all take back the objects you gave your parents as a starting point and go from there.

3. Encourage your aging parents to have household items appraised so there is a record of the value of the items they cherish. They might want to make a detailed list of everything they own and let all the kids review it to see what they might ultimately want. It sounds like a barbaric way to divvy up the spoils, but from an estate-planning perspective it can do a lot to ease the transition.

4. Talk to your parents about charitable gifts and their $10,000 gifting allowance per person if they can afford it to help whittle down any estate taxes if they are likely to have an estate large enough to be subject to estate taxes.

5. Most importantly, make sure your folks have a will and that someone in the family knows where the important financial documents—insurance documents, trust documents, wills, funeral and burial instructions, birth certificates, real estate deeds, financial accounts, and any business accounts—are located.

Talking about death is a downer, but as we age it is important to have these open discussions with our parents as well as our children.

CONCLUSION

Be prepared and the process will be less difficult than you imagine. Helping your parents plan and being forthright about estate planning will make it easier on everyone.

Estate Planning via the Web

So you think you really don't have much of an estate. You've got a house, a retirement plan at work, and a few tchotchkes you have gathered on your travels. Who needs an estate plan? Well, with the stock market pumping and real estate prices gaining strength, you could probably use a bit of estate planning in case you die unexpectedly. Your not having an estate plan could really screw up the lives of those who survive you.

The Internet has made it easier than ever to learn about estate planning. Beware of any estate planning web site that is pushing just one product. Nonetheless, you can find all types of basic will- and trust-writing software on the Web.

Here are some of my favorite sites.

✔ *The American College of Trust and Estate Counsel* (*www.actec.org)*. You can get a referral to an estate lawyer who can help you get a plan jump-started.

✔ *The Nolo.com Self-Help Law Center* (*www.nolo.com)*. You can download or order top-quality will- and trust-writing software here. This is the web site of the 29-year-old Berkeley, California–based publisher of law books. It is a super source for research and is extremely accurate as far as its advice and tax information are concerned.

✔ *Lawyers.com (www.lawyers.com)*. This is the place to go to run a check on a lawyer you are pondering hiring for some estate planning. It is part of the Martindale-Hubbell enterprise. Martindale-Hubbell is the major publisher of legal directories. There are some 420,000 lawyers in the database. You can track their bios and career histories as well as their specialties. Try to focus on those who specialize in estate planning.

✔ *Legal Information Institute (www.law.cornell.edu)*. The Cornell University law school has a splendid site. Go to the estate planning section and you are on your way. There are links to federal and state laws relating to estate planning and more.

✔ *MSN MoneyCentral (www.moneycentral.msn.com)*. This is an easy-to-follow estate planning helper that anyone can grasp. It offers helpful advice on estate planning when your life takes a turn—say, marriage or divorce and so on.

✔ *Rushforth (www.rushforth.org)*. This is a site operated by a Nevada lawyer, Layne T. Rushforth. It is a wonderful source to find checklists and questionnaires to help you prepare to visit your own estate planning attorney.

✔ *The Internal Revenue Service (www.irs.gov)*. You can find any tax forms and pamphlets related to estate planning here.

✔ *NDB University (www.ndb.com)*. There are dozens of topics here, from learning about insurance to wills and trusts. You can also get advice on giving away money while you are still alive and more. It is created by *Money* magazine and even has an interactive quiz to check what you have learned.

Web sites come and go, but you can always check various mutual fund web sites for more help and calculators.

Commonly Asked Questions

1. *What's an estate plan?*

It's a method of figuring out how you want your assets and property to be managed and transferred after your death. It's a fairly broad term that can cover everything from writing a will to naming guardians for your children and reducing any death taxes on your estate. Estate planning is an integral part of anyone's financial plan.

2. *What's a will?*

This is a legal document witnessed by at least two people and signed and dated by you that in the most basic form states how you want your affairs handled and property dispensed in the event that you die. You should revise it periodically especially if you have a life-changing event like a marriage or divorce.

3. *What is probate?*

This is the legal procedure that proves that a will is authentic and watches over the distribution of the assets to heirs and creditors. It can be an expensive and time-consuming process.

4. *What property is considered to be nonprobate?*

In essence, a nonprobate asset is any asset that is held in joint tenancy with right of survivorship. Also nonprobate are life insurance payouts and assets held in a living trust. Retirement plans such as 401(k)s and IRAs that have a named beneficiary are usually considered to be nonprobate assets that do not need to be reported to the court. Any earnings and vacation pay that is due to you at the time of your death is also free from probate in most states.

5. *What do I need to probate a will?*

In sum, you will need a copy of the original will, a listing of all assets from real estate to financial accounts, a list of all debts, tax returns from the past five years, and a list of all retirement plan accounts and insurance policies. Copies of all trusts will also be required. An accounting of any of the estate expenses such as funeral bills and medical bills may also be asked for by the court.

6. *Who is an administrator?*

This is a person picked by the court to handle the disposition of your estate if you have not named someone in your will to do so. This individual may also be referred to as an executor.

7. *Who is a beneficiary?*

This is someone named in a will to receive your assets.

8. *When is an estate subject to federal tax?*

If the taxable estate is less than $675,000 in 2000, gradually increasing to $1 million in 2006, it is exempt from taxation.

9. *If I leave everything to my spouse, will my spouse be hit with an estate tax?*

Every cent you leave your spouse is excluded from your taxable estate, provided that your spouse is a U.S. citizen. This is known as the unlimited marital deduction.

10. *What happens if I die without a will?*

The state decides how to divvy up the proceeds. It may split your estate between spouse and children or give the spouse the entire estate.

The law varies from state to state. In some cases, parents receive a portion as well.

11. *How much can I give away each year tax-free to reduce the size of my estate?*

You can give away up to $10,000 to any person each year without paying a gift tax. You can give this amount to as many people as you want each year. So you and your spouse together can give away $20,000 annually per recipient.

12. *If I die, who will inherit my IRA?*

Individual retirement accounts (IRAs) are among the biggest assets most of us have these days, thanks to a roaring bull market. You must name a beneficiary for your IRA with the financial services company that you have it invested with. If you name someone different in your will to receive the funds, that does not hold water in a court of law. Make sure you have an IRA beneficiary named with your IRA custodian. If you don't pick someone, your IRA will be considered part of your taxable estate. Once liquidated, income taxes must be paid within five years of your death in most cases.

13. *What if I want to name my two-year-old child as my beneficiary?*

No problem. However, you should specify that any minor's share be paid to a custodian under the Uniform Transfers to Minors Act until the child is of age, typically 18. This is the least expensive way to go. You should name a custodian, or state that your executor will pick one.

14. *What are the pitfalls of being an executor?*

Truthfully, it can be a thankless job. It is time-consuming and requires a lot of financial know-how in many cases. Moreover, you could be liable to any heirs if they accuse you of mishandling the estate's funds and making risky or bad investment choices. You really need to have a good working knowledge of the deceased's circumstances to handle an estate properly without running into trouble. It's not unusual for unexpected claims from business transactions and the like to appear out of nowhere.

15. *What are the most important things to consider when writing an estate plan?*

There are a myriad of issues to consider when it comes to setting up an estate plan. First, you need to consider your age and your partner's age. Next, what's your life expectancy and his or hers? Will you inherit money one day? How much income do you and your partner generate each year? What are your current assets and potential growth of those assets? Do you have children? If so, how old are they? Do you have other dependents? Do you own a business?

16. *When do I need to hire a lawyer to help with my estate plan?*

There are plenty of good reasons to hire a pro to help you sort through this process. It is most important if you think there is someone out there who will contest your will. Second, if you have remarried and there are children from a previous marriage, it is probably wise to get things nailed down so that there is no conflict with an ex-spouse in regard to what you have outlined. You should also hire an estate attorney if you think your and your spouse's estate will exceed the federal tax exemption threshold. Finally, hire a lawyer to draft a will for you if you want to place any restrictions on how your estate will be doled out to your beneficiaries.

17. *Where should I store my will?*

It's a good idea to keep your will in an envelope on which you have printed or typed "Will of" plus your name, then place it in a fireproof home safe or filing cabinet. Make sure someone besides you knows where it is as well.

18. *What if I don't have any kids and I want to name a pet as a beneficiary?*

You can't leave assets to a pet per se, so forget about naming a pet in your will to receive your assets. However, you can give a pet away in your will to a friend or relative. And in some states you are able to name a pet as a beneficiary of a trust.

19. *Aren't trusts expensive?*

Not true. You can put a simple trust arrangement together for under $300.

20. *Why would I want to set up a trust?*

There are many good reasons to consider a trust, but perhaps the biggest one is to preserve an inheritance for your kids. They can't get their hands on the funds usually until they are old enough to know how to manage the windfall, and that can be a real advantage to them in the long run.

21. *How can I locate an estate attorney to help me?*

There are many good sources, and one of the best may be just talking to friends and family members and asking for referrals. You might also consider consulting the *Martindale-Hubbell Law Directory*, which is available at most public libraries and law school libraries. It lists attorneys across the country and rates them on their ability and ethical standards.

Epilogue

Planning Ahead

Estate planning takes discipline and an understanding of finances and human nature. While estate planning is different for each one of us, the need to pay attention to it is universal. It's common sense on one level, but the intricacies of the laws from state to state to state do play a key role in what will be the right plan for you.

Moreover, an estate plan, as you have learned, is an ever-changing entity. It must be tweaked and updated throughout your life. For all the reasons I cited earlier—you marry, divorce, remarry and blend families, fall ill, have a windfall, and so on—you'll need to address the various components of an estate plan.

Here are eight key action steps to follow:

1. Sit down and figure out what your estate really is worth. For many people, this can be a real eye-opener. After all, your estate includes everything that you own from stocks and bonds and mutual funds to retirement plans, life insurance policies, your home and more. Take an inventory and see where you stand.

2. Check to be sure you have enough life insurance if you have children or other dependents who will need financial support after you are gone. Landing the right insurance policy can be tricky, but there are loads of places these days to go to research what is currently on the market. Check web sites and personal finance magazines and their web sites for calculators to help you determine how much you need and who offers the best-priced policies.

3. Write a will. All the fancy estate planning tax moves and manipulations you can make are helpful no doubt in the long run, but simply stating in a written document how you want your belongings distributed (make sure that your heirs know the location of that document) is the single most important step you can take. And be sure it is updated at least annually and witnessed by at least two other people. It must be signed and dated by you as well.

A valid will requires that you are of age according to your state law. For instance, you must be 18 in Pennsylvania to write a valid will. You must be mentally sound, so no one can contest that you didn't know what you were doing. You must write the will freely and voluntarily, not because you were pressured by another person to do so.

Remember you can change your will or rewrite portions of it at any given time, provided you are competent. You can also simply amend portions of it with a codicil, or a separate document that is attached to the original will.

4. Name an executor to manage the distribution of your assets, and make sure the executor has a copy of your will or knows where to track down the original document. Your executor should be someone you trust implicitly to manage all your financial affairs and who is knowledgeable about money.

Your executor will have to determine the total value of your assets and have them appraised at the time of your death. He or she will need to pay off any debts or liabilities of your estate, make sure your tax return is filed for the year of your death, and be sure your heirs get what you have left for them.

5. Hire an expert attorney who is up to speed on the estate planning laws of your state and can help you execute your plan. Having the right financial advice and attention to the legal nuances of the estate laws is crucial. Estate law is a complicated animal, and if you don't get the proper guidance, your will can be declared invalid. Your cost for that expert help can be as little as $100 or climb into the thousands, depending on how complicated the plan you have in mind is.

6. Choose a guardian. If you have children under the age of 18 in most states, this is an important decision. Make sure it is someone you feel shares your views of parenting. It is not unusual to choose two guardians—one who will raise your child or children if something should happen to you and another who can manage the property or financial assets you leave behind for your children.

7. Consider setting up a trust. This legal arrangement can protect your estate from probate and more. It can help manage your assets and provide tax savings for your survivors. A trust can be as loose or as strict as you want it to be. Trusts aren't for everyone, but you don't need to be landed gentry to consider one. A trust can reduce estate taxes, manage asset distribution, give charitable donations, and manage funds left to minor children.

8. Draw up a durable power of attorney. This written document hands over the authority to make decisions for you to someone you trust in case you become disabled or incompetent. It must be clear in outlining the duration of the power and the duties of the person you name. You must be mentally competent at the time you authorize a power of attorney, and the document should be drafted by an attorney. By picking someone in advance to handle your financial and medical matters, you can be assured that your affairs are still under your control even if you cannot make the decisions at that time.

The ultimate goal of a successful estate plan is making sure that your goals and objectives for your heirs are met. Particularly as we boomers age, it's imperative to make sure that you decide what happens to your assets, children, and medical care, if you are no longer able to make those decisions. Make an estate plan and implement it.

Appendix A

IRS Forms

IRS Forms

W-9: Request for Taxpayer Identification Number and Certification

706: United States Estate (and Generation-Skipping Transfer) Tax Return

706-A: United States Additional Estate Tax Return

706-CE: Certification of Payment of Foreign Death Tax

706-GS(D): Generation-Skipping Transfer Tax Return for Distributions

706-GS(D-1): Notification of Distribution from a Generation-Skipping Trust

706-GS(T): Generation-Skipping Transfer Tax Return for Terminations

706-NA: United States Estate (and Generation-Skipping Transfer) Tax Return for Nonresident Aliens

709: United States Gift (and Generation-Skipping Transfer) Tax Return

709-(A): United States Short Form Gift Tax Return

712: Life Insurance Statement

1040: U.S. Individual Income Tax Return

1040-C: U.S. Departing Alien Income Tax Return

1041: U.S. Income Tax Return for Estates and Trusts

2848: Power of Attorney and Declaration of Representative

4506: Request for Copy or Transcript of Tax Form

4768: Application for Extension of Time to File a Return and/or Pay U.S. Estate (and Generation-Skipping Transfer) Taxes

Request for Taxpayer
Identification Number and Certification

Give form to the
requester. Do NOT
send to the IRS.

Please print or type

Name (If a joint account or you changed your name, see **Specific Instructions** on page 2.)

Business name, if different from above. (See **Specific Instructions** on page 2.)

Check appropriate box: ☐ Individual/Sole proprietor ☐ Corporation ☐ Partnership ☐ Other ▶ ....

Address (number, street, and apt. or suite no.)

Requester's name and address (optional)

City, state, and ZIP code

Part I   **Taxpayer Identification Number (TIN)**

List account number(s) here (optional)

Enter your TIN in the appropriate box. For individuals, this is your social security number (SSN). However, if you are a resident alien OR a sole proprietor, see the instructions on page 2. For other entities, it is your employer identification number (EIN). If you do not have a number, see **How to get a TIN** on page 2.

Note: *If the account is in more than one name, see the chart on page 2 for guidelines on whose number to enter.*

Social security number

OR

Employer identification number

Part II   **For Payees Exempt From Backup Withholding** (See the instructions on page 2.)

▶

Part III   **Certification**

Under penalties of perjury, I certify that:

1. The number shown on this form is my correct taxpayer identification number (or I am waiting for a number to be issued to me), **and**

2. I am not subject to backup withholding because: **(a)** I am exempt from backup withholding, or **(b)** I have not been notified by the Internal Revenue Service (IRS) that I am subject to backup withholding as a result of a failure to report all interest or dividends, or **(c)** the IRS has notified me that I am no longer subject to backup withholding.

Certification instructions. You must cross out item **2** above if you have been notified by the IRS that you are currently subject to backup withholding because you have failed to report all interest and dividends on your tax return. For real estate transactions, item **2** does not apply. For mortgage interest paid, acquisition or abandonment of secured property, cancellation of debt, contributions to an individual retirement arrangement (IRA), and generally, payments other than interest and dividends, you are not required to sign the Certification, but you must provide your correct TIN. (See the instructions on page 2.)

Sign
Here   Signature ▶   Date ▶

Purpose of form. A person who is required to file an information return with the IRS must get your correct taxpayer identification number (TIN) to report, for example, income paid to you, real estate transactions, mortgage interest you paid, acquisition or abandonment of secured property, cancellation of debt, or contributions you made to an IRA.

Use Form W-9, if you are a U.S. person (including a resident alien), to give your correct TIN to the person requesting it (the requester) and, when applicable, to:

1. Certify the TIN you are giving is correct (or you are waiting for a number to be issued).

2. Certify you are not subject to backup withholding, or

3. Claim exemption from backup withholding if you are an exempt payee.

If you are a foreign person, IRS **prefers** you use a Form W-8 (certificate of foreign status). After December 31, 2000, foreign persons **must** use an appropriate Form W-8.

Note: *If a requester gives you a form other than Form W-9 to request your TIN, you must use the requester's form if it is substantially similar to this Form W-9.*

What is backup withholding? Persons making certain payments to you must withhold and pay to the IRS 31% of such payments under certain conditions. This is called "backup withholding." Payments that may be subject to backup withholding include interest, dividends, broker and barter exchange transactions, rents, royalties, nonemployee pay, and certain payments from fishing boat operators. Real estate transactions are not subject to backup withholding.

If you give the requester your correct TIN, make the proper certifications, and report all your taxable interest and dividends on your tax return, payments you receive will not be subject to backup withholding. Payments you receive **will** be subject to backup withholding if:

1. You do not furnish your TIN to the requester, or

2. You do not certify your TIN when required (see the Part III instructions on page 2 for details), or

3. The IRS tells the requester that you furnished an incorrect TIN, or

4. The IRS tells you that you are subject to backup withholding because you did not report all your interest and dividends on your tax return (for reportable interest and dividends only), or

5. You do not certify to the requester that you are not subject to backup withholding under 3 above (for reportable interest and dividend accounts opened after 1983 only).

Certain payees and payments are exempt from backup withholding. See the Part II instructions and the separate **Instructions for the Requester of Form W-9.**

Penalties

Failure to furnish TIN. If you fail to furnish your correct TIN to a requester, you are subject to a penalty of $50 for each such failure unless your failure is due to reasonable cause and not to willful neglect.

Civil penalty for false information with respect to withholding. If you make a false statement with no reasonable basis that results in no backup withholding, you are subject to a $500 penalty.

Criminal penalty for falsifying information. Willfully falsifying certifications or affirmations may subject you to criminal penalties including fines and/or imprisonment.

Misuse of TINs. If the requester discloses or uses TINs in violation of Federal law, the requester may be subject to civil and criminal penalties.

Cat. No. 10231X

Form **W-9** (Rev. 11-99)

FIGURE A.1   Request for Taxpayer Identification Number and Certification

Specific Instructions

Name. If you are an individual, you must generally enter the name shown on your social security card. However, if you have changed your last name, for instance, due to marriage, without informing the Social Security Administration of the name change, enter your first name, the last name shown on your social security card, and your new last name.

If the account is in joint names, list first and then circle the name of the person or entity whose number you enter in Part I of the form.

Sole proprietor. You must enter your **individual** name as shown on your social security card. You may enter your business, trade, or "doing business as" name on the **business name** line.

Other entities. Enter your business name as shown on required Federal tax documents. This name should match the name shown on the charter or other legal document creating the entity. You may enter any business, trade, or "doing business as" name on the business name line.

Part I—Taxpayer Identification Number (TIN)

You must enter your TIN in the appropriate box. If you are a resident alien and you do not have and are not eligible to get an SSN, your TIN is your IRS individual taxpayer identification number (ITIN). Enter it in the social security number box. If you do not have an ITIN, see **How to get a TIN** below.

If you are a sole proprietor and you have an EIN, you may enter either your SSN or EIN. However, using your EIN may result in unnecessary notices to the requester.

Note: See the chart on this page for further clarification of name and TIN combinations.

How to get a TIN. If you do not have a TIN, apply for one immediately. To apply for an SSN, get **Form SS-5,** Application for a Social Security Card, from your local Social Security Administration office. Get **Form W-7,** Application for IRS Individual Taxpayer Identification Number, to apply for an ITIN or **Form SS-4,** Application for Employer Identification Number, to apply for an EIN. You can get Forms W-7 and SS-4 from the IRS by calling 1-800-TAX-FORM (1-800-829-3676) or from the IRS's Internet Web Site at **www.irs.gov.**

If you do not have a TIN, write "Applied For" in the space for the TIN, sign and date the form, and give it to the requester. For interest and dividend payments, and certain payments made with respect to readily tradable instruments, generally you will have 60 days to get a TIN and give it to the requester. Other payments are subject to backup withholding.

Note: Writing "Applied For" means that you have already applied for a TIN OR that you intend to apply for one soon.

Part II—For Payees Exempt From Backup Withholding

Individuals (including sole proprietors) are **not** exempt from backup withholding. Corporations are exempt from backup withholding for certain payments, such as interest and dividends. For more information on exempt payees, see the separate Instructions for the Requester of Form W-9.

If you are exempt from backup withholding, you should still complete this form to avoid possible erroneous backup withholding. Enter your correct TIN in Part I, write "Exempt" in Part II, and sign and date the form.

If you are a nonresident alien or a foreign entity not subject to backup withholding, give the requester a completed Form W-8 (certification of foreign status).

Part III—Certification

For a joint account, only the person whose TIN is shown in Part I should sign (when required).

1. Interest, dividend, and barter exchange accounts opened before 1984 and broker accounts considered active during 1983. You must give your correct TIN, but you do not have to sign the certification.

2. Interest, dividend, broker, and barter exchange accounts opened after 1983 and broker accounts considered inactive during 1983. You must sign the certification or backup withholding will apply. If you are subject to backup withholding and you are merely providing your correct TIN to the requester, you must cross out item **2** in the certification before signing the form.

3. Real estate transactions. You must sign the certification. You may cross out item **2** of the certification.

4. Other payments. You must give your correct TIN, but you do not have to sign the certification unless you have been notified that you have previously given an incorrect TIN. "Other payments" include payments made in the course of the requester's trade or business for rents, royalties, goods (other than bills for merchandise), medical and health care services (including payments to corporations), payments to a nonemployee for services, payments to certain fishing boat crew members and fishermen, and gross proceeds paid to attorneys (including payments to corporations).

5. Mortgage interest paid by you, acquisition or abandonment of secured property, cancellation of debt, qualified state tuition program payments, IRA or MSA contributions or distributions, and pension distributions. You must give your correct TIN, but you do not have to sign the certification.

Privacy Act Notice

Section 6109 of the Internal Revenue Code requires you to give your correct TIN to persons who must file information returns with the IRS to report interest, dividends, and certain other income paid to you, mortgage interest you paid, the acquisition or abandonment of secured property, cancellation of debt, or contributions you made to an IRA or MSA. The IRS uses the numbers for identification purposes and to help verify the accuracy of your tax return. The IRS may also provide this information to the Department of Justice for civil and criminal litigation, and to cities, states, and the District of Columbia to carry out their tax laws.

You must provide your TIN whether or not you are required to file a tax return. Payers must generally withhold 31% of taxable interest, dividend, and certain other payments to a payee who does not give a TIN to a payer. Certain penalties may also apply.

What Name and Number To Give the Requester

For this type of account:	Give name and SSN of:
1. Individual	The individual
2. Two or more individuals (joint account)	The actual owner of the account or, if combined funds, the first individual on the account [1]
3. Custodian account of a minor (Uniform Gift to Minors Act)	The minor [2]
4. a. The usual revocable savings trust (grantor is also trustee)	The grantor-trustee [1]
b. So-called trust account that is not a legal or valid trust under state law	The actual owner [1]
5. Sole proprietorship	The owner [3]

For this type of account:	Give name and EIN of:
6. Sole proprietorship	The owner [3]
7. A valid trust, estate, or pension trust	Legal entity [4]
8. Corporation	The corporation
9. Association, club, religious, charitable, educational, or other tax-exempt organization	The organization
10. Partnership	The partnership
11. A broker or registered nominee	The broker or nominee
12. Account with the Department of Agriculture in the name of a public entity (such as a state or local government, school district, or prison) that receives agricultural program payments	The public entity

[1] List first and circle the name of the person whose number you furnish. If only one person on a joint account has an SSN, that person's number must be furnished.

[2] Circle the minor's name and furnish the minor's SSN.

[3] You must show your individual name, but you may also enter your business or "doing business as" name. You may use either your SSN or EIN (if you have one).

[4] List first and circle the name of the legal trust, estate, or pension trust. (Do not furnish the TIN of the personal representative or trustee unless the legal entity itself is not designated in the account title.)

Note: If no name is circled when more than one name is listed, the number will be considered to be that of the first name listed.

FIGURE A.1 *Continued*

Form **706**
(Rev. July 1999)

Department of the Treasury
Internal Revenue Service

United States Estate (and Generation-Skipping Transfer) Tax Return

Estate of a citizen or resident of the United States (see separate instructions).
To be filed for decedents dying after December 31, 1998
For Paperwork Reduction Act Notice, see page 1 of the separate instructions.

OMB No. 1545-0015

Part 1.—Decedent and Executor

1a Decedent's first name and middle initial (and maiden name, if any)	1b Decedent's last name	2 Decedent's Social Security No.
3a Legal residence (domicile) at time of death (county, state, and ZIP code, or foreign country)	3b Year domicile established	4 Date of birth	5 Date of death
6a Name of executor (see page 4 of the instructions)	6b Executor's address (number and street including apartment or suite no. or rural route; city, town, or post office; state; and ZIP code)	
6c Executor's social security number (see page 4 of the instructions)		
7a Name and location of court where will was probated or estate administered		7b Case number

8 If decedent died testate, check here ▶ ☐ and attach a certified copy of the will. | 9 If Form 4768 is attached, check here ▶ ☐
10 If Schedule R-1 is attached, check here ▶ ☐

Part 2.—Tax Computation

1	Total gross estate less exclusion (from Part 5, Recapitulation, page 3, item 12)	1
2	Total allowable deductions (from Part 5, Recapitulation, page 3, item 23)	2
3	Taxable estate (subtract line 2 from line 1)	3
4	Adjusted taxable gifts (total taxable gifts (within the meaning of section 2503) made by the decedent after December 31, 1976, other than gifts that are includible in decedent's gross estate (section 2001(b)))	4
5	Add lines 3 and 4	5
6	Tentative tax on the amount on line 5 from Table A on page 12 of the instructions	6
7a	If line 5 exceeds $10,000,000, enter the lesser of line 5 or $17,184,000. If line 5 is $10,000,000 or less, skip lines 7a and 7b and enter -0- on line 7c . **7a**	
b	Subtract $10,000,000 from line 7a **7b**	
c	Enter 5% (.05) of line 7b	7c
8	Total tentative tax (add lines 6 and 7c)	8
9	Total gift tax payable with respect to gifts made by the decedent after December 31, 1976. Include gift taxes by the decedent's spouse for such spouse's share of split gifts (section 2513) only if the decedent was the donor of these gifts and they are includible in the decedent's gross estate (see instructions)	9
10	Gross estate tax (subtract line 9 from line 8)	10
11	Maximum unified credit (applicable credit amount) against estate tax . **11**	
12	Adjustment to unified credit (applicable credit amount). (This adjustment may not exceed $6,000. See page 4 of the instructions.) **12**	
13	Allowable unified credit (applicable credit amount) (subtract line 12 from line 11)	13
14	Subtract line 13 from line 10 (but do not enter less than zero)	14
15	Credit for state death taxes. Do not enter more than line 14. Figure the credit by using the amount on line 3 less $60,000. See Table B in the instructions and **attach credit evidence** (see instructions) .	15
16	Subtract line 15 from line 14	16
17	Credit for Federal gift taxes on pre-1977 gifts (section 2012) (attach computation) . **17**	
18	Credit for foreign death taxes (from Schedule(s) P). (Attach Form(s) 706-CE.) **18**	
19	Credit for tax on prior transfers (from Schedule Q) **19**	
20	Total (add lines 17, 18, and 19)	20
21	Net estate tax (subtract line 20 from line 16)	21
22	Generation-skipping transfer taxes (from Schedule R, Part 2, line 10)	22
23	Total transfer taxes (add lines 21 and 22)	23
24	Prior payments. Explain in an attached statement **24**	
25	United States Treasury bonds redeemed in payment of estate tax . **25**	
26	Total (add lines 24 and 25).	26
27	Balance due (or overpayment) (subtract line 26 from line 23).	27

Under penalties of perjury, I declare that I have examined this return, including accompanying schedules and statements, and to the best of my knowledge and belief, it is true, correct, and complete. Declaration of preparer other than the executor is based on all information of which preparer has any knowledge.

Signature(s) of executor(s)

Date

Signature of preparer other than executor

Address (and ZIP code)

Date

Cat. No. 20548R

FIGURE A.2 United States Estate (and Generation-Skipping Transfer) Tax Return

Estate of: _____

Part 3—Elections by the Executor

Please check the "Yes" or "No" box for each question. (See instructions beginning on page 5.)		Yes	No
1	Do you elect alternate valuation? **1**		
2	Do you elect special use valuation? . . . . If "Yes," you must complete and attach Schedule A–1. **2**		
3	Do you elect to pay the taxes in installments as described in section 6166? . . . . If "Yes," you must attach the additional information described on page 8 of the instructions. **3**		
4	Do you elect to postpone the part of the taxes attributable to a reversionary or remainder interest as described in section 6163? **4**		

Part 4—General Information (Note: Please attach the necessary supplemental documents. **You must attach the death certificate.**)
(See instructions on page 9.)

Authorization to receive confidential tax information under Regs. sec. 601.504(b)(2)(i); to act as the estate's representative before the IRS; and to make written or oral presentations on behalf of the estate if return prepared by an attorney, accountant, or enrolled agent for the executor:

Name of representative (print or type)	State	Address (number, street, and room or suite no., city, state, and ZIP code)

I declare that I am the ☐ attorney/ ☐ certified public accountant/ ☐ enrolled agent (you must check the applicable box) for the executor and prepared this return for the executor. I am not under suspension or disbarment from practice before the Internal Revenue Service and am qualified to practice in the state shown above.

Signature	CAF number	Date	Telephone number

1 Death certificate number and issuing authority (attach a copy of the death certificate to this return).

2 Decedent's business or occupation. If retired, check here ▶ ☐ and state decedent's former business or occupation.

3 Marital status of the decedent at time of death:
   ☐ Married
   ☐ Widow or widower—Name, SSN, and date of death of deceased spouse ▶ ....
   ....
   ☐ Single
   ☐ Legally separated
   ☐ Divorced—Date divorce decree became final ▶

4a Surviving spouse's name	4b Social security number	4c Amount received (see page 9 of the instructions)

5 Individuals (other than the surviving spouse), trusts, or other estates who receive benefits from the estate (do not include charitable beneficiaries shown in Schedule O) (see instructions). For Privacy Act Notice (applicable to individual beneficiaries only), see the Instructions for Form 1040.

Name of individual, trust, or estate receiving $5,000 or more	Identifying number	Relationship to decedent	Amount (see instructions)

All unascertainable beneficiaries and those who receive less than $5,000 . . . . ▶	

Total	

Please check the "Yes" or "No" box for each question.	Yes	No
6 Does the gross estate contain any section 2044 property (qualified terminable interest property (QTIP) from a prior gift or estate) (see page 9 of the instructions)?		

(continued on next page)

Page 2

FIGURE A.2 *Continued*

Part 4—General Information *(continued)*

Please check the "Yes" or "No" box for each question.		Yes	No
7a Have Federal gift tax returns ever been filed? . . . . If "Yes," please attach copies of the returns, if available, and furnish the following information:			
7b Period(s) covered	**7c** Internal Revenue office(s) where filed		

If you answer "Yes" to any of questions 8–16, you must attach additional information as described in the instructions.

8a	Was there any insurance on the decedent's life that is not included on the return as part of the gross estate?		
b	Did the decedent own any insurance on the life of another that is not included in the gross estate?		
9	Did the decedent at the time of death own any property as a joint tenant with right of survivorship in which **(a)** one or more of the other joint tenants was someone other than the decedent's spouse, and **(b)** less than the full value of the property is included on the return as part of the gross estate? If "Yes," you must complete and attach Schedule E		
10	Did the decedent, at the time of death, own any interest in a partnership or unincorporated business or any stock in an inactive or closely held corporation?		
11	Did the decedent make any transfer described in section 2035, 2036, 2037, or 2038 (see the instructions for Schedule G beginning on page 11 of the separate instructions)? If "Yes," you must complete and attach Schedule G		
12	Were there in existence at the time of the decedent's death:		
a	Any trusts created by the decedent during his or her lifetime?		
b	Any trusts not created by the decedent under which the decedent possessed any power, beneficial interest, or trusteeship?		
13	Did the decedent ever possess, exercise, or release any general power of appointment? If "Yes," you must complete and attach Schedule H		
14	Was the marital deduction computed under the transitional rule of Public Law 97-34, section 403(e)(3) (Economic Recovery Tax Act of 1981)? If "Yes," attach a separate computation of the marital deduction, enter the amount on item 20 of the Recapitulation, and note on item 20 "computation attached."		
15	Was the decedent, immediately before death, receiving an annuity described in the "General" paragraph of the instructions for Schedule I? If "Yes," you must complete and attach Schedule I		
16	Was the decedent ever the beneficiary of a trust for which a deduction was claimed by the estate of a pre-deceased spouse under section 2056(b)(7) and which is not reported on this return? If "Yes," attach an explanation		

Part 5—Recapitulation

Item number	Gross estate		Alternate value	Value at date of death
1	Schedule A—Real Estate	1		
2	Schedule B—Stocks and Bonds	2		
3	Schedule C—Mortgages, Notes, and Cash	3		
4	Schedule D—Insurance on the Decedent's Life (attach Form(s) 712) . . .	4		
5	Schedule E—Jointly Owned Property (attach Form(s) 712 for life insurance) .	5		
6	Schedule F—Other Miscellaneous Property (attach Form(s) 712 for life insurance)	6		
7	Schedule G—Transfers During Decedent's Life (att. Form(s) 712 for life insurance)	7		
8	Schedule H—Powers of Appointment	8		
9	Schedule I—Annuities	9		
10	Total gross estate (add items 1 through 9)	10		
11	Schedule U—Qualified Conservation Easement Exclusion	11		
12	Total gross estate less exclusion (subtract item 11 from item 10). Enter here and on line 1 of Part 2—Tax Computation	12		

Item number	Deductions		Amount	
13	Schedule J—Funeral Expenses and Expenses Incurred in Administering Property Subject to Claims . . .	13		
14	Schedule K—Debts of the Decedent	14		
15	Schedule K—Mortgages and Liens	15		
16	Total of items 13 through 15	16		
17	Allowable amount of deductions from item 16 (see the instructions for item 17 of the Recapitulation) .	17		
18	Schedule L—Net Losses During Administration	18		
19	Schedule L—Expenses Incurred in Administering Property Not Subject to Claims	19		
20	Schedule M—Bequests, etc., to Surviving Spouse	20		
21	Schedule O—Charitable, Public, and Similar Gifts and Bequests	21		
22	Schedule T—Qualified Family-Owned Business Interest Deduction	22		
23	Total allowable deductions (add items 17 through 22). Enter here and on line 2 of the Tax Computation	23		

Page 3

FIGURE A.2 *Continued*

Estate of:

SCHEDULE A—Real Estate

- *For jointly owned property that must be disclosed on Schedule E, see the instructions on the reverse side of Schedule E.*
- *Real estate that is part of a sole proprietorship should be shown on Schedule F.*
- *Real estate that is included in the gross estate under section 2035, 2036, 2037, or 2038 should be shown on Schedule G.*
- *Real estate that is included in the gross estate under section 2041 should be shown on Schedule H.*
- *If you elect section 2032A valuation, you must complete Schedule A and Schedule A-1.*

Item number	Description	Alternate valuation date	Alternate value	Value at date of death
1				
	Total from continuation schedules or additional sheets attached to this schedule . . .			
	TOTAL. (Also enter on Part 5, Recapitulation, page 3, at item 1.)			

(If more space is needed, attach the continuation schedule from the end of this package or additional sheets of the same size.)

(See the instructions on the reverse side.)

Schedule A—Page 4

FIGURE A.2 *Continued*

133

Form 706 (Rev. 7-99)

Instructions for Schedule A—Real Estate

If the total gross estate contains any real estate, you must complete Schedule A and file it with the return. On Schedule A list real estate the decedent owned or had contracted to purchase. Number each parcel in the left-hand column.

Describe the real estate in enough detail so that the IRS can easily locate it for inspection and valuation. For each parcel of real estate, report the area and, if the parcel is improved, describe the improvements. For city or town property, report the street and number, ward, subdivision, block and lot, etc. For rural property, report the township, range, landmarks, etc.

If any item of real estate is subject to a mortgage for which the decedent's estate is liable; that is, if the indebtedness may be charged against other property of the estate that is not subject to that mortgage, or if the decedent was personally liable for that mortgage, you must report the full value of the property in the value column. Enter the amount of the mortgage under "Description" on this schedule. The unpaid amount of the mortgage may be deducted on Schedule K.

If the decedent's estate is NOT liable for the amount of the mortgage, report only the value of the equity of redemption (or value of the property less the indebtedness) in the value column as part of the gross estate. Do not enter any amount less than zero. Do not deduct the amount of indebtedness on Schedule K.

Also list on Schedule A real property the decedent contracted to purchase. Report the full value of the property and not the equity in the value column. Deduct the unpaid part of the purchase price on Schedule K.

Report the value of real estate without reducing it for homestead or other exemption, or the value of dower, curtesy, or a statutory estate created instead of dower or curtesy.

Explain how the reported values were determined and attach copies of any appraisals.

Schedule A Examples

In this example, alternate valuation is not adopted; the date of death is January 1, 1999.

Item number	Description	Alternate valuation date	Alternate value	Value at date of death
1	House and lot, 1921 William Street NW, Washington, DC (lot 6, square 481). Rent of $2,700 due at end of each quarter, February 1, May 1, August 1, and November 1. Value based on appraisal, copy of which is attached			$108,000
	Rent due on item 1 for quarter ending November 1, 1998, but not collected at date of death			2,700
	Rent accrued on item 1 for November and December 1998			1,800
2	House and lot, 304 Jefferson Street, Alexandria, VA (lot 18, square 40). Rent of $600 payable monthly. Value based on appraisal, copy of which is attached			96,000
	Rent due on item 2 for December 1998, but not collected at date of death			600

In this example, alternate valuation is adopted; the date of death is January 1, 1999.

Item number	Description	Alternate valuation date	Alternate value	Value at date of death
1	House and lot, 1921 William Street NW, Washington, DC (lot 6, square 481). Rent of $2,700 due at end of each quarter, February 1, May 1, August 1, and November 1. Value based on appraisal, copy of which is attached. Not disposed of within 6 months following death	7/1/99	90,000	$108,000
	Rent due on item 1 for quarter ending November 1, 1998, but not collected until February 1, 1999	2/1/99	2,700	2,700
	Rent accrued on item 1 for November and December 1998, collected on February 1, 1999	2/1/99	1,800	1,800
2	House and lot, 304 Jefferson Street, Alexandria, VA (lot 18, square 40). Rent of $600 payable monthly. Value based on appraisal, copy of which is attached. Property exchanged for farm on May 1, 1999	5/1/99	90,000	96,000
	Rent due on item 2 for December 1998, but not collected until February 1, 1999 .	2/1/99	600	600

Schedule A—Page 5

FIGURE A.2 *Continued*

134

Instructions for Schedule A-1. Section 2032A Valuation

The election to value certain farm and closely held business property at its special use value is made by checking "Yes" to line 2 of Part 3, Elections by the Executor, Form 706. Schedule A-1 is used to report the additional information that must be submitted to support this election. In order to make a valid election, you must complete Schedule A-1 and attach all of the required statements and appraisals.

For definitions and additional information concerning special use valuation, see section 2032A and the related regulations.

Part 1. Type of Election

Estate and GST Tax Elections. If you elect special use valuation for the estate tax, you must also elect special use valuation for the GST tax and vice versa.

You must value each specific property interest at the same value for GST tax purposes that you value it at for estate tax purposes.

Protective Election. To make the protective election described in the separate instructions for line 2 of Part 3, Elections by the Executor, you must check this box, enter the decedent's name and social security number in the spaces provided at the top of Schedule A-1, and complete line 1 and column A of lines 3 and 4 of Part 2. For purposes of the protective election, list on line 3 all of the real property that passes to the qualified heirs even though some of the property will be shown on line 2 when the additional notice of election is subsequently filed. You need not complete columns B–D of lines 3 and 4. You need not complete any other line entries on Schedule A-1. Completing Schedule A-1 as described above constitutes a Notice of Protective Election as described in Regulations section 20.2032A-8(b).

Part 2. Notice of Election

Line 10. Because the special use valuation election creates a potential tax liability for the recapture tax of section 2032A(c), you must list each person who receives an interest in the specially valued property on Schedule A-1. If there are more than eight persons who receive interests, use an additional sheet that follows the format of line 10. In the columns "Fair market value" and "Special use value," you should enter the total respective values of all the specially valued property interests received by each person.

GST Tax Savings

To compute the additional GST tax due upon disposition (or cessation of qualified use) of the property, each "skip person" (as defined in the instructions to Schedule R) who receives an interest in the specially valued property must know the total GST tax savings on all of the interests in specially valued property received. This GST tax savings is the difference between the total GST tax that was imposed on all of the interests in specially valued property received by the skip person valued at their special use value and the total GST tax that would have been imposed on the same interests received by the skip person had they been valued at their fair market value.

Because the GST tax depends on the executor's allocation of the GST exemption and the grandchild exclusion, the skip person who receives the interests is unable to compute this GST tax savings. Therefore, for each skip person who receives an interest in specially valued property, you must attach worksheets showing the total GST tax savings attributable to all of that person's interests in specially valued property.

How To Compute the GST Tax Savings. Before computing each skip person's GST tax savings, you must complete Schedules R and R-1 for the entire estate (using the special use values).

For each skip person, you must complete two Schedules R (Parts 2 and 3 only) as worksheets, one showing the interests in

specially valued property received by the skip person at their special use value and one showing the same interests at their fair market value.

If the skip person received interests in specially valued property that were shown on Schedule R-1, show these interests on the Schedule R, Parts 2 and 3 worksheets, as appropriate. Do not use Schedule R-1 as a worksheet.

Completing the Special Use Value Worksheets. On lines 2–4 and 6, enter -0-.

Completing the Fair Market Value Worksheets. Lines 2 and 3, fixed taxes and other charges. If valuing the interests at their fair market value (instead of special use value) causes any of these taxes and charges to increase, enter the increased amount (only) on these lines and attach an explanation of the increase. Otherwise, enter -0-.

Line 6—GST exemption. If you completed line 10 of Schedule R, Part 1, enter on line 6 the amount shown for the skip person on the line 10 special use allocation schedule you attached to Schedule R. If you did not complete line 10 of Schedule R, Part 1, enter -0- on line 6.

Total GST Tax Savings. For each skip person, subtract the tax amount on line 10, Part 2 of the special use value worksheet from the tax amount on line 10, Part 2 of the fair market value worksheet. This difference is the skip person's total GST tax savings.

Part 3. Agreement to Special Valuation Under Section 2032A

The agreement to special valuation by persons with an interest in property is required under section 2032A(a)(1)(B) and (d)(2) and must be signed by all parties who have any interest in the property being valued based on its qualified use as of the date of the decedent's death.

An interest in property is an interest that, as of the date of the decedent's death, can be asserted under applicable local law so as to affect the disposition of the specially valued property by the estate. Any person who at the decedent's death has any such interest in the property, whether present or future, or vested or contingent, must enter into the agreement. Included are owners of remainder and executory interests; the holders of general or special powers of appointment; beneficiaries of a gift over in default of exercise of any such power; joint tenants and holders of similar undivided interests when the decedent held only a joint or undivided interest in the property or when only an undivided interest is specially valued; and trustees of trusts and representatives of other entities holding title to, or holding any interests in the property. An heir who has the power under local law to caveat (challenge) a will and thereby affect disposition of the property is not, however, considered to be a person with an interest in property under section 2032A solely by reason of that right. Likewise, creditors of an estate are not such persons solely by reason of their status as creditors.

If any person required to enter into the agreement either desires that an agent act for him or her or cannot legally bind himself or herself due to infancy or other incompetency, or due to death before the election under section 2032A is timely exercised, a representative authorized by local law to bind the person in an agreement of this nature may sign the agreement on his or her behalf.

The Internal Revenue Service will contact the agent designated in the agreement on all matters relating to continued qualification under section 2032A of the specially valued real property and on all matters relating to the special lien arising under section 6324B. It is the duty of the agent as attorney-in-fact for the parties with interests in the specially valued property to furnish the IRS with any requested information and to notify the IRS of any disposition or cessation of qualified use of any part of the property.

Schedule A-1—Page 6

FIGURE A.2 *Continued*

135

Checklist for Section 2032A Election. *If you are going to make the special use valuation election on Schedule A-1, please use this checklist to ensure that you are providing everything necessary to make a valid election.*

To have a valid special use valuation election under section 2032A, you must file, in addition to the Federal estate tax return, **(a)** a notice of election (Schedule A-1, Part 2), and **(b)** a fully executed agreement (Schedule A-1, Part 3). You must include certain information in the notice of election. To ensure that the notice of election includes all of the information required for a valid election, use the following checklist. The checklist is for your use only. Do not file it with the return.

1. Does the notice of election include the decedent's name and social security number as they appear on the estate tax return?

2. Does the notice of election include the relevant qualified use of the property to be specially valued?

3. Does the notice of election describe the items of real property shown on the estate tax return that are to be specially valued and identify the property by the Form 706 schedule and item number?

4. Does the notice of election include the fair market value of the real property to be specially valued and also include its value based on the qualified use (determined without the adjustments provided in section 2032A(b)(3)(B))?

5. Does the notice of election include the adjusted value (as defined in section 2032A(b)(3)(B)) of **(a)** all real property that both passes from the decedent and is used in a qualified use, without regard to whether it is to be specially valued, and **(b)** all real property to be specially valued?

6. Does the notice of election include **(a)** the items of personal property shown on the estate tax return that pass from the decedent to a qualified heir and that are used in qualified use and **(b)** the total value of such personal property adjusted under section 2032A(b)(3)(B)?

7. Does the notice of election include the adjusted value of the gross estate? (See section 2032A(b)(3)(A).)

8. Does the notice of election include the method used to determine the special use value?

9. Does the notice of election include copies of written appraisals of the fair market value of the real property?

10. Does the notice of election include a statement that the decedent and/or a member of his or her family has owned all of the specially valued property for at least 5 years of the 8 years immediately preceding the date of the decedent's death?

11. Does the notice of election include a statement as to whether there were any periods during the 8-year period preceding the decedent's date of death during which the decedent or a member of his or her family did not **(a)** own the property to be specially valued, **(b)** use it in a qualified use, or **(c)** materially participate in the operation of the farm or other business? (See section 2032A(e)(6).)

12. Does the notice of election include, for each item of specially valued property, the name of every person taking an interest in that item of specially valued property and the following information about each such person: **(a)** the person's address, **(b)** the person's taxpayer identification number, **(c)** the person's relationship to the decedent, and **(d)** the value of the property interest passing to that person based on both fair market value and qualified use?

13. Does the notice of election include affidavits describing the activities constituting material participation and the identity of the material participants?

14. Does the notice of election include a legal description of each item of specially valued property?

(In the case of an election made for qualified woodlands, the information included in the notice of election must include the reason for entitlement to the woodlands election.)

Any election made under section 2032A will not be valid unless a properly executed agreement (Schedule A-1, Part 3) is filed with the estate tax return. To ensure that the agreement satisfies the requirements for a valid election, use the following checklist.

1. Has the agreement been signed by each and every qualified heir having an interest in the property being specially valued?

2. Has every qualified heir expressed consent to personal liability under section 2032A(c) in the event of an early disposition or early cessation of qualified use?

3. Is the agreement that is actually signed by the qualified heirs in a form that is binding on all of the qualified heirs having an interest in the specially valued property?

4. Does the agreement designate an agent to act for the parties to the agreement in all dealings with the IRS on matters arising under section 2032A?

5. Has the agreement been signed by the designated agent and does it give the address of the agent?

FIGURE A.2 *Continued*

	Decedent's Social Security Number

Estate of:

SCHEDULE A-1—Section 2032A Valuation

Part 1. Type of Election (Before making an election, see the checklist on page 7.):

☐ **Protective election (Regulations section 20.2032A-8(b)).** Complete Part 2, line 1, and column A of lines 3 and 4. (See instructions.)
☐ **Regular election.** Complete all of Part 2 (including line 11, if applicable) and Part 3. (See instructions.)

Before completing Schedule A-1, see the checklist on page 7 for the information and documents that must be included to make a valid election.

The election is not valid unless the agreement (i.e., Part 3—Agreement to Special Valuation Under Section 2032A)—
● Is signed by each and every qualified heir with an interest in the specially valued property, and
● Is attached to this return when it is filed.

Part 2. Notice of Election (Regulations section 20.2032A-8(a)(3))
  Note: *All real property entered on lines 2 and 3 must also be entered on Schedules A, E, F, G, or H, as applicable.*

1 Qualified use—check one ▶ ☐ Farm used for farming, or
                          ▶ ☐ Trade or business other than farming
2 Real property used in a qualified use, passing to qualified heirs, and to be specially valued on this Form 706.

A	B	C	D
Schedule and item number from Form 706	Full value (without section 2032A(b)(3)(B) adjustment)	Adjusted value (with section 2032A(b)(3)(B) adjustment)	Value based on qualified use (without section 2032A(b)(3)(B) adjustment)

Totals . . . .

Attach a legal description of all property listed on line 2.
Attach copies of appraisals showing the column B values for all property listed on line 2.

3 Real property used in a qualified use, passing to qualified heirs, but not specially valued on this Form 706.

A	B	C	D
Schedule and item number from Form 706	Full value (without section 2032A(b)(3)(B) adjustment)	Adjusted value (with section 2032A(b)(3)(B) adjustment)	Value based on qualified use (without section 2032A(b)(3)(B) adjustment)

Totals . . . .

If you checked "Regular election," you must attach copies of appraisals showing the column B values for all property listed on line 3.

(continued on next page)   Schedule A-1—Page 8

FIGURE A.2 *Continued*

137

4 Personal property used in a qualified use and passing to qualified heirs.

A Schedule and item number from Form 706	B Adjusted value (with section 2032A(b)(3)(B) adjustment)	A (continued) Schedule and item number from Form 706	B (continued) Adjusted value (with section 2032A(b)(3)(B) adjustment)
		"Subtotal" from Col. B, below left	. . . .

Subtotal . . . .   Total adjusted value . . .

5 Enter the value of the total gross estate as adjusted under section 2032A(b)(3)(A). ▶ _____

6 Attach a description of the method used to determine the special value based on qualified use.

7 Did the decedent and/or a member of his or her family own all property listed on line 2 for at least 5 of the 8 years immediately preceding the date of the decedent's death? . . . . ☐ Yes ☐ No

8 Were there any periods during the 8-year period preceding the date of the decedent's death during which the decedent or a member of his or her family: | Yes | No |

a Did not own the property listed on line 2 above? . . . .

b Did not use the property listed on line 2 above in a qualified use? . . . .

c Did not materially participate in the operation of the farm or other business within the meaning of section 2032A(e)(6)?. . . . .

If "Yes" to any of the above, you must attach a statement listing the periods. If applicable, describe whether the exceptions of sections 2032A(b)(4) or (5) are met.

9 Attach affidavits describing the activities constituting material participation and the identity and relationship to the decedent of the material participants.

10 Persons holding interests. Enter the requested information for each party who received any interest in the specially valued property. **(Each of the qualified heirs receiving an interest in the property must sign the agreement, and the agreement must be filed with this return.)**

	Name	Address
A		
B		
C		
D		
E		
F		
G		
H		

	Identifying number	Relationship to decedent	Fair market value	Special use value
A				
B				
C				
D				
E				
F				
G				
H				

You must attach a computation of the GST tax savings attributable to direct skips for each person listed above who is a skip person. (See instructions.)

11 Woodlands election. Check here ▶ ☐ if you wish to make a woodlands election as described in section 2032A(e)(13). Enter the Schedule and item numbers from Form 706 of the property for which you are making this election ▶.......................................
You must attach a statement explaining why you are entitled to make this election. The IRS may issue regulations that require more information to substantiate this election. You will be notified by the IRS if you must supply further information.

Schedule A-1—Page 9

FIGURE A.2 *Continued*

Part 3. Agreement to Special Valuation Under Section 2032A

Estate of:	Date of Death	Decedent's Social Security Number

There cannot be a valid election unless:

● The agreement is executed by each and every one of the qualified heirs, and

● The agreement is included with the estate tax return when the estate tax return is filed.

We (list all qualified heirs and other persons having an interest in the property required to sign this agreement)

_____ ,
_____

being all the qualified heirs and _____ ,
_____ ,

being all other parties having interests in the property which is qualified real property and which is valued under section 2032A of the Internal Revenue Code, do hereby approve of the election made by _____ ,
Executor/Administrator of the estate of _____ ,
pursuant to section 2032A to value said property on the basis of the qualified use to which the property is devoted and do hereby enter into this agreement pursuant to section 2032A(d).

The undersigned agree and consent to the application of subsection (c) of section 2032A of the Code with respect to all the property described on line 2 of Part 2 of Schedule A-1 of Form 706, attached to this agreement. More specifically, the undersigned heirs expressly agree and consent to personal liability under subsection (c) of 2032A for the additional estate and GST taxes imposed by that subsection with respect to their respective interests in the above-described property in the event of certain early dispositions of the property or early cessation of the qualified use of the property. It is understood that if a qualified heir disposes of any interest in qualified real property to any member of his or her family, such member may thereafter be treated as the qualified heir with respect to such interest upon filing a Form 706-A and a new agreement.

The undersigned interested parties who are not qualified heirs consent to the collection of any additional estate and GST taxes imposed under section 2032A(c) of the Code from the specially valued property.

If there is a disposition of any interest which passes, or has passed to him or her, or if there is a cessation of the qualified use of any specially valued property which passes or passed to him or her, each of the undersigned heirs agrees to file a **Form 706-A,** United States Additional Estate Tax Return, and pay any additional estate and GST taxes due within 6 months of the disposition or cessation.

It is understood by all interested parties that this agreement is a condition precedent to the election of special use valuation under section 2032A of the Code and must be executed by every interested party even though that person may not have received the estate (or GST) tax benefits or be in possession of such property.

Each of the undersigned understands that by making this election, a lien will be created and recorded pursuant to section 6324B of the Code on the property referred to in this agreement for the adjusted tax differences with respect to the estate as defined in section 2032A(c)(2)(C).

As the interested parties, the undersigned designate the following individual as their agent for all dealings with the Internal Revenue Service concerning the continued qualification of the specially valued property under section 2032A of the Code and on all issues regarding the special lien under section 6324B. The agent is authorized to act for the parties with respect to all dealings with the Service on matters affecting the qualified real property described earlier. This authority includes the following:

● To receive confidential information on all matters relating to continued qualification under section 2032A of the specially valued real property and on all matters relating to the special lien arising under section 6324B.

● To furnish the Internal Revenue Service with any requested information concerning the property.

● To notify the Internal Revenue Service of any disposition or cessation of qualified use of any part of the property.

● To receive, but not to endorse and collect, checks in payment of any refund of Internal Revenue taxes, penalties, or interest.

● To execute waivers (including offers of waivers) of restrictions on assessment or collection of deficiencies in tax and waivers of notice of disallowance of a claim for credit or refund.

● To execute closing agreements under section 7121.

(continued on next page)

Schedule A-1— Page 10

FIGURE A.2 *Continued*

Form 706 (Rev. 7-99)

Part 3. Agreement to Special Valuation Under Section 2032A *(Continued)*

Estate of:	Date of Death	Decedent's Social Security Number

● Other acts (specify) ▶ _____

By signing this agreement, the agent agrees to provide the Internal Revenue Service with any requested information concerning this property and to notify the Internal Revenue Service of any disposition or cessation of the qualified use of any part of this property.

Name of Agent	Signature	Address

The property to which this agreement relates is listed in Form 706, United States Estate (and Generation-Skipping Transfer) Tax Return, and in the Notice of Election, along with its fair market value according to section 2031 of the Code and its special use value according to section 2032A. The name, address, social security number, and interest (including the value) of each of the undersigned in this property are as set forth in the attached Notice of Election.

IN WITNESS WHEREOF, the undersigned have hereunto set their hands at _____ ,

this _____ day of _____ .

SIGNATURES OF EACH OF THE QUALIFIED HEIRS:

Signature of qualified heir | Signature of qualified heir

Signature of qualified heir | Signature of qualified heir

Signature of qualified heir | Signature of qualified heir

Signature of qualified heir | Signature of qualified heir

Signature of qualified heir | Signature of qualified heir

Signature of qualified heir | Signature of qualified heir

Signatures of other interested parties

Signatures of other interested parties

Schedule A-1—Page 11

FIGURE A.2 *Continued*

140

Estate of:

SCHEDULE B—Stocks and Bonds

(For jointly owned property that must be disclosed on Schedule E, see the instructions for Schedule E.)

Item number	Description including face amount of bonds or number of shares and par value where needed for identification. Give 9-digit CUSIP number.	Unit value	Alternate valuation date	Alternate value	Value at date of death
	CUSIP number				
1					

Total from continuation schedules (or additional sheets) attached to this schedule . . .

TOTAL. (Also enter on Part 5, Recapitulation, page 3, at item 2.) . . . .

(If more space is needed, attach the continuation schedule from the end of this package or additional sheets of the same size.)
(The instructions to Schedule B are in the separate instructions.)

Schedule B—Page 12

FIGURE A.2 *Continued*

141

Estate of:

SCHEDULE C—Mortgages, Notes, and Cash

(For jointly owned property that must be disclosed on Schedule E, see the instructions for Schedule E.)

Item number	Description	Alternate valuation date	Alternate value	Value at date of death
1				
	Total from continuation schedules (or additional sheets) attached to this schedule . .			
	TOTAL. (Also enter on Part 5, Recapitulation, page 3, at item 3.).			

(If more space is needed, attach the continuation schedule from the end of this package or additional sheets of the same size.)
(See the instructions on the reverse side.)

Schedule C—Page 13

FIGURE A.2 *Continued*

142

Instructions for Schedule C.—
Mortgages, Notes, and Cash

Complete Schedule C and file it with your return if the total gross estate contains any:

- mortgages,
- notes, or
- cash.

List on Schedule C:

- Mortgages and notes payable **to the decedent** at the time of death.
- Cash the decedent had at the date of death.

Do not list on Schedule C:

- Mortgages and notes payable **by the decedent.** (If these are deductible, list them on Schedule K.)

List the items on Schedule C in the following order:

- mortgages,
- promissory notes,
- contracts by decedent to sell land,
- cash in possession, and
- cash in banks, savings and loan associations, and other types of financial organizations.

What to enter in the "Description" column:

For mortgages, list:

- face value,
- unpaid balance,
- date of mortgage,
- date of maturity,
- name of maker,
- property mortgaged,
- interest dates, and
- interest rate.

Example to enter in "Description" column:

"Bond and mortgage of $50,000, unpaid balance: $24,000; dated: January 1, 1981; John Doe to Richard Roe; premises: 22 Clinton Street, Newark, NJ; due: January 1, 1999; interest payable at 10% a year--January 1 and July 1."

For promissory notes, list:

- in the same way as mortgages.

For contracts by the decedent to sell land, list:

- name of purchaser,
- contract date,
- property description,
- sale price,
- initial payment,
- amounts of installment payment,
- unpaid balance of principal, and
- interest rate.

For cash in possession, list:

- such cash separately from bank deposits.

For cash in banks, savings and loan associations, and other types of financial organizations, list:

- name and address of each financial organization,
- amount in each account,
- serial or account number,
- nature of account--checking, savings, time deposit, etc., and
- unpaid interest accrued from date of last interest payment to the date of death.

Important: If you obtain statements from the financial organizations, keep them for IRS inspection.

Schedule C—Page 14

FIGURE A.2 *Continued*

143

Estate of:

SCHEDULE D—Insurance on the Decedent's Life

You must list **all** policies on the life of the decedent and attach a Form 712 for each policy.

Item number	Description	Alternate valuation date	Alternate value	Value at date of death
1				

Total from continuation schedules (or additional sheets) attached to this schedule . .

TOTAL. (Also enter on Part 5, Recapitulation, page 3, at item 4.). . . . .

(If more space is needed, attach the continuation schedule from the end of this package or additional sheets of the same size.)

(See the instructions on the reverse side.)

Schedule D—Page 15

FIGURE A.2 *Continued*

144

Instructions for Schedule D—Insurance on the Decedent's Life

If you are required to file Form 706 and there was any insurance on the decedent's life, whether or not included in the gross estate, you must complete Schedule D and file it with the return.

Insurance you must include on Schedule D. Under section 2042 you must include in the gross estate:

- Insurance on the decedent's life receivable by or for the benefit of the estate; and
- Insurance on the decedent's life receivable by beneficiaries other than the estate, as described below.

The term "insurance" refers to life insurance of every description, including death benefits paid by fraternal beneficiary societies operating under the lodge system, and death benefits paid under no-fault automobile insurance policies if the no-fault insurer was unconditionally bound to pay the benefit in the event of the insured's death.

Insurance in favor of the estate. Include on Schedule D the full amount of the proceeds of insurance on the life of the decedent receivable by the executor or otherwise payable to or for the benefit of the estate. Insurance in favor of the estate includes insurance used to pay the estate tax, and any other taxes, debts, or charges that are enforceable against the estate. The manner in which the policy is drawn is immaterial as long as there is an obligation, legally binding on the beneficiary, to use the proceeds to pay taxes, debts, or charges. You must include the full amount even though the premiums or other consideration may have been paid by a person other than the decedent.

Insurance receivable by beneficiaries other than the estate. Include on Schedule D the proceeds of all insurance on the life of the decedent not receivable by or for the benefit of the decedent's estate if the decedent possessed at death any of the incidents of ownership, exercisable either alone or in conjunction with any person.

Incidents of ownership in a policy include:

- The right of the insured or estate to its economic benefits;
- The power to change the beneficiary;
- The power to surrender or cancel the policy;
- The power to assign the policy or to revoke an assignment;
- The power to pledge the policy for a loan;
- The power to obtain from the insurer a loan against the surrender value of the policy;
- A reversionary interest if the value of the reversionary interest was more than 5% of the value of the policy immediately before the decedent died. (An interest in an insurance policy is considered a reversionary interest if, for example, the proceeds become payable to the insured's estate or payable as the insured directs if the beneficiary dies before the insured.)

Life insurance not includible in the gross estate under section 2042 may be includible under some other section of the Code. For example, a life insurance policy could be transferred by the decedent in such a way that it would be includible in the gross estate under section 2036, 2037, or 2038. (See the instructions to Schedule G for a description of these sections.)

Completing the Schedule

You must list every policy of insurance on the life of the decedent, whether or not it is included in the gross estate.

Under "Description" list:

- Name of the insurance company and
- Number of the policy.

For every policy of life insurance listed on the schedule, you must request a statement on **Form 712,** Life Insurance Statement, from the company that issued the policy. Attach the Form 712 to the back of Schedule D.

If the policy proceeds are paid in one sum, enter the net proceeds received (from Form 712, line 24) in the value (and alternate value) columns of Schedule D. If the policy proceeds are not paid in one sum, enter the value of the proceeds as of the date of the decedent's death (from Form 712, line 25).

If part or all of the policy proceeds are not included in the gross estate, you must explain why they were not included.

FIGURE A.2 *Continued*

Estate of:

SCHEDULE E—Jointly Owned Property
(If you elect section 2032A valuation, you must complete Schedule E and Schedule A-1.)

PART 1.—Qualified Joint Interests—Interests Held by the Decedent and His or Her Spouse as the Only Joint Tenants (Section 2040(b)(2))

Item number	Description For securities, give CUSIP number.	Alternate valuation date	Alternate value	Value at date of death
	Total from continuation schedules (or additional sheets) attached to this schedule			
1a Totals	**1a**		
1b Amounts included in gross estate (one-half of line 1a)	**1b**		

PART 2.—All Other Joint Interests

2a State the name and address of each surviving co-tenant. If there are more than three surviving co-tenants, list the additional co-tenants on an attached sheet.

Name	Address (number and street, city, state, and ZIP code)
A.	
B.	
C.	

Item number	Enter letter for co-tenant	Description (including alternate valuation date if any) For securities, give CUSIP number.	Percentage includible	Includible alternate value	Includible value at date of death
		Total from continuation schedules (or additional sheets) attached to this schedule			
2b		Total other joint interests			
3		**Total includible joint interests** (add lines 1b and 2b). Also enter on Part 5, Recapitulation, page 3, at item 5			

(If more space is needed, attach the continuation schedule from the end of this package or additional sheets of the same size.)
(See the instructions on the reverse side.)   **Schedule E—Page 17**

FIGURE A.2 *Continued*

Instructions for Schedule E. Jointly Owned Property

If you are required to file Form 706, you must complete Schedule E and file it with the return if the decedent owned any joint property at the time of death, whether or not the decedent's interest is includible in the gross estate.

Enter on this schedule all property of whatever kind or character, whether real estate, personal property, or bank accounts, in which the decedent held at the time of death an interest either as a joint tenant with right to survivorship or as a tenant by the entirety.

Do not list on this schedule property that the decedent held as a tenant in common, but report the value of the interest on Schedule A if real estate, or on the appropriate schedule if personal property. Similarly, community property held by the decedent and spouse should be reported on the appropriate Schedules A through I. The decedent's interest in a partnership should not be entered on this schedule unless the partnership interest itself is jointly owned. Solely owned partnership interests should be reported on Schedule F, "Other Miscellaneous Property."

Part 1—Qualified joint interests held by decedent and spouse. Under section 2040(b)(2), a joint interest is a qualified joint interest if the decedent and the surviving spouse held the interest as:

- Tenants by the entirety, or
- Joint tenants with right of survivorship if the decedent and the decedent's spouse are the only joint tenants.

Interests that meet either of the two requirements above should be entered in Part 1. Joint interests that do not meet either of the two requirements above should be entered in Part 2.

Under "Description," describe the property as required in the instructions for Schedules A, B, C, and F for the type of property involved. For example, jointly held stocks and bonds should be described using the rules given in the instructions to Schedule B.

Under "Alternate value" and "Value at date of death," enter the full value of the property.

Note: *You cannot claim the special treatment under section 2040(b) for property held jointly by a decedent and a surviving spouse who is not a U.S. citizen. You must report these joint interests on Part 2 of Schedule E, not Part 1.*

Part 2—Other joint interests. All joint interests that were not entered in Part 1 must be entered in Part 2.

For each item of property, enter the appropriate letter A, B, C, etc., from line 2a to indicate the name and address of the surviving co-tenant.

Under "Description," describe the property as required in the instructions for Schedules A, B, C, and F for the type of property involved.

In the "Percentage includible" column, enter the percentage of the total value of the property that you intend to include in the gross estate.

Generally, you must include the full value of the jointly owned property in the gross estate. However, the full value should not be included if you can show that a part of the property originally belonged to the other tenant or tenants and was never received or acquired by the other tenant or tenants from the decedent for less than adequate and full consideration in money or money's worth, or unless you can show that any part of the property was acquired with consideration originally belonging to the surviving joint tenant or tenants. In this case, you may exclude from the value of the property an amount proportionate to the consideration furnished by the other tenant or tenants. Relinquishing or promising to relinquish dower, curtesy, or statutory estate created instead of dower or curtesy, or other marital rights in the decedent's property or estate is not consideration in money or money's worth. See the Schedule A instructions for the value to show for real property that is subject to a mortgage.

If the property was acquired by the decedent and another person or persons by gift, bequest, devise, or inheritance as joint tenants, and their interests are not otherwise specified by law, include only that part of the value of the property that is figured by dividing the full value of the property by the number of joint tenants.

If you believe that less than the full value of the entire property is includible in the gross estate for tax purposes, you must establish the right to include the smaller value by attaching proof of the extent, origin, and nature of the decedent's interest and the interest(s) of the decedent's co-tenant or co-tenants.

In the "Includible alternate value" and "Includible value at date of death" columns, you should enter only the values that you believe are includible in the gross estate.

FIGURE A.2 *Continued*

147

Estate of:

SCHEDULE F—Other Miscellaneous Property Not Reportable Under Any Other Schedule
(For jointly owned property that must be disclosed on Schedule E, see the instructions for Schedule E.)
(If you elect section 2032A valuation, you must complete Schedule F and Schedule A-1.)

		Yes	No
1	Did the decedent at the time of death own any articles of artistic or collectible value in excess of $3,000 or any collections whose artistic or collectible value combined at date of death exceeded $10,000? . . . . If "Yes," submit full details on this schedule and attach appraisals.		
2	Has the decedent's estate, spouse, or any other person, received (or will receive) any bonus or award as a result of the decedent's employment or death? . . . . If "Yes," submit full details on this schedule.		
3	Did the decedent at the time of death have, or have access to, a safe deposit box? . . . . If "Yes," state location, and if held in joint names of decedent and another, state name and relationship of joint depositor.		

If any of the contents of the safe deposit box are omitted from the schedules in this return, explain fully why omitted.

Item number	Description For securities, give CUSIP number.	Alternate valuation date	Alternate value	Value at date of death
1				

Total from continuation schedules (or additional sheets) attached to this schedule . .

TOTAL. (Also enter on Part 5, Recapitulation, page 3, at item 6.) . . . .

(If more space is needed, attach the continuation schedule from the end of this package or additional sheets of the same size.)
(See the instructions on the reverse side.)

Schedule F—Page 19

FIGURE A.2 *Continued*

148

Form 706 (Rev. 7-99)

Instructions for Schedule F—Other Miscellaneous Property

You must complete Schedule F and file it with the return.

On Schedule F list all items that must be included in the gross estate that are not reported on any other schedule, including:

- Debts due the decedent (other than notes and mortgages included on Schedule C)
- Interests in business
- Insurance on the life of another (obtain and attach **Form 712,** Life Insurance Statement, for each policy)

Note for single premium or paid-up policies: *In certain situations, for example where the surrender value of the policy exceeds its replacement cost, the true economic value of the policy will be greater than the amount shown on line 56 of Form 712. In these situations, you should report the full economic value of the policy on Schedule F. See Rev. Rul. 78-137, 1978-1 C.B. 280 for details.*

- Section 2044 property (see **Decedent Who Was a Surviving Spouse** below)
- Claims (including the value of the decedent's interest in a claim for refund of income taxes or the amount of the refund actually received)
- Rights
- Royalties
- Leaseholds
- Judgments
- Reversionary or remainder interests
- Shares in trust funds (attach a copy of the trust instrument)
- Household goods and personal effects, including wearing apparel
- Farm products and growing crops
- Livestock
- Farm machinery
- Automobiles

If the decedent owned any interest in a partnership or unincorporated business, attach a statement of assets and liabilities for the valuation date and for the 5 years before the valuation date. Also attach statements of the net earnings for the same 5 years.

You must account for goodwill in the valuation. In general, furnish the same information and follow the methods used to value close corporations. See the instructions for Schedule B.

All partnership interests should be reported on Schedule F unless the partnership interest, itself, is jointly owned. Jointly owned partnership interests should be reported on Schedule E.

If real estate is owned by the sole proprietorship, it should be reported on Schedule F and not on Schedule A. Describe the real estate with the same detail required for Schedule A.

Line 1. If the decedent owned at the date of death articles with artistic or intrinsic value (e.g., jewelry, furs, silverware, books, statuary, vases, oriental rugs, coin or stamp collections), check the "Yes" box on line 1 and provide full details. If any one article is valued at more than $3,000, or any collection of similar articles is valued at more than $10,000, attach an appraisal by an expert under oath and the required statement regarding the appraiser's qualifications (see Regulations section 20.2031-6(b)).

Decedent Who Was a Surviving Spouse

If the decedent was a surviving spouse, he or she may have received qualified terminable interest property (QTIP) from the predeceased spouse for which the marital deduction was elected either on the predeceased spouse's estate tax return or on a gift tax return, Form 709. The election was available for gifts made and decedents dying after December 31, 1981. List such property on Schedule F.

If this election was made and the surviving spouse retained his or her interest in the QTIP property at death, the full value of the QTIP property is includible in his or her estate, even though the qualifying income interest terminated at death. It is valued as of the date of the surviving spouse's death, or alternate valuation date, if applicable. Do not reduce the value by any annual exclusion that may have applied to the transfer creating the interest.

The value of such property included in the surviving spouse's gross estate is treated as passing from the surviving spouse. It therefore qualifies for the charitable and marital deductions on the surviving spouse's estate tax return if it meets the other requirements for those deductions.

For additional details, see Regulations section 20.2044-1.

Schedule F—Page 20

FIGURE A.2 *Continued*

149

Estate of:

SCHEDULE G—Transfers During Decedent's Life
(If you elect section 2032A valuation, you must complete Schedule G and Schedule A-1.)

Item number	Description For securities, give CUSIP number.	Alternate valuation date	Alternate value	Value at date of death
A.	Gift tax paid by the decedent or the estate for all gifts made by the decedent or his or her spouse within 3 years before the decedent's death (section 2035(b))	X X X X X		
B.	Transfers includible under section 2035(a), 2036, 2037, or 2038:			
1				
	Total from continuation schedules (or additional sheets) attached to this schedule . .			
	TOTAL. (Also enter on Part 5, Recapitulation, page 3, at item 7.).			

SCHEDULE H—Powers of Appointment
(Include "5 and 5 lapsing" powers (section 2041(b)(2)) held by the decedent.)
(If you elect section 2032A valuation, you must complete Schedule H and Schedule A-1.)

Item number	Description	Alternate valuation date	Alternate value	Value at date of death
1				
	Total from continuation schedules (or additional sheets) attached to this schedule . .			
	TOTAL. (Also enter on Part 5, Recapitulation, page 3, at item 8.).			

(If more space is needed, attach the continuation schedule from the end of this package or additional sheets of the same size.)
(The instructions to Schedules G and H are in the separate instructions.)

Schedules G and H—Page 21

FIGURE A.2 *Continued*

150

Estate of:

SCHEDULE I—Annuities

Note: *Generally, no exclusion is allowed for the estates of decedents dying after December 31, 1984 (see page 15 of the instructions).*

	Yes	No
A Are you excluding from the decedent's gross estate the value of a lump-sum distribution described in section 2039(f)(2)? . . . . If "Yes," you must attach the information required by the instructions.		

Item number	Description Show the entire value of the annuity before any exclusions.	Alternate valuation date	Includible alternate value	Includible value at date of death
1				
	Total from continuation schedules (or additional sheets) attached to this schedule . .			
	TOTAL. (Also enter on Part 5, Recapitulation, page 3, at item 9.)			

(If more space is needed, attach the continuation schedule from the end of this package or additional sheets of the same size.)

Schedule I—Page 22

(The instructions to Schedule I are in the separate instructions.)

FIGURE A.2 *Continued*

151

Estate of:

SCHEDULE J—Funeral Expenses and Expenses Incurred in Administering Property Subject to Claims

Note: *Do not list on this schedule expenses of administering property not subject to claims. For those expenses, see the instructions for Schedule L.*

If executors' commissions, attorney fees, etc., are claimed and allowed as a deduction for estate tax purposes, they are not allowable as a deduction in computing the taxable income of the estate for Federal income tax purposes. They are allowable as an income tax deduction on Form 1041 if a waiver is filed to waive the deduction on Form 706 (see the Form 1041 instructions).

Item number	Description	Expense amount	Total amount
1	**A. Funeral expenses:**		
	Total funeral expenses . . . . ▶		....
	B. Administration expenses:		
1	Executors' commissions—amount estimated/agreed upon/paid. (Strike out the words that do not apply.)		....
2	Attorney fees—amount estimated/agreed upon/paid. (Strike out the words that do not apply.). .		....
3	Accountant fees—amount estimated/agreed upon/paid. (Strike out the words that do not apply.).		....
4	Miscellaneous expenses:	*Expense amount*	
	Total miscellaneous expenses from continuation schedules (or additional sheets) attached to this schedule		
	Total miscellaneous expenses . . . . ▶		
	TOTAL. (Also enter on Part 5, Recapitulation, page 3, at item 13.) . . . . ▶		

(If more space is needed, attach the continuation schedule from the end of this package or additional sheets of the same size.)
(See the instructions on the reverse side.)

FIGURE A.2 *Continued*

Instructions for Schedule J—Funeral Expenses and Expenses Incurred in Administering Property Subject to Claims

General. You must complete and file Schedule J if you claim a deduction on item 13 of Part 5, Recapitulation.

On Schedule J, itemize funeral expenses and expenses incurred in administering property subject to claims. List the names and addresses of persons to whom the expenses are payable and describe the nature of the expense. **Do not list expenses incurred in administering property not subject to claims on this schedule. List them on Schedule L instead.**

The deduction is limited to the amount paid for these expenses that is allowable under local law but may not exceed:

1. The value of property subject to claims included in the gross estate, plus

2. The amount paid out of property included in the gross estate but not subject to claims. This amount must actually be paid by the due date of the estate tax return.

The applicable local law under which the estate is being administered determines which property is and is not subject to claims. If under local law a particular property interest included in the gross estate would bear the burden for the payment of the expenses, then the property is considered property subject to claims.

Unlike certain claims against the estate for debts of the decedent (see the instructions for Schedule K in the separate instructions), you cannot deduct expenses incurred in administering property subject to claims on both the estate tax return and the estate's income tax return. If you choose to deduct them on the estate tax return, you cannot deduct them on a Form 1041 filed for the estate. Funeral expenses are only deductible on the estate tax return.

Funeral Expenses. Itemize funeral expenses on line A. Deduct from the expenses any amounts that were reimbursed, such as death benefits payable by the Social Security Administration and the Veterans Administration.

Executors' Commissions. When you file the return, you may deduct commissions that have actually been paid to you or that you expect will be paid. You may not deduct commissions if none will be collected. If the amount of the commissions has not been fixed by decree of the proper court, the deduction will be allowed on the final examination of the return, provided that:

- The District Director is reasonably satisfied that the commissions claimed will be paid;

- The amount entered as a deduction is within the amount allowable by the laws of the jurisdiction where the estate is being administered;

- It is in accordance with the usually accepted practice in that jurisdiction for estates of similar size and character.

If you have not been paid the commissions claimed at the time of the final examination of the return, you must support the amount you deducted with an affidavit or statement signed under the penalties of perjury that the amount has been agreed upon and will be paid.

You may not deduct a bequest or devise made to you instead of commissions. If, however, the decedent fixed by will the compensation payable to you for services to be rendered in the administration of the estate, you may deduct this amount to the extent it is not more than the compensation allowable by the local law or practice.

Do not deduct on this schedule amounts paid as trustees' commissions whether received by you acting in the capacity of a trustee or by a separate trustee. If such amounts were paid in administering property not subject to claims, deduct them on Schedule L.

Note: *Executors' commissions are taxable income to the executors. Therefore, be sure to include them as income on your individual income tax return.*

Attorney Fees. Enter the amount of attorney fees that have actually been paid or that you reasonably expect to be paid. If on the final examination of the return the fees claimed have not been awarded by the proper court and paid, the deduction will be allowed provided the District Director is reasonably satisfied that the amount claimed will be paid and that it does not exceed a reasonable payment for the services performed, taking into account the size and character of the estate and the local law and practice. If the fees claimed have not been paid at the time of final examination of the return, the amount deducted must be supported by an affidavit, or statement signed under the penalties of perjury, by the executor or the attorney stating that the amount has been agreed upon and will be paid.

Do not deduct attorney fees incidental to litigation incurred by the beneficiaries. These expenses are charged against the beneficiaries personally and are not administration expenses authorized by the Code.

Interest Expense. Interest expenses incurred after the decedent's death are generally allowed as a deduction if they are reasonable, necessary to the administration of the estate, and allowable under local law.

Interest incurred as the result of a Federal estate tax deficiency is a deductible administrative expense. Penalties are not deductible even if they are allowable under local law.

Note: *If you elect to pay the tax in installments under section 6166, you may* **not** *deduct the interest payable on the installments.*

Miscellaneous Expenses. Miscellaneous administration expenses necessarily incurred in preserving and distributing the estate are deductible. These expenses include appraiser's and accountant's fees, certain court costs, and costs of storing or maintaining assets of the estate.

The expenses of selling assets are deductible only if the sale is necessary to pay the decedent's debts, the expenses of administration, or taxes, or to preserve the estate or carry out distribution.

FIGURE A.2 *Continued*

Estate of:

SCHEDULE K—Debts of the Decedent, and Mortgages and Liens

Item number	Debts of the Decedent—Creditor and nature of claim, and allowable death taxes	Amount unpaid to date	Amount in contest	Amount claimed as a deduction
1				

Total from continuation schedules (or additional sheets) attached to this schedule . . . .

TOTAL. (Also enter on Part 5, Recapitulation, page 3, at item 14.) . . . .

Item number	Mortgages and Liens—Description	Amount
1		

Total from continuation schedules (or additional sheets) attached to this schedule . . . .

TOTAL. (Also enter on Part 5, Recapitulation, page 3, at item 15.) . . . .

(If more space is needed, attach the continuation schedule from the end of this package or additional sheets of the same size.)
(The instructions to Schedule K are in the separate instructions.)

Schedule K—Page 25

FIGURE A.2 *Continued*

154

Estate of:

SCHEDULE L—Net Losses During Administration and
Expenses Incurred in Administering Property Not Subject to Claims

Item number	Net losses during administration (**Note:** *Do not deduct losses claimed on a Federal income tax return.*)	Amount
1		
	Total from continuation schedules (or additional sheets) attached to this schedule.	
	TOTAL. (Also enter on Part 5, Recapitulation, page 3, at item 18.)	

Item number	Expenses incurred in administering property not subject to claims (Indicate whether estimated, agreed upon, or paid.)	Amount
1		
	Total from continuation schedules (or additional sheets) attached to this schedule.	
	TOTAL. (Also enter on Part 5, Recapitulation, page 3, at item 19.)	

(If more space is needed, attach the continuation schedule from the end of this package or additional sheets of the same size.)

Schedule L—Page 26 (The instructions to Schedule L are in the separate instructions.)

FIGURE A.2 *Continued*

Estate of:

SCHEDULE M—Bequests, etc., to Surviving Spouse

Election To Deduct Qualified Terminable Interest Property Under Section 2056(b)(7). If a trust (or other property) meets the requirements of qualified terminable interest property under section 2056(b)(7), and

  a. The trust or other property is listed on Schedule M, and

  b. The value of the trust (or other property) is entered in whole or in part as a deduction on Schedule M,

then unless the executor specifically identifies the trust (all or a fractional portion or percentage) or other property to be excluded from the election, the executor shall be deemed to have made an election to have such trust (or other property) treated as qualified terminable interest property under section 2056(b)(7).

  If less than the entire value of the trust (or other property) that the executor has included in the gross estate is entered as a deduction on Schedule M, the executor shall be considered to have made an election only as to a fraction of the trust (or other property). The numerator of this fraction is equal to the amount of the trust (or other property) deducted on Schedule M. The denominator is equal to the total value of the trust (or other property).

Election To Deduct Qualified Domestic Trust Property Under Section 2056A. If a trust meets the requirements of a qualified domestic trust under section 2056A(a) and this return is filed no later than 1 year after the time prescribed by law (including extensions) for filing the return, and

  a. The entire value of a trust or trust property is listed on Schedule M, and

  b. The entire value of the trust or trust property is entered as a deduction on Schedule M,

then unless the executor specifically identifies the trust to be excluded from the election, the executor shall be deemed to have made an election to have the entire trust treated as qualified domestic trust property.

		Yes	No
1	Did any property pass to the surviving spouse as a result of a qualified disclaimer? **1**		
	If "Yes," attach a copy of the written disclaimer required by section 2518(b).		
2a	In what country was the surviving spouse born? _____		
b	What is the surviving spouse's date of birth? _____		
c	Is the surviving spouse a U.S. citizen? **2c**		
d	If the surviving spouse is a naturalized citizen, when did the surviving spouse acquire citizenship?_____		
e	If the surviving spouse is not a U.S. citizen, of what country is the surviving spouse a citizen? _____		
3	**Election Out of QTIP Treatment of Annuities**—Do you elect under section 2056(b)(7)(C)(ii) **not** to treat as qualified terminable interest property any joint and survivor annuities that are included in the gross estate and would otherwise be treated as qualified terminable interest property under section 2056(b)(7)(C)? (see instructions) **3**		

Item number	Description of property interests passing to surviving spouse	Amount
1		
	Total from continuation schedules (or additional sheets) attached to this schedule	
4	**Total** amount of property interests listed on Schedule M **4**	
5a	Federal estate taxes payable out of property interests listed on Schedule M . . **5a**	
b	Other death taxes payable out of property interests listed on Schedule M . . . **5b**	
c	Federal and state GST taxes payable out of property interests listed on Schedule M **5c**	
d	Add items 5a, b, and c **5d**	
6	Net amount of property interests listed on Schedule M (subtract 5d from 4). Also enter on Part 5, Recapitulation, page 3, at item 20 . . . . **6**	

(If more space is needed, attach the continuation schedule from the end of this package or additional sheets of the same size.)
(See the instructions on the reverse side.)

Schedule M—Page 27

FIGURE A.2 *Continued*

156

Examples of Listing of Property Interests on Schedule M

Item number	Description of property interests passing to surviving spouse	Amount
1	One-half the value of a house and lot, 256 South West Street, held by decedent and surviving spouse as joint tenants with right of survivorship under deed dated July 15, 1957 (Schedule E, Part I, item 1)	$132,500
2	Proceeds of Gibraltar Life Insurance Company policy No. 104729, payable in one sum to surviving spouse (Schedule D, item 3)	200,000
3	Cash bequest under Paragraph Six of will	100,000

Instructions for Schedule M—Bequests, etc., to Surviving Spouse (Marital Deduction)

General

You must complete Schedule M and file it with the return if you claim a deduction on item 20 of Part 5, Recapitulation.

The marital deduction is authorized by section 2056 for certain property interests that pass from the decedent to the surviving spouse. You may claim the deduction only for property interests that are included in the decedent's gross estate (Schedules A through I).

Note: *The marital deduction is generally not allowed if the surviving spouse is not a U.S. citizen. The marital deduction is allowed for property passing to such a surviving spouse in a "qualified domestic trust" or if such property is transferred or irrevocably assigned to such a trust before the estate tax return is filed. The executor must elect qualified domestic trust status on this return. See the instructions that follow, on pages 29–30, for details on the election.*

Property Interests That You May List on Schedule M

Generally, you may list on Schedule M all property interests that pass from the decedent to the surviving spouse and are included in the gross estate. However, you should not list any "Nondeductible terminable interests" (described below) unless you are making a QTIP election. The property for which you make this election must be included on Schedule M. See "Qualified terminable interest property" on the following page.

For the rules on common disaster and survival for a limited period, see section 2056(b)(3).

You may list on Schedule M only those interests that the surviving spouse takes:

1. As the decedent's legatee, devisee, heir, or donee;

2. As the decedent's surviving tenant by the entirety or joint tenant;

3. As an appointee under the decedent's exercise of a power or as a taker in default at the decedent's nonexercise of a power;

4. As a beneficiary of insurance on the decedent's life;

5. As the surviving spouse taking under dower or curtesy (or similar statutory interest); and

6. As a transferee of a transfer made by the decedent at any time.

Property Interests That You May Not List on Schedule M

You should not list on Schedule M:

1. The value of any property that does not pass from the decedent to the surviving spouse;

2. Property interests that are not included in the decedent's gross estate;

3. The full value of a property interest for which a deduction was claimed on Schedules J through L. The value of the property interest should be reduced by the deductions claimed with respect to it;

4. The full value of a property interest that passes to the surviving spouse subject to a mortgage or other encumbrance or an obligation of the surviving spouse. Include on Schedule M only the net value of the interest after reducing it by the amount of the mortgage or other debt;

5. Nondeductible terminable interests (described below);

6. Any property interest disclaimed by the surviving spouse.

Terminable Interests

Certain interests in property passing from a decedent to a surviving spouse are referred to as *terminable interests*. These are interests that will terminate or fail after the passage of time, or on the occurrence or nonoccurrence of some contingency. Examples are: life estates, annuities, estates for terms of years, and patents.

The ownership of a bond, note, or other contractual obligation, which when discharged would not have the effect of an annuity for life or for a term, is not considered a terminable interest.

Nondeductible terminable interests. A terminable interest is *nondeductible*, and should not be entered on Schedule M (unless you are making a QTIP election) if:

1. Another interest in the same property passed from the decedent to some other person for less than adequate and full consideration in money or money's worth; and

2. By reason of its passing, the other person or that person's heirs may enjoy part of the property after the termination of the surviving spouse's interest.

This rule applies even though the interest that passes from the decedent to a person other than the surviving spouse is not included in the gross estate, and regardless of when the interest passes. The rule also applies regardless of whether the surviving spouse's interest and the other person's interest pass from the decedent at the same time.

Property interests that are considered to pass to a person other than the surviving spouse are any property interest that: **(a)** passes under a decedent's will or intestacy; **(b)** was transferred by a decedent during life; or **(c)** is held by or passed on to any person as a decedent's joint tenant, as appointee under a decedent's exercise of a power, as taker in default at a decedent's release or nonexercise of a power, or as a beneficiary of insurance on the decedent's life.

For example, a decedent devised real property to his wife for life, with remainder to his children. The life interest that passed to the wife does not qualify for the marital deduction because it will terminate at her death and the children will thereafter possess or enjoy the property.

However, if the decedent purchased a joint and survivor annuity for himself and his wife who survived him, the value of the survivor's annuity, to the extent that it is included in the gross estate, qualifies for the marital deduction because even though the interest will terminate on the wife's death, no one else will possess or enjoy any part of the property.

The marital deduction is not allowed for an interest that the decedent directed the executor or a trustee to convert, after death, into a terminable interest for the surviving spouse. The marital deduction is not allowed for such an interest even if there was no interest

Page 28

FIGURE A.2 *Continued*

157

in the property passing to another person and even if the terminable interest would otherwise have been deductible under the exceptions described below for life estate and life insurance and annuity payments with powers of appointment. For more information, see Regulations sections 20.2056(b)-1(f) and 20.2056(b)-1(g), Example (7).

If any property interest passing from the decedent to the surviving spouse may be paid or otherwise satisfied out of any of a group of assets, the value of the property interest is, for the entry on Schedule M, reduced by the value of any asset or assets that, if passing from the decedent to the surviving spouse, would be nondeductible terminable interests. Examples of property interests that may be paid or otherwise satisfied out of any of a group of assets are a bequest of the residue of the decedent's estate, or of a share of the residue, and a cash legacy payable out of the general estate.

Example: A decedent bequeathed $100,000 to the surviving spouse. The general estate includes a term for years (valued at $10,000 in determining the value of the gross estate) in an office building, which interest was retained by the decedent under a deed of the building by gift to a son. Accordingly, the value of the specific bequest entered on Schedule M is $90,000.

Life Estate With Power of Appointment in the Surviving Spouse.
A property interest, whether or not in trust, will be treated as passing to the surviving spouse, and will not be treated as a nondeductible terminable interest if: **(a)** the surviving spouse is entitled for life to all of the income from the entire interest; **(b)** the income is payable annually or at more frequent intervals; **(c)** the surviving spouse has the power, exercisable in favor of the surviving spouse or of the estate of the surviving spouse, to appoint the entire interest; **(d)** the power is exercisable by the surviving spouse alone and (whether exercisable by will or during life) is exercisable by the surviving spouse in all events; and **(e)** no part of the entire interest is subject to a power in any other person to appoint any part to any person other than the surviving spouse (or the surviving spouse's legal representative or relative if the surviving spouse is disabled. See Rev. Rul. 85-35, 1985-1 C.B. 328). If these five conditions are satisfied only for a specific portion of the entire interest, see the section 2056(b) regulations to determine the amount of the marital deduction.

Life Insurance, Endowment, or Annuity Payments, With Power of Appointment in Surviving Spouse. A property interest consisting of the entire proceeds under

a life insurance, endowment, or annuity contract is treated as passing from the decedent to the surviving spouse, and will not be treated as a nondeductible terminable interest if: **(a)** the surviving spouse is entitled to receive the proceeds in installments, or is entitled to interest on them, with all amounts payable during the life of the spouse, payable only to the surviving spouse; **(b)** the installment or interest payments are payable annually, or more frequently, beginning not later than 13 months after the decedent's death; **(c)** the surviving spouse has the power, exercisable in favor of the surviving spouse or of the estate of the surviving spouse, to appoint all amounts payable under the contract; **(d)** the power is exercisable by the surviving spouse alone and (whether exercisable by will or during life) is exercisable by the surviving spouse in all events; and **(e)** no part of the amount payable under the contract is subject to a power in any other person to appoint any part to any person other than the surviving spouse. If these five conditions are satisfied only for a specific portion of the proceeds, see the section 2056(b) regulations to determine the amount of the marital deduction.

Charitable Remainder Trusts. An interest in a charitable remainder trust will **not** be treated as a nondeductible terminable interest if:

1. The interest in the trust passes from the decedent to the surviving spouse; and

2. The surviving spouse is the only beneficiary of the trust other than charitable organizations described in section 170(c).

A "charitable remainder trust" is either a charitable remainder annuity trust or a charitable remainder unitrust. (See section 664 for descriptions of these trusts.)

Election To Deduct Qualified Terminable Interests (QTIP)

You may elect to claim a marital deduction for qualified terminable interest property or property interests. You make the QTIP election simply by listing the qualified terminable interest property on Schedule M and deducting its value. You are presumed to have made the QTIP election if you list the property and deduct its value on Schedule M. If you make this election, the surviving spouse's gross estate will include the value of the "qualified terminable interest property." See the instructions for line 6 of General Information for more details. **The election is irrevocable.**

If you file a Form 706 in which you do not make this election, you may not file an amended return to make the election

unless you file the amended return on or before the due date for filing the original Form 706.

The effect of the election is that the property (interest) will be treated as passing to the surviving spouse and will not be treated as a nondeductible terminable interest. All of the other marital deduction requirements must still be satisfied before you may make this election. For example, you may not make this election for property or property interests that are not included in the decedent's gross estate.

Qualified terminable interest property is property **(a)** that passes from the decedent, and **(b)** in which the surviving spouse has a qualifying income interest for life.

The surviving spouse has a *qualifying income interest for life* if the surviving spouse is entitled to all of the income from the property payable annually or at more frequent intervals, or has a usufruct interest for life in the property, and during the surviving spouse's lifetime no person has a power to appoint any part of the property to any person other than the surviving spouse. An annuity is treated as an income interest regardless of whether the property from which the annuity is payable can be separately identified.

Amendments to Regulations sections 20.2044-1, 20.2056(b)-7 and 20.2056(b)-10 clarify that an interest in property is eligible for QTIP treatment if the income interest is contingent upon the executor's election even if that portion of the property for which no election is made will pass to or for the benefit of beneficiaries other than the surviving spouse.

The QTIP election may be made for all or any part of qualified terminable interest property. A partial election must relate to a fractional or percentile share of the property so that the elective part will reflect its proportionate share of the increase or decline in the whole of the property when applying sections 2044 or 2519. Thus, if the interest of the surviving spouse in a trust (or other property in which the spouse has a qualified life estate) is qualified terminable interest property, you may make an election for a part of the trust (or other property) only if the election relates to a defined fraction or percentage of the entire trust (or other property). The fraction or percentage may be defined by means of a formula.

Qualified Domestic Trust Election (QDOT)

The marital deduction is allowed for transfers to a surviving spouse who is not a U.S. citizen only if the property passes to the surviving spouse in a "qualified domestic trust" (QDOT) or if

Page 29

FIGURE A.2 *Continued*

158

such property is transferred or irrevocably assigned to a QDOT before the decedent's estate tax return is filed.

A QDOT is any trust:

1. That requires at least one trustee to be either an individual who is a citizen of the United States or a domestic corporation;

2. That requires that no distribution of corpus from the trust can be made unless such a trustee has the right to withhold from the distribution the tax imposed on the QDOT;

3. That meets the requirements of any applicable regulations; and

4. For which the executor has made an election on the estate tax return of the decedent.

Note: *For trusts created by an instrument executed before November 5, 1990, paragraphs 1 and 2 above will be treated as met if the trust instrument requires that all trustees be individuals who are citizens of the United States or domestic corporations.*

You make the QDOT election simply by listing the qualified domestic trust or the **entire value** of the trust property on Schedule M and deducting its value. You are presumed to have made the QDOT election if you list the trust or trust property and deduct its value on Schedule M. **Once made, the election is irrevocable.**

If an election is made to deduct qualified domestic trust property under section 2056A(d), the following information should be provided for each qualified domestic trust on an attachment to this schedule:

1. The name and address of every trustee;

2. A description of each transfer passing from the decedent that is the source of the property to be placed in trust; and

3. The employer identification number (EIN) for the trust.

The election must be made for an entire trust. In listing a trust for which you are making a QDOT election, unless you specifically identify the trust as not subject to the election, the election will be considered made for the entire trust.

The determination of whether a trust qualifies as a QDOT will be made as of the date the decedent's Form 706 is filed. If, however, judicial proceedings are brought before the Form 706's due date (including extensions) to have the trust revised to meet the QDOT requirements, then the determination will not be made until the court-ordered changes to the trust are made.

Page 30

Line 1

If property passes to the surviving spouse as the result of a qualified disclaimer, check "Yes" and attach a copy of the written disclaimer required by section 2518(b).

Line 3

Section 2056(b)(7) creates an automatic QTIP election for certain joint and survivor annuities that are includible in the estate under section 2039. To qualify, only the surviving spouse can have the right to receive payments before the death of the surviving spouse.

The executor can elect out of QTIP treatment, however, by checking the "Yes" box on line 3. Once made, the election is irrevocable. If there is more than one such joint and survivor annuity, you are not required to make the election for all of them.

If you make the election out of QTIP treatment by checking "Yes" on line 3, you cannot deduct the amount of the annuity on Schedule M. If you do not make the election out, you must list the joint and survivor annuities on Schedule M.

Listing Property Interests on Schedule M

List each property interest included in the gross estate that passes from the decedent to the surviving spouse and for which a marital deduction is claimed. This includes otherwise nondeductible terminable interest property for which you are making a QTIP election. Number each item in sequence and describe each item in detail. Describe the instrument (including any clause or paragraph number) or provision of law under which each item passed to the surviving spouse. If possible, show where each item appears (number and schedule) on Schedules A through I.

In listing otherwise nondeductible property for which you are making a QTIP election, unless you specifically identify a fractional portion of the trust or other property as not subject to the election, the election will be considered made for all of the trust or other property.

Enter the value of each interest before taking into account the Federal estate tax or any other death tax. The valuation dates used in determining the value of the gross estate apply also on Schedule M.

If Schedule M includes a bequest of the residue or a part of the residue of the decedent's estate, attach a copy of the computation showing how the value of the residue was determined. Include a statement showing:

● The value of all property that is included in the decedent's gross estate (Schedules A through I) but is not a part of the decedent's probate estate, such as lifetime transfers, jointly owned property that passed to the survivor on decedent's death, and the insurance payable to specific beneficiaries.

● The values of all specific and general legacies or devises, with reference to the applicable clause or paragraph of the decedent's will or codicil. (If legacies are made to each member of a class; for example, $1,000 to each of decedent's employees, only the number in each class and the total value of property received by them need be furnished.)

● The date of birth of all persons, the length of whose lives may affect the value of the residuary interest passing to the surviving spouse.

● Any other important information such as that relating to any claim to any part of the estate not arising under the will.

Lines 5a, b, and c—The total of the values listed on Schedule M must be reduced by the amount of the Federal estate tax, the Federal GST tax, and the amount of state or other death and GST taxes paid out of the property interest involved. If you enter an amount for state or other death or GST taxes on lines 5b or 5c, identify the taxes and attach your computation of them.

Attachments. If you list property interests passing by the decedent's will on Schedule M, attach a certified copy of the order admitting the will to probate. If, when you file the return, the court of probate jurisdiction has entered any decree interpreting the will or any of its provisions affecting any of the interests listed on Schedule M, or has entered any order of distribution, attach a copy of the decree or order. In addition, the District Director may request other evidence to support the marital deduction claimed.

FIGURE A.2 *Continued*

159

Estate of:

SCHEDULE O—Charitable, Public, and Similar Gifts and Bequests

		Yes	No
1a If the transfer was made by will, has any action been instituted to have interpreted or to contest the will or any of its provisions affecting the charitable deductions claimed in this schedule? . . . . If "Yes," full details must be submitted with this schedule.			
b According to the information and belief of the person or persons filing this return, is any such action planned? If "Yes," full details must be submitted with this schedule.			
2 Did any property pass to charity as the result of a qualified disclaimer? . . . . If "Yes," attach a copy of the written disclaimer required by section 2518(b).			

Item number	Name and address of beneficiary	Character of institution	Amount
1			

Total from continuation schedules (or additional sheets) attached to this schedule . . . .

3 Total	**3**		
4a Federal estate tax payable out of property interests listed above	**4a**		
b Other death taxes payable out of property interests listed above	**4b**		
c Federal and state GST taxes payable out of property interests listed above	**4c**		
d Add items 4a, b, and c	**4d**		
5 Net value of property interests listed above (subtract 4d from 3). Also enter on Part 5, Recapitulation, page 3, at item 21	**5**		

(If more space is needed, attach the continuation schedule from the end of this package or additional sheets of the same size.)
(The instructions to Schedule O are in the separate instructions.)

Schedule O—Page 31

FIGURE A.2 *Continued*

160

Estate of:

SCHEDULE P—Credit for Foreign Death Taxes

List all foreign countries to which death taxes have been paid and for which a credit is claimed on this return.

If a credit is claimed for death taxes paid to more than one foreign country, compute the credit for taxes paid to one country on this sheet and attach a separate copy of Schedule P for each of the other countries.

The credit computed on this sheet is for the ....
(Name of death tax or taxes)

.... imposed in ....
(Name of country)

Credit is computed under the ....
(Insert title of treaty or "statute")

Citizenship (nationality) of decedent at time of death

(All amounts and values must be entered in United States money.)

1 Total of estate, inheritance, legacy, and succession taxes imposed in the country named above attributable to property situated in that country, subjected to these taxes, and included in the gross estate (as defined by statute)	**1**
2 Value of the gross estate (adjusted, if necessary, according to the instructions for item 2)	**2**
3 Value of property situated in that country, subjected to death taxes imposed in that country, and included in the gross estate (adjusted, if necessary, according to the instructions for item 3)	**3**
4 Tax imposed by section 2001 reduced by the total credits claimed under sections 2010, 2011, and 2012 (see instructions).	**4**
5 Amount of Federal estate tax attributable to property specified at item 3. (Divide item 3 by item 2 and multiply the result by item 4.)	**5**
6 Credit for death taxes imposed in the country named above (the smaller of item 1 or item 5). Also enter on line 18 of Part 2, Tax Computation	**6**

SCHEDULE Q—Credit for Tax on Prior Transfers

Part 1—Transferor Information

	Name of transferor	Social security number	IRS office where estate tax return was filed	Date of death
A				
B				
C				

Check here ▶ ☐ if section 2013(f) (special valuation of farm, etc., real property) adjustments to the computation of the credit were made (see page 18 of the instructions).

Part 2—Computation of Credit (see instructions beginning on page 18)

Item	Transferor			Total A, B, & C
	A	B	C	
1 Transferee's tax as apportioned (from worksheet, (line 7 ÷ line 8) × line 35 for each column) . .				
2 Transferor's tax (from each column of worksheet, line 20)				
3 Maximum amount before percentage requirement (for each column, enter amount from line 1 or 2, whichever is smaller)				
4 Percentage allowed (each column) (see instructions)	%	%	%	
5 Credit allowable (line 3 × line 4 for each column)				
6 TOTAL credit allowable (add columns A, B, and C of line 5). Enter here and on line 19 of Part 2, Tax Computation				

Schedules P and Q—Page 32   (The instructions to Schedules P and Q are in the separate instructions.)

FIGURE A.2 *Continued*

161

Form 706 (Rev. 7-99)

SCHEDULE R—Generation-Skipping Transfer Tax

Note: *To avoid application of the deemed allocation rules, Form 706 and Schedule R should be filed to allocate the GST exemption to trusts that may later have taxable terminations or distributions under section 2612 even if the form is not required to be filed to report estate or GST tax.*

*The GST tax is imposed on taxable transfers of interests in property located **outside the United States** as well as property located inside the United States.*

See instructions beginning on page 19.

Part 1—GST Exemption Reconciliation (Section 2631) and Section 2652(a)(3) (Special QTIP) Election

You no longer need to check a box to make a section 2652(a)(3) (special QTIP) election. If you list qualifying property in Part 1, line 9, below, you will be considered to have made this election. See page 21 of the separate instructions for details.

1 Maximum allowable GST exemption . . . . | **1** |

2 Total GST exemption allocated by the decedent against decedent's lifetime transfers . . . . | **2** |

3 Total GST exemption allocated by the executor, using Form 709, against decedent's lifetime transfers . . . . | **3** |

4 GST exemption allocated on line 6 of Schedule R, Part 2 . . . . | **4** |

5 GST exemption allocated on line 6 of Schedule R, Part 3 . . . . | **5** |

6 Total GST exemption allocated on line 4 of Schedule(s) R-1 . . . . | **6** |

7 Total GST exemption allocated to intervivos transfers and direct skips (add lines 2–6) . . . . | **7** |

8 GST exemption available to allocate to trusts and section 2032A interests (subtract line 7 from line 1) . . . . | **8** |

9 Allocation of GST exemption to trusts (as defined for GST tax purposes):

A Name of trust	B Trust's EIN (if any)	C GST exemption allocated on lines 2–6, above (see instructions)	D Additional GST exemption allocated (see instructions)	E Trust's inclusion ratio (optional—see instructions)

9D Total. May not exceed line 8, above . . . . | **9D** |

10 GST exemption available to allocate to section 2032A interests received by individual beneficiaries (subtract line 9D from line 8). You must attach special use allocation schedule (see instructions) | **10** |

(The instructions to Schedule R are in the separate instructions.) **Schedule R—Page 33**

FIGURE A.2 *Continued*

162

Estate of:

Part 2—Direct Skips Where the Property Interests Transferred Bear the GST Tax on the Direct Skips

Name of skip person	Description of property interest transferred	Estate tax value

1 Total estate tax values of all property interests listed above	1	
2 Estate taxes, state death taxes, and other charges borne by the property interests listed above .	2	
3 GST taxes borne by the property interests listed above but imposed on direct skips other than those shown on this Part 2 (see instructions)	3	
4 Total fixed taxes and other charges (add lines 2 and 3).	4	
5 Total tentative maximum direct skips (subtract line 4 from line 1)	5	
6 GST exemption allocated	6	
7 Subtract line 6 from line 5	7	
8 GST tax due (divide line 7 by 2.818182).	8	
9 Enter the amount from line 8 of Schedule R, Part 3	9	
10 **Total GST taxes payable by the estate** (add lines 8 and 9). Enter here and on line 22 of Part 2—Tax Computation, on page 1.	10	

Schedule R—Page 34

FIGURE A.2 *Continued*

163

Estate of:

Part 3—Direct Skips Where the Property Interests Transferred Do Not Bear the GST
Tax on the Direct Skips

Name of skip person	Description of property interest transferred	Estate tax value

1 Total estate tax values of all property interests listed above	**1**	
2 Estate taxes, state death taxes, and other charges borne by the property interests listed above .	**2**	
3 GST taxes borne by the property interests listed above but imposed on direct skips other than those shown on this Part 3 (see instructions)	**3**	
4 Total fixed taxes and other charges (add lines 2 and 3).	**4**	
5 Total tentative maximum direct skips (subtract line 4 from line 1)	**5**	
6 GST exemption allocated	**6**	
7 Subtract line 6 from line 5	**7**	
8 GST tax due (multiply line 7 by .55). Enter here and on Schedule R, Part 2, line 9	**8**	

Schedule R—Page 35

FIGURE A.2 *Continued*

164

Generation-Skipping Transfer Tax

Direct Skips From a Trust

Payment Voucher

OMB No. 1545-0015

Executor: File one copy with Form 706 and send two copies to the fiduciary. Do not pay the tax shown. See the separate instructions.

Fiduciary: See instructions on the following page. Pay the tax shown on line 6.

Name of trust		Trust's EIN
Name and title of fiduciary	Name of decedent	
Address of fiduciary (number and street)	Decedent's SSN	Service Center where Form 706 was filed
City, state, and ZIP code	Name of executor	
Address of executor (number and street)	City, state, and ZIP code	
Date of decedent's death	Filing due date of Schedule R, Form 706 (with extensions)	

Part 1—Computation of the GST Tax on the Direct Skip

Description of property interests subject to the direct skip	Estate tax value

1	Total estate tax value of all property interests listed above	1
2	Estate taxes, state death taxes, and other charges borne by the property interests listed above.	2
3	Tentative maximum direct skip from trust (subtract line 2 from line 1)	3
4	GST exemption allocated	4
5	Subtract line 4 from line 3	5
6	**GST tax due from fiduciary** (divide line 5 by 2.818182) **(See instructions if property will not bear the GST tax.)**	6

Under penalties of perjury, I declare that I have examined this return, including accompanying schedules and statements, and to the best of my knowledge and belief, it is true, correct, and complete.

	Date
Signature(s) of executor(s)	
	Date
	Date
Signature of fiduciary or officer representing fiduciary	

Schedule R-1 (Form 706)—Page 36

FIGURE A.2 *Continued*

165

Instructions for the Trustee

Introduction

Schedule R-1 (Form 706) serves as a payment voucher for the Generation-Skipping Transfer (GST) tax imposed on a direct skip from a trust, which you, the trustee of the trust, must pay. The executor completes the Schedule R-1 (Form 706) and gives you 2 copies. File one copy and keep one for your records.

How to pay

You can pay by check or money order.
- Make it payable to the "United States Treasury."
- Make the check or money order for the amount on line 6 of Schedule R-1.
- Write "GST Tax" and the trust's EIN on the check or money order.

Signature

You must sign the Schedule R-1 in the space provided.

What to mail

Mail your check or money order and the copy of Schedule R-1 that you signed.

Where to mail

Mail to the Service Center shown on Schedule R-1.

When to pay

The GST tax is due and payable 9 months after the decedent's date of death (shown on the Schedule R-1). You will owe interest on any GST tax not paid by that date.

Automatic extension

You have an automatic extension of time to file Schedule R-1 and pay the GST tax. The automatic extension allows you to file and pay by 2 months after the due date (with extensions) for filing the decedent's Schedule R (shown on the Schedule R-1).

If you pay the GST tax under the automatic extension, you will be charged interest (but no penalties).

Additional information

For more information, see Code section 2603(a)(2) and the instructions for Form 706, United States Estate (and Generation-Skipping Transfer) Tax Return.

Schedule R-1 (Form 706)—Page 37

FIGURE A.2 *Continued*

Estate of:

SCHEDULE T—Qualified Family-Owned Business Interest Deduction

For details on the deduction, including trades and businesses that do not qualify, see page 22 of the separate Instructions for Form 706.

Part 1—Election

Note: *The executor is deemed to have made the election under section 2057 if he or she files Schedule T and deducts any qualifying business interests from the gross estate.*

Part 2—General Qualifications

1 Did the decedent and/or a member of the decedent's family own the business interests listed on line 5 of this schedule for at least 5 of the 8 years immediately preceding the date of the decedent's death?   ☐ **Yes** ☐ **No**

2 Were there any periods during the 8-year period preceding the date of the decedent's death during which the decedent or a member of his or her family:

	Yes	No
a Did not own the business interests listed on this schedule?		
b Did not materially participate, within the meaning of section 2032A(e)(6), in the operation of the business to which such interests relate?.		

If "Yes" to either of the above, you must attach a statement listing the periods. If applicable, describe whether the exceptions of sections 2032A(b)(4) or (5) are met.

Attach affidavits describing the activities constituting material participation and the identity and relationship to the decedent of the material participants.

3 Check the applicable box(es). The qualified family-owned business interest(s) is:

☐ An interest as a proprietor in a trade or business carried on as a proprietorship.

☐ An interest in an entity, at least 50% of which is owned (directly or indirectly) by the decedent and members of the decedent's family.

☐ An interest in an entity, at least 70% of which is owned (directly or indirectly) by members of 2 families and at least 30% of which is owned (directly or indirectly) by the decedent and members of the decedent's family.

☐ An interest in an entity, at least 90% of which is owned (directly or indirectly) by members of 3 families and at least 30% of which is owned (directly or indirectly) by the decedent and members of the decedent's family.

4 Persons holding interests. Enter the requested information for each party who received any interest in the family-owned business. If any qualified heir is not a U.S. citizen, see the line 4 instructions beginning on page 23 of the separate instructions.

(Each of the qualified heirs receiving an interest in the business must sign the agreement that begins on the following page 40, and the agreement must be filed with this return.)

	Name	Address
A		
B		
C		
D		
E		
F		
G		
H		

	Identifying number	Relationship to decedent	Value of interest
A			
B			
C			
D			
E			
F			
G			
H			

Schedule T (Form 706)—Page 38

FIGURE A.2 *Continued*

Part 3—Adjusted Value of Qualified Family-Owned Business Interests

5 Qualified family-owned business interests reported on this return.
Note: *All property listed on line 5 must also be entered on Schedules A, B, C, E, F, G, or H, as applicable.*

A Schedule and item number from Form 706	B Description of business interest and principal place of business	C Reported value

6 **Total** reported value	**6**	
7 Amount of claims or mortgages deductible under section 2053(a)(3) or (4) (see separate instructions).	**7**	
8a Enter the amount of any indebtedness on qualified residence of the decedent (see separate instructions)	**8a**	
b Enter the amount of any indebtedness used for educational or medical expenses (see separate instructions)	**8b**	
c Enter the amount of any indebtedness other than that listed on line 8a or 8b, but do not enter more than $10,000 (see separate instructions)	**8c**	
d Total (add lines 8a through 8c).	**8d**	
9 Subtract line 8d from line 7	**9**	
10 Adjusted value of qualified family-owned business interests (subtract line 9 from line 6) . .	**10**	

Part 4—Qualifying Estate

11 Includible gifts of qualified family-owned business interests (see separate instructions):		
a Amount of gifts taken into account under section 2001(b)(1)(B) .	**11a**	
b Amount of such gifts excluded under section 2503(b)	**11b**	
c Add lines 11a and 11b	**11c**	
12 Add lines 10 and 11c.	**12**	
13 Adjusted gross estate (see separate instructions):		
a Amount of gross estate	**13a**	
b Enter the amount from line 7 . . .	**13b**	
c Subtract line 13b from line 13a . . .	**13c**	
d Enter the amount from line 11c . . .	**13d**	
e Enter the amount of transfers, if any, to the decedent's spouse (see inst.)	**13e**	
f Enter the amount of other gifts (see inst.)	**13f**	
g Add the amounts on lines 13d, 13e, and 13f	**13g**	
h Enter any amounts from line 13g that are otherwise includible in the gross estate	**13h**	
i Subtract line 13h from line 13g	**13i**	
j Adjusted gross estate (add lines 13c and 13i).	**13j**	
14 Enter one-half of the amount on line 13j	**14**	
	Note: *If line 12 does not exceed line 14, stop here; the estate does not qualify for the deduction. Otherwise, complete line 15.*	
15 Net value of qualified family-owned business interests you elect to deduct (line 10 reduced by any marital or other deductions)—**DO NOT** enter more than $675,000—(see instructions) (attach schedule)—enter here and on Part 5, Recapitulation, page 3, at item 22	**15**	

Schedule T—Page 39

FIGURE A.2 *Continued*

Part 5—Agreement to Family-Owned Business Interest Deduction Under Section 2057

Estate of:	Date of Death	Decedent's Social Security Number
		: :

There cannot be a valid election unless:
- The agreement is executed by each and every one of the qualified heirs, and
- The agreement is included with the estate tax return when the estate tax return is filed.

We (list all qualified heirs and other persons having an interest in the business required to sign this agreement)

_____ ,

_____ ,

being all the qualified heirs and _____ ,

_____ ,

being all other parties having interests in the business(es) which are deducted under section 2057 of the Internal Revenue Code, do hereby approve of the election made by _____ ,

Executor/Administrator of the estate of _____ ,

pursuant to section 2057 to deduct said interests from the gross estate and do hereby enter into this agreement pursuant to section 2057(h).

The undersigned agree and consent to the application of subsection (f) of section 2057 of the Code with respect to all the qualified family-owned business interests deducted on Schedule T of Form 706, attached to this agreement. More specifically, the undersigned heirs expressly agree and consent to personal liability under subsection (c) of 2032A (as made applicable by section 2057(i)(3)(F) of the Code) for the additional estate tax imposed by that subsection with respect to their respective interests in the above-described business interests in the event of certain early dispositions of the interests or the occurrence of any of the disqualifying acts described in section 2057(f)(1) of the Code. It is understood that if a qualified heir disposes of any deducted interest to any member of his or her family, such member may thereafter be treated as the qualified heir with respect to such interest upon filing a new agreement and any other form required by the Internal Revenue Service.

The undersigned interested parties who are not qualified heirs consent to the collection of any additional estate tax imposed under section 2057(f) of the Code from the deducted interests.

If there is a disposition of any interest which passes or has passed to him or her, each of the undersigned heirs agrees to file the appropriate form and pay any additional estate tax due within 6 months of the disposition or other disqualifying act.

It is understood by all interested parties that this agreement is a condition precedent to the election of the qualified family-owned business deduction under section 2057 of the Code and must be executed by every interested party even though that person may not have received the estate tax benefits or be in possession of such property.

Each of the undersigned understands that by making this election, a lien will be created and recorded pursuant to section 6324B of the Code on the interests referred to in this agreement for the applicable percentage of the adjusted tax differences with respect to the estate as defined in section 2057(f)(2)(C).

As the interested parties, the undersigned designate the following individual as their agent for all dealings with the Internal Revenue Service concerning the continued qualification of the deducted property under section 2057 of the Code and on all issues regarding the special lien under section 6324B. The agent is authorized to act for all the parties with respect to all dealings with the Service on matters affecting the qualified interests described earlier. This authority includes the following:

- To receive confidential information on all matters relating to continued qualification under section 2057 of the deducted interests and on all matters relating to the special lien arising under section 6324B.

- To furnish the Service with any requested information concerning the interests.

- To notify the Service of any disposition or other disqualifying events specified in section 2057(f)(1) of the Code.

- To receive, but not to endorse and collect, checks in payment of any refund of Internal Revenue taxes, penalties, or interest.

- To execute waivers (including offers of waivers) of restrictions on assessment or collection of deficiencies in tax and waivers of notice of disallowance of a claim for credit or refund.

- To execute closing agreements under section 7121.

(continued on next page)

FIGURE A.2 *Continued*

Part 5. Agreement to Family-Owned Business Interest Deduction Under Section 2057 (continued)

Estate of:	Date of Death	Decedent's Social Security Number

● Other acts (specify) ▶ _____

By signing this agreement, the agent agrees to provide the Internal Revenue Service with any requested information concerning the qualified business interests and to notify the Internal Revenue Service of any disposition or other disqualifying events with regard to said interests.

Name of Agent	Signature	Address

The interests to which this agreement relates are listed in Form 706, United States Estate (and Generation-Skipping Transfer) Tax Return, along with their fair market value according to section 2031 (or, if applicable, section 2032A) of the Code. The name, address, social security number, and interest (including the value) of each of the undersigned in this business(es) are as set forth in the attached Schedule T.

IN WITNESS WHEREOF, the undersigned have hereunto set their hands at _____ ,

this _____ day of _____ .

SIGNATURES OF EACH OF THE QUALIFIED HEIRS:

Signature of qualified heir	Signature of qualified heir
Signature of qualified heir	Signature of qualified heir
Signature of qualified heir	Signature of qualified heir
Signature of qualified heir	Signature of qualified heir
Signature of qualified heir	Signature of qualified heir
Signature of qualified heir	Signature of qualified heir

Signature(s) of other interested parties

Signature(s) of other interested parties

FIGURE A.2 *Continued*

Estate of:

SCHEDULE U. Qualified Conservation Easement Exclusion

Part 1—Election

Note: *The executor is deemed to have made the election under section 2031(c)(6) if he or she files Schedule U and excludes any qualifying conservation easements from the gross estate.*

Part 2—General Qualifications

1 Describe the land subject to the qualified conservation easement (see separate instructions) _____

2 Did the decedent or a member of the decedent's family own the land described above during the 3-year period ending on the date of the decedent's death? . . . . ☐ **Yes** ☐ **No**

3 The land described above is located (check whichever applies) (see separate instructions):
   ☐ In or within 25 miles of an area which, on the date of the decedent's death, is a metropolitan area.
   ☐ In or within 25 miles of an area which, on the date of the decedent's death, is a national park or wilderness area.
   ☐ In or within 10 miles of an area which, on the date of the decedent's death, is an Urban National Forest.

4 Describe the conservation easement with regard to which the exclusion is being claimed (see separate instructions).

Part 3—Computation of Exclusion

5 Estate tax value of the land subject to the qualified conservation easement (see separate instructions)	**5**	
6 Date of death value of any easements granted prior to decedent's death and included on line 11 below (see instructions)	**6**	
7 Add lines 5 and 6	**7**	
8 Value of retained development rights on the land (see instructions)	**8**	
9 Subtract line 8 from line 7	**9**	
10 Multiply line 9 by 30% (.30).	**10**	
11 Value of qualified conservation easement for which the exclusion is being claimed (see instructions)	**11**	
Note: *If line 11 is less than line 10, continue with line 12. If line 11 is equal to or more than line 10, skip lines 12 through 14, enter ".40" on line 15, and complete the schedule.*		
12 Divide line 11 by line 9. Figure to 3 decimal places (e.g., .123) . .	**12**	
If line 12 is equal to or less than .100, stop here; the estate does not qualify for the conservation easement exclusion.		
13 Subtract line 12 from .300. Enter the answer in hundredths by rounding any thousandths up to the next higher hundredth (i.e., .030 = .03; but .031 = .04).	**13**	
14 Multiply line 13 by 2	**14**	
15 Subtract line 14 from .40	**15**	
16 Deduction under section 2055(f) for the conservation easement (see separate instructions).	**16**	
17 Amount of indebtedness on the land (see separate instructions)	**17**	
18 Total reductions in value (add lines 8, 16, and 17)	**18**	
19 Net value of land (subtract line 18 from line 5)	**19**	
20 Multiply line 19 by line 15	**20**	
21 Enter the smaller of line 20 or the exclusion limitation (see instructions). Also enter this amount on item 11, Part 5, Recapitulation, Page 3.	**21**	

Schedule U—Page 42

FIGURE A.2 *Continued*

(Make copies of this schedule before completing it if you will need more than one schedule.)

Estate of:

CONTINUATION SCHEDULE

Continuation of Schedule _____
(Enter letter of schedule you are continuing.)

Item number	Description For securities, give CUSIP number.	Unit value (Sch. B, E, or G only)	Alternate valuation date	Alternate value	Value at date of death or amount deductible

TOTAL. (Carry forward to main schedule.) . . . .

See the instructions on the reverse side.

Continuation Schedule—Page 43

FIGURE A.2 *Continued*

172

Instructions for Continuation Schedule

When you need to list more assets or deductions than you have room for on one of the main schedules, use the Continuation Schedule on page 43. It provides a uniform format for listing additional assets from Schedules A through I and additional deductions from Schedules J, K, L, M, and O.

Please keep the following points in mind:

● Use a separate Continuation Schedule for each main schedule you are continuing. Do not combine assets or deductions from different schedules on one Continuation Schedule.

● Make copies of the blank schedule before completing it if you expect to need more than one.

● Use as many Continuation Schedules as needed to list all the assets or deductions.

● Enter the letter of the schedule you are continuing in the space at the top of the Continuation Schedule.

● Use the *Unit value* column <u>only</u> if continuing Schedule B, E, or G. For all other schedules, use this space to continue the description.

● Carry the total from the Continuation Schedules forward to the appropriate line on the main schedule.

If continuing	Report	Where on Continuation Schedule
Schedule E, Pt. 2	*Percentage includible*	*Alternate valuation date*
Schedule K	*Amount unpaid to date*	*Alternate valuation date*
Schedule K	*Amount in contest*	*Alternate value*
Schedules J, L, M	*Description of deduction continuation*	*Alternate valuation date* **and** *Alternate value*
Schedule O	*Character of institution*	*Alternate valuation date* **and** *Alternate value*
Schedule O	*Amount of each deduction*	*Amount deductible*

FIGURE A.2 *Continued*

Form **706-A**

(Rev. August 1999)
Department of the Treasury
Internal Revenue Service

United States Additional Estate Tax Return
(To report dispositions or cessations of qualified use under
section 2032A of the Internal Revenue Code)

For Privacy Act and Paperwork Reduction Act Notice, see page 4 of the separate instructions.

OMB No. 1545-0016

Part I General Information

1a Name of qualified heir	2 Heir's social security number

1b Address of qualified heir (number and street, including apartment number, P.O. Box, or rural route)	3 Commencement date (see instructions)

1c City, town or post office, state, and ZIP code

4 Decedent's name reported on Form 706	5 Decedent's social security number	6 Date of death

Part II Tax Computation (First complete Schedules A and B—see instructions.)

1	Value at date of death (or alternate valuation date) of all specially valued property that passed from decedent to qualified heir:			
a	Without section 2032A election	1a		
b	With section 2032A election	1b		
c	Balance (subtract line 1b from line 1a)		1c	
2	Value at date of death (or alternate valuation date) of all specially valued property in decedent's estate:			
a	Without section 2032A election	2a		
b	With section 2032A election	2b		
c	Balance (subtract line 2b from line 2a)		2c	
3	Decedent's estate tax:			
a	Recomputed without section 2032A election (attach computation)	3a		
b	Reported on Form 706 with section 2032A election	3b		
c	Balance (subtract line 3b from line 3a)		3c	
4	Divide line 1c by line 2c and enter the result as a percentage		4	%
5	Total estate tax saved (multiply line 3c by percentage on line 4)		5	
6	Value, without section 2032A election, at date of death (or alternate valuation date) of specially valued property shown on Schedule A of this Form 706-A	6		
7	Divide line 6 by line 1a and enter the result as a percentage		7	%
8	Multiply line 5 by percentage on line 7		8	
9	Total estate tax recaptured on previous Form(s) 706-A (attach copies of 706-A)		9	
10	Remaining estate tax savings (subtract line 9 from line 5) (do not enter less than zero)		10	
11	Enter the lesser of line 8 or line 10		11	
12	Enter the total of column D, Schedule A, page 2	12		
13	Enter the total of column E, Schedule A, page 2	13		
14	Balance (subtract line 13 from line 12) (but enter the line 12 amount in the case of a disposition of standing timber on qualified woodland)		14	
15	Enter the lesser of line 11 or line 14		15	

If you completed Schedule B, complete lines 16–19. If you did not complete Schedule B, skip lines 16–18 and enter the amount from line 15 on line 19.

16	Enter the total cost (or FMV) from Schedule B		16	
17	Divide line 16 by line 12 and enter the result as a percentage (do not enter more than 100%)		17	%
18	Multiply line 15 by percentage on line 17		18	
19	**Additional estate tax,** subtract line 18 from line 15 (do not enter less than zero)		19	

Under penalties of perjury, I declare that I have examined this return, and to the best of my knowledge and belief, it is true, correct, and complete. Declaration of preparer other than taxpayer is based on all information of which preparer has any knowledge.

Signature of taxpayer/qualified heir   Date

Signature of preparer other than taxpayer/qualified heir   Date

Address (and ZIP code)

Cat. No. 10141S   Form **706-A** (Rev. 8-99)

FIGURE A.3 United States Additional Estate Tax Return

Schedule A.—Disposition of Specially Valued Property or Cessation of Qualified Use
List property in chronological order of disposition or cessation

A Item number	B Description of specially valued property and schedule and item number where reported on the decedent's Form 706	C Date of disposition (or date qualified use ceased)	D Amount received (or fair market value if applicable) (see instructions)		E Special use value (see instructions)	
1	Form 706, Schedule ...., Item .... Description—					

Totals:
Enter total of column D on line 12 of the Tax Computation, and total of column E on line 13 of the Tax Computation.

FIGURE A.3 *Continued*

Schedule B.—Involuntary Conversions or Exchanges

Check if for: ☐ Involuntary conversion ☐ Exchange

Qualified replacement (or exchange) property

A Item	B Description of qualified replacement (or exchange) property	C Cost (or FMV)
1		

Total cost (or FMV) (enter here and on line 16 of the Tax Computation) . . . .

FIGURE A.3 *Continued*

Schedule C.—Dispositions to Family Members of the Qualified Heir

Each transferee must enter into an agreement to be personally liable for any additional taxes imposed by section 2032A(c) and the agreement must be attached to this Form 706-A. (See instructions.)

Transferee #1:

Last name	First name	Middle initial
Social security number	Relationship to the qualified heir	

Description of property transferred

A Item number	B Description of specially valued property and schedule and item number where reported on the decedent's Form 706	C Date of disposition
1	Form 706, Schedule ...., Item .... Description—	

Transferee #2:

Last name	First name	Middle initial
Social security number	Relationship to the qualified heir	

Description of property transferred

A Item number	B Description of specially valued property and schedule and item number where reported on the decedent's Form 706	C Date of disposition
1	Form 706, Schedule ...., Item .... Description—	

If there are more than two transferees, attach additional sheets using the same format.   Form **706-A** (Rev. 8-99)

FIGURE A.3 *Continued*

Certificate of Payment of Foreign Death Tax

▶ **For Paperwork Reduction Act Notice, see the back of this form.**

OMB No. 1545-0260

District Director of Internal Revenue (city, state, and ZIP code) for the district in which decedent had his or her legal residence (domicile) at time of death

Decedent's first name and middle initial	Decedent's last name	Social security number

Country of citizenship at time of death	Legal residence (domicile) at time of death	Date of death

Last address (number and street, city, state, and ZIP code)

Name of executor, administrator, etc.

Address (number and street, apt. or suite no., city, state, and ZIP code)

1 Name of foreign government imposing the tax	2 Death tax finally determined by that government. Do not include any interest or penalty. Show amount in foreign currency.

3 Was the amount on line 2 figured under the provisions of a death tax convention? . . . . ☐ **Yes** ☐ **No**

4 The amounts paid (other than interest or penalty) and payment dates of the death tax are (show amounts in foreign currency):

5 The description, location, and value (as established and accepted by the death tax officials of the government named above) of the property subjected to the death tax are as follows:

Item Number	Description and location	Value shown in foreign currency
1		

(If necessary, attach additional sheets and follow the same format.) Cat. No. 10149C Form **706-CE** (Rev. 9-97)

FIGURE A.4 Certification of Payment of Foreign Death Tax

178

6 Has any refund of part or all of the death tax on line 2 been claimed or allowed? . . . . ☐ **Yes** ☐ **No**

If "Yes," check the statement below that applies:

☐ Refund was allowed (show that amount in foreign currency). ▶ ....
☐ Claim was rejected in full.
☐ Consideration is pending.

7 Explain below if **(a)** any credit against or reduction of the death tax shown on line 2 is pending or was allowed, **(b)** property was taxed at more than one rate, or **(c)** more than one inheritance was taxed. If you need more space, attach additional sheets.

8 Will you claim a refund or credit (except as shown on line 6) for any of the amount shown on line 2? . . . . ☐ **Yes** ☐ **No**

Under penalties of perjury, I declare that I have examined this statement, including any attached sheets, and to the best of my knowledge and belief, it is true, correct, and complete.

(Signature of executor, administrator, etc.)   (Date)

(Signature of executor, administrator, etc.)   (Date)

Certification
(For use of authorized tax official of the foreign government imposing the death tax)

The information contained on lines **1** through **7** above, including any attached schedules, ☐ without exception (or) ☐ except as indicated is certified to be correct in my attached statement.

(Signature)   (Title)

(Government)   (Date)
Forward a certified copy to the District Director of Internal Revenue shown on the front of this form.

Instructions

You must file Form 706-CE before IRS can allow a credit for foreign death taxes claimed on **Form 706,** United States Estate (and Generation-Skipping Transfer) Tax Return. See the Form 706 instructions for how to figure the credit.

Prepare three copies of Form 706-CE for each foreign death tax for which you are claiming credit. Send the original form and one copy to the foreign government to whom you paid the tax. Ask that office to certify the form and send it to the District Director of Internal Revenue shown on the front. Keep the third copy for your records.

If the foreign government refuses to certify Form 706-CE, you, as executor, must file it directly with the District Director shown on the front. Complete the entire form, except the certification. Attach a statement under penalties of perjury to explain why the foreign government did not certify it. In addition, attach a copy of the foreign death tax return. Also attach a copy of the receipt or cancelled check for the payment of the foreign death tax.

If you or any other person receives a refund of any of the foreign death tax for which you are claiming this credit, you or the person receiving the refund must notify the District Director within 30 days. Section 20.2016-1 of the Estate Tax Regulations describes what information to include in this notice. The persons who received the refund must pay any additional Federal estate tax due.

For a decedent who was a nonresident U.S. citizen, the District Director's address is: Internal Revenue Service, Assistant Commissioner (International), 950 L'Enfant Plaza S.W., Washington, DC 20024, U.S.A.

Death tax conventions are in effect with the countries listed below:

Australia	Germany	Norway
Austria	Greece	Republic of South Africa
Canada	Ireland	Sweden
Denmark	Italy	Switzerland
Finland	Japan	United Kingdom
France	Netherlands	

Paperwork Reduction Act Notice.—We ask for the information on this form to carry out the Internal Revenue laws of the United States. You are required to give us the information. We need it to ensure that you are complying with these laws and to allow us to figure and collect the right amount of tax.

You are not required to provide the information requested on a form that is subject to the Paperwork Reduction Act unless the form displays a valid OMB control number. Books or records relating to a form or its instructions must be retained as long as their contents may become material in the administration of any Internal Revenue law. Generally, tax returns and return information are confidential, as required by Code section 6103.

The time needed to complete and file this form will vary depending on individual circumstances. The estimated average time is:

Recordkeeping	46 min.
Learning about the law or the form	5 min.
Preparing the form.	25 min.
Copying, assembling, and sending the form to the IRS	28 min.

If you have comments concerning the accuracy of these time estimates or suggestions for making this form simpler, we would be happy to hear from you. You can write to the Tax Forms Committee, Western Area Distribution Center, Rancho Cordova, CA 95743-0001. **DO NOT** send the tax form to this address. Instead, see the instructions above for information on where to file.

FIGURE A.4 *Continued*

Form **706-GS(D)**
(Rev. June 1999)

Department of the Treasury
Internal Revenue Service

Generation-Skipping Transfer Tax Return
For Distributions

For calendar year ....

OMB No. 1545-1144

Attach a copy of all Forms 706-GS(D-1) to this return.

Part I   **General Information**

1a Name of skip person distributee	1b Social security number of individual distributee (see instructions)

2a Name and title of person filing return (if different from 1a, see instructions)	1c Employer identification number of trust distributee (see instructions)

2b   Address of distributee or person filing return (see instructions) (number and street or P.O. box; city, town, or post office; state; and ZIP code)

Part II   **Distributions**

a Trust EIN (from line 2a, Form 706-GS(D-1))	b Item no. (from line 3, column a, Form 706-GS(D-1))	c Amount of Transfer (from Tentative transfer, line 3, column f, Form 706-GS(D-1))

3 Total transfers (add amounts in column **c**)	**3**	

Part III   **Tax Computation**

4 Adjusted allowable expenses (see instructions)	**4**	
5 Taxable amount (subtract line 4 from line 3)	**5**	
6 Maximum Federal estate tax rate (see instructions)	**6**	%
7 Gross GST tax (multiply line 5 by line 6)	**7**	
8 Creditable state GST tax (if any) **8**		
9 Multiply line 7 by 5% (.05) **9**		
10 Allowable credit (enter the smaller of line 8 or line 9)	**10**	
11 Net GST tax (subtract line 10 from line 7).	**11**	
12 Payment, if any, made with Form 2758	**12**	
13 **TAX DUE**—if line 11 is larger than line 12, enter amount owed . . . . ▶	**13**	
(*Make the check payable to the United States Treasury.*)		
14 **Overpayment**—if line 12 is larger than line 11, enter amount to be refunded . . . . . . ▶	**14**	

Under penalties of perjury, I declare that I have examined this return, including accompanying schedules and statements, and to the best of my knowledge and belief, it is true, correct, and complete. Declaration of preparer other than taxpayer is based on all information of which preparer has any knowledge.

Please **Sign** **Here**	▶		
	Signature of taxpayer or person filing on behalf of taxpayer		Date

Paid **Preparer's** **Use Only**	Preparer's signature ▶		Date
	Firm's name (or yours if self-employed) and address ▶		ZIP code ▶

For Privacy Act and Paperwork Reduction Act Notice, see page 3 of separate instructions.   Cat. No. 10327Q   Form **706-GS(D)** (Rev. 6-99)

FIGURE A.5   Generation-Skipping Transfer Tax Return for Distributions

Form **706-GS(D-1)**
(Rev. June 1999)

Department of The Treasury
Internal Revenue Service

Notification of Distribution From a Generation-Skipping Trust
(Complete for each skip person distributee—see separate instructions.)
For calendar year ....

OMB No. 1545-1143

Copy A—Send to IRS

Part I   General Information

1a Skip person distributee's identifying number (see instructions)	2a **Trust's employer identification number** (see instructions)
1b Skip person distributee's name, address, and ZIP code	2b Trust's name, address, and ZIP code

Part II   Distributions

3   Describe each distribution below (see instructions).

a Item no.	b Description of property	c Date of distribution	d Inclusion ratio	e Value (see instructions)	f Tentative transfer (multiply col. e by col. d)
1					

Part III   Trust Information (see instructions)

		Yes	No
4	If this is not an explicit trust, check the box and attach a statement describing the arrangement that makes its effect substantially similar to an explicit trust . . . . ▶ ☐		
5	Has any property been contributed to this trust since the last Form 706-GS(T) or (D-1) was filed? If "Yes," attach a schedule showing how the trust's inclusion ratio has been refigured		
6	Have any contributions been made to this trust since the last Form 706-GS(T) or (D-1) was filed that were not included in calculating the trust's inclusion ratio? If "Yes," attach a statement explaining why the contributions were not included		
7	Has any exemption been allocated to this trust by reason of the deemed allocation rules?		

Under penalties of perjury, I declare that I have examined this return, including accompanying schedules and statements, and to the best of my knowledge and belief, it is true, correct, and complete. Declaration of preparer other than trustee is based on all information of which preparer has any knowledge.

Signature of trustee ▶ .... Date ▶ ....

Signature of preparer other than trustee ▶ .... Date ▶ ....

Address ▶

For Paperwork Reduction Act Notice, see page 5 of the separate trustee's instructions.   Cat. No. 10328B   Form **706-GS(D-1)** (Rev. 6-99)

FIGURE A.6   Notification of Distribution from a Generation-Skipping Trust

Form **706-GS(D-1)**
(Rev. June 1999)
Department of The Treasury
Internal Revenue Service

Notification of Distribution From a Generation-Skipping Trust
(Complete for each skip person distributee—see separate instructions.)
For calendar year ....

OMB No. 1545-1143

Copy B—For Distributee

Part I	General Information

1a Skip person distributee's identifying number (see instructions)	**2a** Trust's employer identification number (see instructions)
1b Skip person distributee's name, address, and ZIP code	**2b** Trust's name, address, and ZIP code

Part II	Distributions

3 Describe each distribution below (see instructions).

a Item no.	b Description of property	c Date of distribution	d Inclusion ratio	e Value (see instructions)	f Tentative transfer (multiply col. e by col. d)
1					

Skip Person Distributee—To report this distribution, you must file Form 706-GS(D), Generation-Skipping Transfer Tax Return for Distributions, at the following Internal Revenue Service Center. ▶

For Paperwork Reduction Act Notice, see page 5 of the separate trustee's instructions.

Form **706-GS(D-1)** (Rev. 6-99)

FIGURE A.6 *Continued*

Instructions for Skip Person Distributee

General Instructions

Purpose of form.—Form 706-GS(D-1) is used by a trustee to report to the distributee and to the Internal Revenue Service distributions from a trust that are subject to the generation-skipping transfer tax. The skip person distributee uses the information on Form 706-GS(D-1) to complete **Form 706-GS(D), Generation-Skipping Transfer Tax Return for Distributions.**

Attach a copy of each Form 706-GS(D-1) you received during the year to your Form 706-GS(D). You should also keep a copy for your records.

Errors.—If you believe the trustee has made an error on your Form 706-GS(D-1), notify the trustee and ask for a corrected Form 706-GS(D-1). Do not change any items on your copy. Be sure that the trustee sends a copy of the corrected Form 706-GS(D-1) to the IRS.

Specific Instructions

Part I

Line 2a.—Enter the trust's employer identification number from Part I of this form in Part II, column **a,** of your Form 706-GS(D).

Part II

Column a.—Use the same item number used here for the corresponding entry in Part II, column **b,** of your Form 706-GS(D).

Column c.—The date of distribution is the date the title to the property distributed passed from the trustee to the distributee. This is the date used to determine the value of the distribution.

Column f.—Enter the tentative transfer amount in Part II, column **c,** of your Form 706-GS(D).

Form **706-GS(D-1)** (Rev. 6-99)

FIGURE A.6 *Continued*

Form **706-GS(T)**
(Rev. July 1999)
Department of the Treasury
Internal Revenue Service

Generation-Skipping Transfer Tax Return
For Terminations

For calendar year ......

Part I General Information

1a Name of trust	1b Trust's employer identification number (see instructions)

2a Name of trustee

2b Trustee's address (number and street or P.O. box; apt. or suite no.; city, town or post office; state and ZIP code)

Part II Trust Information (see page 3 of the instructions)

		Yes	No	Sch. A number(s)
3	Has any exemption been allocated to this trust by reason of the deemed allocation rules of section 2632 (b) and (c)? If "Yes," describe the allocation on the line 7, Schedule A attachment showing how the inclusion ratio was calculated			
4	Has property been contributed to this trust since the last Form 706-GS(T) or 706-GS(D-1) was filed? If "Yes," attach a schedule showing how the inclusion ratio was calculated			
5	Have any terminations occurred that are not reported on this return because of the exceptions in section 2611(b)(1) or (2) relating to medical and educational exclusions and prior payment of GST tax? If "Yes," attach a statement describing the termination.			
6	Have any contributions been made to this trust that were not included in calculating the trust's inclusion ratio? If "Yes," attach a statement explaining why the contribution was not included .			
7	Has the special QTIP election in section 2652(a)(3) been made for this trust?.			
8	If this is not an explicit trust (see page 1 of the instructions under **Who Must File**), check box and attach a statement describing the trust arrangement that makes its effect substantially similar to an explicit trust . . . . ▶			

Part III Tax Computation

9a Summary of attached Schedules A (see instructions for line 9b on page 6)

Schedule A No.		Net GST tax (from Sch. A, line 14)
1	. . . . **9a1**	
2	. . . . **9a2**	
3	. . . . **9a3**	
4	. . . . **9a4**	
5	. . . . **9a5**	
6	. . . . **9a6**	

9b	Total from all additional Schedules A attached to this form . . . . ▶	**9b**	
10	**Total** net GST tax (add lines 9a1–9b)	**10**	
11	Payment, if any, made with Form 2758	**11**	
12	**TAX DUE**—if line 10 is larger than line 11, enter amount owed	**12**	
13	**Overpayment**—if line 11 is larger than line 10, enter amount to be refunded	**13**	

Please Sign Here

Under penalties of perjury, I declare that I have examined this return, including accompanying schedules and statements, and to the best of my knowledge and belief, it is true, correct, and complete. Declaration of preparer other than fiduciary is based on all information of which preparer has any knowledge.

▶ _____
Signature of fiduciary or officer representing fiduciary   Date

Paid Preparer's Use Only

Preparer's signature ▶		Date
Firm's name (or yours if self-employed) and address ▶		ZIP code

For Paperwork Reduction Act Notice, see page 1 of separate instructions.   Cat. No. 10329M   Form **706-GS(T)** (Rev. 7-99)

FIGURE A.7 Generation-Skipping Transfer Tax Return for Terminations

Name of trust	EIN of trust

Schedule A No.	**Note:** *Make copies of this schedule before completing it if you will need more than one Schedule A.*

Schedule A—Taxable Terminations
(See page 4 of the instructions before completing this schedule.)

1	a Name of skip persons	b SSN or EIN of skip person	c Item no. from line **4** below in which interest held

2   Describe the terminating power or interest. If you need more space, attach an additional sheet.

3   If you elect alternate valuation, check here (see page 4 of the instructions) . . . . ▶ ☐

4   Describe each taxable termination below (see page 4 of the instructions)

a Item no.	b Description of property subject to termination	c Date of termination	d Valuation date	e Value
1				

Total. . . . . ▶	**4**	
5 Total deductions applicable to this Schedule A (from attached Schedule B, line 5)	**5**	
6 Taxable amount (subtract line 5 from line 4)	**6**	
7 Inclusion ratio (attach separate schedule showing computation)	**7**	
8 Maximum Federal estate tax rate (see page 6 of the instructions).	**8**	%
9 Applicable rate (multiply line 7 by line 8)	**9**	
10 Gross GST tax (multiply line 6 by line 9)	**10**	
11 Creditable state GST tax, if any (attach credit evidence) **11**		
12 Multiply line 10 by 5% (.05) **12**		
13 Allowable credit (enter the smaller of line 11 or line 12)	**13**	
14 Net GST tax (subtract line 13 from line 10) (enter here and on line 9, Part III, page 1)	**14**	

Schedule A (Form 706-GS(T)) (Rev. 7-99)

FIGURE A.7 *Continued*

Name of trust	Schedule A No. ▶
	EIN of trust

Note: *Make copies of this schedule before completing it if you will need more than one Schedule B.*

Schedule B(1)—General Trust Debts, Expenses, and Taxes
(Section 2622(b)) (Enter only items related to the entire trust; see page 4 of the instructions.)

a Item no.	**b** Description	**c** Amount
1		

1	Total of Schedule B(1)	**1**	
2	Percentage allocated to corresponding Schedule A	**2**	%
3	Net deduction (multiply line 1 by line 2)	**3**	

Schedule B(2)—Specific Termination-Related Debts, Expenses, and Taxes
(Section 2622(b)) (Enter only items related solely to terminations appearing on corresponding Schedule A; see page 5 of the instructions.)

a Item no.	**b** Description	**c** Amount
1		

4	Total of Schedule B(2)	**4**	
5	**Total**—Add lines 3 and 4 (enter here and on line 5 of the corresponding Schedule A)	**5**	

Schedules B(1) and B(2) (Form 706-GS(T)) (Rev. 7-99)

FIGURE A.7 *Continued*

Form **706-NA**	United States Estate (and Generation-Skipping Transfer) Tax Return	
(Rev. September 1999)	**Estate of nonresident not a citizen of the United States**	OMB No. 1545-0531
Department of the Treasury Internal Revenue Service	(To be filed for decedents dying after December 31, 1997.) (See separate instructions. Section references are to the Internal Revenue Code.)	

Attach supplemental documents and translations. Show amounts in U.S. dollars.

Part I   Decedent, Executor, and Attorney

1a Decedent's first (given) name and middle initial	**b** Decedent's last (family) name	2 U.S. social security number (if any)

3 Place of death	4 Domicile at time of death	5 Citizenship (nationality)	6 Date of death

7a Date of birth	**b** Place of birth	8 Business or occupation

	9a Name of executor	10a Name of attorney for estate
In United States	**b** Address	**b** Address

	11a Name of executor	12a Name of attorney for estate
Outside United States	**b** Address	**b** Address

Part II   Tax Computation

1	Taxable estate (from Schedule B, line 8)	**1**
2	Total taxable gifts of tangible or intangible property located in the U.S., transferred (directly or indirectly) by the decedent after December 31, 1976, and not included in the gross estate (see section 2511)	**2**
3	Total (add lines 1 and 2)	**3**
4	Tentative tax on the amount on line 3 (see page 3 of instructions)	**4**
5	Tentative tax on the amount on line 2 (see page 3 of instructions)	**5**
6	Gross estate tax (subtract line 5 from line 4)	**6**
7	Unified credit—enter smaller of line 6 amount or maximum allowed (see page 3 of instructions) .	**7**
8	Balance (subtract line 7 from line 6)	**8**
9	Credit for state death taxes (see page 4 of instructions and attach credit evidence)	**9**
10	Balance (subtract line 9 from line 8)	**10**
11	Other credits (see page 4 of instructions) **11**	
12	Credit for tax on prior transfers (attach Schedule Q, Form 706) **12**	
13	Total (add lines 11 and 12)	**13**
14	Net estate tax (subtract line 13 from line 10)	**14**
15	Total generation-skipping transfer tax (attach Schedule R, Form 706)	**15**
16	**Total transfer taxes** (add lines 14 and 15)	**16**
17	Earlier payments (see page 4 of instructions and attach explanation) . . **17**	
18	U.S. Treasury bonds redeemed to pay estate tax **18**	
19	Total (add lines 17 and 18)	**19**
20	Balance due (subtract line 19 from line 16) (see page 4 of instructions)	**20**

Under penalties of perjury, I declare that I have examined this return, including any additional sheets attached, and to the best of my knowledge and belief, it is true, correct, and complete. I understand that a complete return requires listing all property constituting the part of the decedent's gross estate (as defined by the statute) situated in the United States.

(Signature of executor)   (Date)

(Signature of preparer (other than executor))   (Address)   (Date)

For Paperwork Reduction Act Notice, see the separate instructions.   Cat. No. 10145K   Form **706-NA** (Rev. 9-99)

FIGURE A.8   United States Estate (and Generation-Skipping Transfer) Tax Return

Part III General Information

		Yes	No			Yes	No
1a	Did the decedent die testate?			**7**	Did the decedent make any transfer (of property that was located in the United States at either the time of the transfer or the time of death) described in sections 2035, 2036, 2037, or 2038 (see the instructions for Form 706, Schedule G)? . . . . *If "Yes," attach Schedule G, Form 706.*		
b	Were letters testamentary or of administration granted for the estate? . . . . *If granted to persons other than those filing the return, include names and addresses on page 1.*						
2	Did the decedent, at the time of death, own any:			**8**	At the date of death, were there any trusts in existence that were created by the decedent and that included property located in the United States either when the trust was created or when the decedent died? . . . *If "Yes," attach Schedule G, Form 706.*		
a	Real property located in the United States? .						
b	U.S. corporate stock?						
c	Debt obligations of (1) a U.S. person, or (2) the United States, a state or any political subdivision, or the District of Columbia? . .						
d	Other property located in the United States?			**9**	At the date of death, did the decedent:		
3	Was the decedent engaged in business in the United States at the date of death? . . .			**a**	Have a general power of appointment over any property located in the United States? .		
4	At the date of death, did the decedent have access, personally or through an agent, to a safe deposit box located in the United States?			**b**	Or, at any time, exercise or release the power? *If "Yes" to either a or b, attach Schedule H, Form 706.*		
5	At the date of death, did the decedent own any property located in the United States as a joint tenant with right of survivorship; as a tenant by the entirety; or, with surviving spouse, as community property? . . . . *If "Yes," attach Schedule E, Form 706.*			**10a**	Have Federal gift tax returns ever been filed?		
				b	Periods covered ▶		
				c	IRS offices where filed ▶		
6a	Had the decedent ever been a citizen or resident of the United States (see page 2 of instructions)?			**11**	Does the gross estate in the United States include any interests in property transferred to a "skip person" as defined in the instructions to Schedule R of Form 706? . *If "Yes," attach Schedules R and/or R-1, Form 706.*		
b	If "Yes," did the decedent lose U.S. citizenship or residency within 10 years of death? . .						

Schedule A—Gross Estate in the United States (see page 2 of instructions)

	Yes	No
Do you elect to value the decedent's gross estate at a date or dates after the decedent's death (as authorized by section 2032)?		

To make the election, you must check this box "Yes." If you check "Yes," complete all columns. If you check "No," complete columns (a), (b), and (e). You may leave columns (c) and (d) blank or you may use them to expand your column (b) description.

(a) Item no.	(b) Description of property and securities For securities, give CUSIP number.	(c) Alternate valuation date	(d) Alternate value in U.S. dollars	(e) Value at date of death in U.S. dollars
1				
	(If you need more space, attach additional sheets of same size.)			
Total				

Schedule B—Taxable Estate
You must document lines 2 and 4 for the deduction on line 5 to be allowed.

1	Gross estate in the United States (Schedule A total)	**1**	
2	Gross estate outside the United States (see page 3 of instructions)	**2**	
3	Entire gross estate wherever located (add amounts on lines 1 and 2)	**3**	
4	Amount of funeral expenses, administration expenses, decedent's debts, mortgages and liens, and losses during administration (attach itemized schedule) (see page 3 of instructions)	**4**	
5	Deduction for expenses, claims, etc. (divide line 1 by line 3 and multiply the result by line 4)	**5**	
6	Charitable deduction (attach Schedule O, Form 706) and marital deduction (attach Schedule M, Form 706, and computation)	**6**	
7	Total deductions (add lines 5 and 6)	**7**	
8	Taxable estate (subtract line 7 from line 1) (enter here and on line 1 of the Tax Computation) . . .	**8**	

Form **706-NA** (Rev. 9-99)

FIGURE A.8 *Continued*

Form **709**		United States Gift (and Generation-Skipping Transfer) Tax Return		OMB No. 1545-0020

(Section 6019 of the Internal Revenue Code) (For gifts made during calendar year 1999)

1999

Department of the Treasury
Internal Revenue Service

► See separate instructions. For Privacy Act Notice, see the Instructions for Form 1040.

1 Donor's first name and middle initial	2 Donor's last name	3 Donor's social security number
4 Address (number, street, and apartment number)		5 Legal residence (domicile) (county and state)
6 City, state, and ZIP code		7 Citizenship

Part 1—General Information

		Yes	No
8	If the donor died during the year, check here ► ☐ and enter date of death................. , ...		
9	If you received an extension of time to file this Form 709, check here ► ☐ and attach the Form 4868, 2688, 2350, or extension letter		
10	Enter the total number of separate donees listed on Schedule A—count each person only once. ►		
11a	Have you (the donor) previously filed a Form 709 (or 709-A) for any other year? If the answer is "No," do not complete line 11b .		
11b	If the answer to line 11a is "Yes," has your address changed since you last filed Form 709 (or 709-A)?		
12	Gifts by husband or wife to third parties.—Do you consent to have the gifts (including generation-skipping transfers) made by you and by your spouse to third parties during the calendar year considered as made one-half by each of you? (See instructions.) (If the answer is "Yes," the following information must be furnished and your spouse must sign the consent shown below. **If the answer is "No," skip lines 13–18 and go to Schedule A.**)		
13	Name of consenting spouse **14** SSN		
15	Were you married to one another during the entire calendar year? (see instructions)		
16	If the answer to 15 is "No," check whether ☐ married ☐ divorced or ☐ widowed, and give date (see instructions) ►		
17	Will a gift tax return for this calendar year be filed by your spouse?		
18	**Consent of Spouse**—I consent to have the gifts (and generation-skipping transfers) made by me and by my spouse to third parties during the calendar year considered as made one-half by each of us. We are both aware of the joint and several liability for tax created by the execution of this consent.		

Consenting spouse's signature ► Date ►

Part 2—Tax Computation

1	Enter the amount from Schedule A, Part 3, line 15	**1**	
2	Enter the amount from Schedule B, line 3	**2**	
3	Total taxable gifts (add lines 1 and 2)	**3**	
4	Tax computed on amount on line 3 (see Table for Computing Tax in separate instructions) . . .	**4**	
5	Tax computed on amount on line 2 (see Table for Computing Tax in separate instructions) . . .	**5**	
6	Balance (subtract line 5 from line 4)	**6**	
7	Maximum unified credit (nonresident aliens, see instructions)	**7**	211,300 00
8	Enter the unified credit against tax allowable for all prior periods (from Sch. B, line 1, col. C) . .	**8**	
9	Balance (subtract line 8 from line 7)	**9**	
10	Enter 20% (.20) of the amount allowed as a specific exemption for gifts made after September 8, 1976, and before January 1, 1977 (see instructions)	**10**	
11	Balance (subtract line 10 from line 9)	**11**	
12	Unified credit (enter the smaller of line 6 or line 11)	**12**	
13	Credit for foreign gift taxes (see instructions)	**13**	
14	Total credits (add lines 12 and 13)	**14**	
15	Balance (subtract line 14 from line 6) (do not enter less than zero)	**15**	
16	Generation-skipping transfer taxes (from Schedule C, Part 3, col. H, Total)	**16**	
17	Total tax (add lines 15 and 16)	**17**	
18	Gift and generation-skipping transfer taxes prepaid with extension of time to file	**18**	
19	If line 18 is less than line 17, enter BALANCE DUE (see instructions)	**19**	
20	If line 18 is greater than line 17, enter AMOUNT TO BE REFUNDED	**20**	

Under penalties of perjury, I declare that I have examined this return, including any accompanying schedules and statements, and to the best of my knowledge and belief it is true, correct, and complete. Declaration of preparer (other than donor) is based on all information of which preparer has any knowledge.

Donor's signature ► Date ►

Preparer's signature (other than donor) ► Date ►

Preparer's address (other than donor) ►

Attach check or money order here.

For Paperwork Reduction Act Notice, see page 8 of the separate instructions for this form. Cat. No. 16783M Form **709** (1999)

FIGURE A.9 United States Gift (and Generation-Skipping Transfer) Tax Return

| SCHEDULE A | Computation of Taxable Gifts (Including Transfers in Trust) |

A Does the value of any item listed on Schedule A reflect any valuation discount? If the answer is "Yes," see instructions . .Yes ☐ No ☐

B ☐ ◄ Check here if you elect under section 529(c)(2)(B) to treat any transfers made this year to a qualified state tuition program as made ratably over a 5-year period beginning this year. See instructions. Attach explanation.

Part 1—Gifts Subject Only to Gift Tax. *Gifts less political organization, medical, and educational exclusions—see instructions*

A Item number	B • Donee's name and address • Relationship to donor (if any) • Description of gift • If the gift was made by means of a trust, enter trust's identifying number and attach a copy of the trust instrument • If the gift was of securities, give CUSIP number	C Donor's adjusted basis of gift	D Date of gift	E Value at date of gift
1				

Total of Part 1 (add amounts from Part 1, column E) . . . . ►

Part 2—Gifts That are Direct Skips and are Subject to Both Gift Tax and Generation-Skipping Transfer Tax. You must list the gifts in chronological order. *Gifts less political organization, medical, and educational exclusions—see instructions. (Also list here direct skips that are subject only to the GST tax at this time as the result of the termination of an "estate tax inclusion period." See instructions.)*

A Item number	B • Donee's name and address • Relationship to donor (if any) • Description of gift • If the gift was made by means of a trust, enter trust's identifying number and attach a copy of the trust instrument • If the gift was of securities, give CUSIP number	C Donor's adjusted basis of gift	D Date of gift	E Value at date of gift
1				

Total of Part 2 (add amounts from Part 2, column E) . . . . ►

Part 3—Taxable Gift Reconciliation

1	Total value of gifts of donor (add totals from column E of Parts 1 and 2)	1	
2	One-half of items ....attributable to spouse (see instructions)	2	
3	Balance (subtract line 2 from line 1)	3	
4	Gifts of spouse to be included (from Schedule A, Part 3, line 2 of spouse's return—see instructions) . .	4	
	If any of the gifts included on this line are also subject to the generation-skipping transfer tax, check here ► ☐ and enter those gifts also on Schedule C, Part 1.		
5	Total gifts (add lines 3 and 4)	5	
6	Total annual exclusions for gifts listed on Schedule A (including line 4, above) (see instructions) . . .	6	
7	Total included amount of gifts (subtract line 6 from line 5)	7	

Deductions (see instructions)

8	Gifts of interests to spouse for which a marital deduction will be claimed, based on items .... of Schedule A	8		
9	Exclusions attributable to gifts on line 8	9		
10	Marital deduction—subtract line 9 from line 8	10		
11	Charitable deduction, based on items ....less exclusions . .	11		
12	Total deductions—add lines 10 and 11		12	
13	Subtract line 12 from line 7		13	
14	Generation-skipping transfer taxes payable with this Form 709 (from Schedule C, Part 3, col. H, Total) .		14	
15	Taxable gifts (add lines 13 and 14). Enter here and on line 1 of the Tax Computation on page 1 . . .		15	

(If more space is needed, attach additional sheets of same size.)   Form **709** (1999)

FIGURE A.9 *Continued*

190

SCHEDULE A	Computation of Taxable Gifts *(continued)*

16 Terminable Interest (QTIP) Marital Deduction. (See instructions for line 8 of Schedule A.)

If a trust (or other property) meets the requirements of qualified terminable interest property under section 2523(f), and

   a. The trust (or other property) is listed on Schedule A, and

   b. The value of the trust (or other property) is entered in whole or in part as a deduction on line 8, Part 3 of Schedule A,

then the donor shall be deemed to have made an election to have such trust (or other property) treated as qualified terminable interest property under section 2523(f).

If less than the entire value of the trust (or other property) that the donor has included in Part 1 of Schedule A is entered as a deduction on line 8, the donor shall be considered to have made an election only as to a fraction of the trust (or other property). The numerator of this fraction is equal to the amount of the trust (or other property) deducted on line 10 of Part 3, Schedule A. The denominator is equal to the total value of the trust (or other property) listed in Part 1 of Schedule A.

If you make the QTIP election (see instructions for line 8 of Schedule A), the terminable interest property involved will be included in your spouse's gross estate upon his or her death (section 2044). If your spouse disposes (by gift or otherwise) of all or part of the qualifying life income interest, he or she will be considered to have made a transfer of the entire property that is subject to the gift tax (see Transfer of Certain Life Estates on page 3 of the instructions).

17 Election Out of QTIP Treatment of Annuities

☐ ◄ Check here if you elect under section 2523(f)(6) **NOT** to treat as qualified terminable interest property any joint and survivor annuities that are reported on Schedule A and would otherwise be treated as qualified terminable interest property under section 2523(f). (See instructions.)
Enter the item numbers (from Schedule A) for the annuities for which you are making this election ► _____

SCHEDULE B	Gifts From Prior Periods

If you answered "Yes" on line 11a of page 1, Part 1, see the instructions for completing Schedule B. If you answered "No," skip to the Tax Computation on page 1 (or Schedule C, if applicable).

A Calendar year or calendar quarter (see instructions)	B Internal Revenue office where prior return was filed	C Amount of unified credit against gift tax for periods after December 31, 1976	D Amount of specific exemption for prior periods ending before January 1, 1977	E Amount of taxable gifts	

1	Totals for prior periods (without adjustment for reduced specific exemption)	**1**				
2	Amount, if any, by which total specific exemption, line 1, column D, is more than $30,000			**2**		
3	Total amount of taxable gifts for prior periods (add amount, column E, line 1, and amount, if any, on line 2). (Enter here and on line 2 of the Tax Computation on page 1.)			**3**		

(If more space is needed, attach additional sheets of same size.)

Form **709** (1999)

FIGURE A.9 *Continued*

SCHEDULE C	Computation of Generation-Skipping Transfer Tax

Note: *Inter vivos direct skips that are completely excluded by the GST exemption must still be fully reported (including value and exemptions claimed) on Schedule C.*

Part 1—Generation-Skipping Transfers

A Item No. (from Schedule A, Part 2, col. A)	B Value (from Schedule A, Part 2, col. E)	C Split Gifts (enter ½ of col. B) (see instructions)	D Subtract col. C from col. B	E Nontaxable portion of transfer	F Net Transfer (subtract col. E from col. D)
1					
2					
3					
4					
5					
6					

If you elected gift splitting and your spouse was required to file a separate Form 709 (see the instructions for "Split Gifts"), you must enter all of the gifts shown on Schedule A, Part 2, of your spouse's Form 709 here. In column C, enter the item number of each gift in the order it appears in column A of your spouse's Schedule A, Part 2. We have preprinted the prefix "S-" to distinguish your spouse's item numbers from your own when you complete column A of Schedule C, Part 3. In column D, for each gift, enter the amount reported in column C, Schedule C, Part 1, of your spouse's Form 709.	Split gifts from spouse's Form 709 (enter item number) S- S- S- S- S- S- S- S-	Value included from spouse's Form 709	Nontaxable portion of transfer	Net transfer (subtract col. E from col. D)

Part 2—GST Exemption Reconciliation (Section 2631) and Section 2652(a)(3) Election

Check box ▶ ☐ if you are making a section 2652(a)(3) (special QTIP) election (see instructions)

Enter the item numbers (from Schedule A) of the gifts for which you are making this election ▶ ....

1	Maximum allowable exemption (see instructions)	1	
2	Total exemption used for periods before filing this return	2	
3	Exemption available for this return (subtract line 2 from line 1)	3	
4	Exemption claimed on this return (from Part 3, col. C total, below)	4	
5	Exemption allocated to transfers not shown on Part 3, below. **You must attach a Notice of Allocation.** (See instructions.)	5	
6	Add lines 4 and 5	6	
7	Exemption available for future transfers (subtract line 6 from line 3)	7	

Part 3—Tax Computation

A Item No. (from Schedule C, Part 1)	B Net transfer (from Schedule C, Part 1, col. F)	C GST Exemption Allocated	D Divide col. C by col. B	E Inclusion Ratio (subtract col. D from 1.000)	F Maximum Estate Tax Rate	G Applicable Rate (multiply col. E by col. F)	H Generation-Skipping Transfer Tax (multiply col. B by col. G)
1					55% (.55)		
2					55% (.55)		
3					55% (.55)		
4					55% (.55)		
5					55% (.55)		
6					55% (.55)		
					55% (.55)		
					55% (.55)		
					55% (.55)		
					55% (.55)		

Total exemption claimed. Enter here and on line 4, Part 2, above. May not exceed line 3, Part 2, above		**Total generation-skipping transfer tax.** Enter here, on line 14 of Schedule A, Part 3, and on line 16 of the Tax Computation on page 1	

(If more space is needed, attach additional sheets of same size.)   ✳

FIGURE A.9 *Continued*

Form **709-A**	United States Short Form Gift Tax Return	OMB No. 1545-0021

Form 709-A
(Rev. November 1999)

Department of the Treasury
Internal Revenue Service

United States Short Form Gift Tax Return
(For "Privacy Act" notice, see the Form 1040 instructions)

OMB No. 1545-0021

Calendar year ....

1 Donor's first name and middle initial	2 Donor's last name	3 Donor's social security number
4 Address (number, street, and apartment number)		5 Legal residence (domicile)
6 City, state, and ZIP code		7 Citizenship

8 Did you file any gift tax returns for prior periods? . . . . ☐ Yes ☐ No

If "Yes," state when and where earlier returns were filed ▶

9 Name of consenting spouse	10 Consenting spouse's social security number

Note: *Do not use this form to report gifts of closely held stock, partnership interests, fractional interests in real estate, or gifts for which the value has been reduced to reflect a valuation discount. Instead, use Form 709.*

List of Gifts

(a) Donee's name and address and description of gift	(b) Donor's adjusted basis of gift	(c) Date of gift	(d) Value at date of gift

Consent

I consent to have the gifts made by my spouse to third parties during the calendar year considered as made one-half by each of us.

Consenting spouse's signature ▶

Date ▶

Under penalties of perjury, I declare that I have examined this return, and to the best of my knowledge and belief it is true, correct, and complete. Declaration of preparer (other than donor) is based on all information of which preparer has any knowledge.

Donor's signature ▶ .... Date ▶ ....

Preparer's signature
(other than donor's) ▶ .... Date ▶ ....

Preparer's address
(other than donor's) ▶

For Paperwork Reduction Act Notice, see the instructions on the reverse side of this form. Cat. No. 10171G Form **709-A** (Rev. 11-99)

FIGURE A.10 United States Short Form Gift Tax Return

General Instructions

For Privacy Act notice, see the Form 1040 instructions.

Form 709-A is an annual short form gift tax return that certain married couples may use instead of **Form 709**, United States Gift (and Generation-Skipping Transfer) Tax Return, to report nontaxable gifts that they consent to split.

Who May File

Gifts to your spouse. For gifts to your spouse who is a U.S. citizen, you must only file a gift tax return to report certain gifts of terminable interests. For details on this and for filing rules for gifts to a spouse who is not a U.S. citizen, see the Instructions for Form 709.

Gifts to donee other than your spouse. You must file a gift tax return if you gave either of the following gifts to someone other than your spouse:

1. Gifts of future interests of any amount; or

2. Gifts of present interests of more than $10,000 (annual exclusion) to any one donee. The amount of the annual exclusion is indexed for inflation and is announced annually in a revenue procedure published by the IRS.

Exceptions. You do not have to file a gift tax return for any year in which the only gifts you made were for any of the following:

1. Gifts that were paid on behalf of an individual as tuition to an educational organization;

2. Gifts that were paid on behalf of an individual as payment for medical care to a provider of medical care; or

3. Gifts to charity if:

• The gifts were of your entire interest in property,

• The entire transfer qualifies for the gift tax charitable deduction, and

• You have never previously transferred another interest in the property other than as a gift that qualified for the gift tax charitable deduction.

However, if you are required to file a return to report noncharitable gifts and you made gifts to charities, you must include all of your gifts to charities on the return.

You may use Form 709-A if you meet all of the following requirements:

1. You are a citizen or resident of the United States, and were married during the entire calendar year to one individual who is also a citizen or resident of the United States. Both you and your spouse were alive at the end of the calendar year.

2. Your only gifts (other than qualifying gifts for tuition or medical care) to a third party consisted entirely of present interests in tangible personal property, cash, U.S. Savings Bonds, or stocks and bonds listed on a stock exchange. A "third-party donee" is any donee other than your spouse.

3. Your gifts to any one third-party donee (other than qualifying gifts for tuition or medical care) during the calendar year did not total more than $20,000. If the donee is a charity, no part of that gift may be given to a noncharitable donee.

4. During the calendar year, you did not make any gifts of terminable interests to your spouse.

5. During the calendar year, your spouse did not make any gifts to any of the donees listed on this form, did not make gifts of terminable interests to you, did not make gifts (other than qualifying gifts for tuition or medical care) of over $10,000 to any other donee, and did not make any gifts of future interests to any other donee.

6. You and your spouse agree to split all of the gifts either of you made during the calendar year.

7. You did not file a Form 709 for this calendar year.

If you meet all seven requirements above, you may also use Form 709-A to report gifts made under the Uniform Gifts to Minors Act.

Note: *Gifts include transfers of property when no money changes hands and also transfers when some payment was made, but the payment made was less than the value of the item transferred.*

When To File

Form 709-A is a calendar-year return to be filed on or after January 1 but not later than April 15 of the year following the year when the nontaxable gifts were made.

If the due date falls on a Saturday, Sunday, or legal holiday, file on the next business day.

Any extension of time granted to file your calendar year income tax return will also extend the time to file Form 709-A. Income tax extensions are made using Forms 4868, 2688, or 2350. See Form 4868 to get an automatic 4-month extension by phone. If you received an extension, attach a copy of it to Form 709-A.

You may not file Form 709-A later than April 15 (or the extension due date). Instead, you must file Form 709.

Where To File

File Form 709-A with the Internal Revenue Service Center where you would file your Federal income tax return. See the Form 1040 instructions for a list of filing locations.

Additional Help

The Instructions for Form 709 contain further information on the gift tax, including information about the following matters:

1. Annual exclusion.

2. Present and future interest.

3. Fair market value.

4. Adjusted basis. See **Pub. 551**, Basis of Assets, and the instructions for Schedule D (Form 1040).

5. Extension of time to file.

6. Terminable interest.

7. Gifts for tuition or medical care.

Specific Instructions

Column (a). List the names and addresses of all third party donees to whom you made gifts (other than qualifying gifts for tuition or medical care) totaling more than $10,000 during the calendar year. Do not list the names of donees to whom you gave only qualifying gifts for tuition, medical care, or to whom you gave gifts of present interests of $10,000 or less.

Describe the gifts in enough detail so they may be easily identified.

If you list **bonds**, include in your description:

• The number of bonds transferred;

• The principal amount of the bonds;

• The name of the obligor;

• The date of maturity of the bonds;

• The rate of interest;

• The date or dates on which interest is payable;

• The series number (if there is more than one issue);

• The exchange where the bond is listed; and

• The CUSIP number. The CUSIP number is a nine-digit number assigned by the American Banking Association to traded securities.

If you list **stocks,** you should include:

• The number of shares transferred;

• Whether the stocks are common or preferred. (If the stocks are preferred, list the issue and par value.);

• Exact name of corporation;

• Principal exchange where the stocks are sold; and

• The CUSIP number (see "bonds" above).

If you list **tangible personal property** (such as a car), describe the property in enough detail so that its fair market value (FMV) can be accurately figured.

Column (b). Show the basis you would use for income tax purposes if you sold or exchanged the property.

Column (d). If you make the gift in property other than money, determine the FMV as of the date the gift was made.

Consent

Your spouse must consent to split all gifts made by either of you. Your spouse gives this consent by signing in the space provided. You give your consent by signing in the space for the donor's signature. The guardian of a legally incompetent spouse may sign the consent. The executor for a deceased spouse may sign the consent if the spouse died after the close of the calendar year. Although a properly filed Form 709-A will not result in any gift tax liability, you should know that if you and your spouse consent to split gifts, either or both of you will be liable in the event any gift tax is later determined to be due.

Signature

You, as a donor, must sign the return. If you pay another person, firm, or corporation to prepare your return, that person must also sign the return as preparer unless he or she is your regular, full-time employee.

FIGURE A.10 *Continued*

Form **712**		**Life Insurance Statement**	OMB No. 1545-0022

Form **712**
(Rev. October 1997)
Department of the Treasury
Internal Revenue Service

Life Insurance Statement

OMB No. 1545-0022

Part I **Decedent—Insured** (To be filed by the executor with **Form 706**, United State Estate (and Generation-Skipping Transfer) Tax Return, or **Form 706-NA**, United States Estate (and Generation-Skipping Transfer) Tax Return, Estate of nonresident not a citizen of the United States.)

1 Decedent's first name and middle initial	2 Decedent's last name	3 Decedent's social security number (if known)	4 Date of death

5 Name and address of insurance company

6 Type of policy	7 Policy number

8 Owner's name. If decedent is not owner, attach copy of application.	9 Date issued	10 Assignor's name. Attach copy of assignment.	11 Date assigned

12 Value of the policy at the time of assignment	13 Amount of premium (see instructions)	14 Name of beneficiaries

15 Face amount of policy . . . . $ _____
16 Indemnity benefits . . . . $ _____
17 Additional insurance . . . . $ _____
18 Other benefits. . . . . $ _____
19 Principal of any indebtedness to the company that is deductible in determining net proceeds . . . $ _____
20 Interest on indebtedness (line 19) accrued to date of death . . . . $ _____
21 Amount of accumulated dividends . . . . $ _____
22 Amount of post-mortem dividends . . . . $ _____
23 Amount of returned premium . . . . $ _____
24 Amount of proceeds if payable in one sum . . . . $ _____
25 Value of proceeds as of date of death (if not payable in one sum) . . . . $ _____
26 Policy provisions concerning deferred payments or installments.
   Note: *If other than lump-sum settlement is authorized for a surviving spouse, attach a copy of the insurance policy.*
   ....
   ....
27 Amount of installments .... $ _____
28 Date of birth, sex, and name of any person the duration of whose life may measure the number of payments.
   ....
   ....
29 Amount applied by the insurance company as a single premium representing the purchase of installment benefits . . . . $ _____
30 Basis (mortality table and rate of interest) used by insurer in valuing installment benefits.
   ....
31 Was the insured the annuitant or beneficiary of any annuity contract issued by the company?. . . . ☐ **Yes** ☐ **No**
32 Names of companies with which decedent carried other policies and amount of such policies if this information is disclosed by your records.
   ....
   ....

The undersigned officer of the above-named insurance company (or appropriate Federal agency or retirement system official) hereby certifies that this statement sets forth true and correct information.

Signature ▶   Title ▶   Date of Certification ▶

Instructions

Statement of insurer.—This statement must be made, on behalf of the insurance company that issued the policy, by an officer of the company having access to the records of the company. For purposes of this statement, a facsimile signature may be used in lieu of a manual signature and if used, shall be binding as a manual signature.

Separate statements.—File a separate Form 712 for each policy.

Line 13.—Report on line 13 the annual premium, not the cumulative premium to date of death. If death occurred after the end of the premium period, report the last annual premium.

Paperwork Reduction Act Notice.—We ask for the information on this form to carry out the Internal Revenue laws of the United States. You are required to give us the information. We need it to ensure that you are complying with these laws and to allow us to figure and collect the right amount of tax.

You are not required to provide the information requested on a form that is subject to the Paperwork Reduction Act unless the form displays a valid OMB control number. Books or records relating to a form or its instructions must be retained as long as their contents may become material in the administration of any Internal Revenue law. Generally, tax returns and return information are confidential, as required by section 6103.

The time needed to complete and file this form will vary depending on individual circumstances. The estimated average time is: **Recordkeeping,** 18 hours, 25 minutes; **Learning about the form,** 6 minutes; **Preparing the form,** 18 minutes.

If you have comments concerning the accuracy of these time estimates or suggestions for making this form simpler, we would be happy to hear from you. See the instructions for the tax return with which this form is filed. **DO NOT** send the tax form to that office. Instead, return it to the executor or representative who requested it.

Cat. No. 10170V   Form **712** (Rev. 10-97)

FIGURE A.11 Life Insurance Statement

Part II   Living Insured

(File with **Form 709,** United States Gift (and Generation-Skipping Transfer) Tax Return. May also be filed with **Form 706,** United States Estate (and Generation-Skipping Transfer) Tax Return, or **Form 706-NA,** United States Estate (and Generation-Skipping Transfer) Tax Return, Estate of nonresident not a citizen of the United States, where decedent owned insurance on life of another.)

SECTION A—General Information

33 First name and middle initial of donor (or decedent)	34 Last name	35 Social security number

36 Date of gift for which valuation data submitted . . . . ▶	
37 Date of decedent's death for which valuation data submitted . . . . ▶	

SECTION B—Policy Information

38 Name of insured	39 Sex	40 Date of birth

41 Name and address of insurance company

42 Type of policy	43 Policy number	44 Face amount	45 Issue date

46 Gross premium	47 Frequency of payment

48 Assignee's name	49 Date assigned

50 If irrevocable designation of beneficiary made, name of beneficiary	51 Sex	52 Date of birth, if known	53 Date designated

54 If other than simple designation, quote in full. (Attach additional sheets if necessary.)

55 If policy is not paid up:
  a Interpolated terminal reserve on date of death, assignment, or irrevocable designation of beneficiary . . . .
  b Add proportion of gross premium paid beyond date of death, assignment, or irrevocable designation of beneficiary . . . . . .
  c Add adjustment on account of dividends to credit of policy. . . . .
  d **Total** (add lines a, b, and c) . . . .
  e Outstanding indebtedness against policy . . . .
  f Net total value of the policy (for gift or estate tax purposes) (subtract line e from line d) . . . . . .
56 If policy is either paid up or a single premium:
  a Total cost, on date of death, assignment, or irrevocable designation of beneficiary, of a single-premium policy on life of insured at attained age, for original face amount plus any additional paid-up insurance (additional face amount $ _____)

  (If a single-premium policy for the total face amount would not have been issued on the life of the insured as of the date specified, nevertheless, assume that such a policy could then have been purchased by the insured and state the cost thereof, using for such purpose the same formula and basis employed, on the date specified, by the company in calculating single premiums.)

  b Adjustment on account of dividends to credit of policy . . . .
  c **Total** (add lines 56a and 56b). . . . .
  d Outstanding indebtedness against policy . . . .
  e Net total value of policy (for gift or estate tax purposes) (subtract line 56d from line 56c) . . . .

The undersigned officer of the above-named insurance company (or appropriate Federal agency or retirement system official) hereby certifies that this statement sets forth true and correct information.

Signature ▶	Title ▶	Date of Certification ▶

FIGURE A.11 *Continued*

196

Form 1040

Department of the Treasury—Internal Revenue Service

U.S. Individual Income Tax Return 1999 | (99) IRS Use Only—Do not write or staple in this space.

For the year Jan. 1–Dec. 31, 1999, or other tax year beginning ____ 1999, ending ____ | OMB No. 1545-0074

Label
(See instructions on page 18.)

Use the IRS label. Otherwise, please print or type.

LABEL HERE

Your first name and initial | Last name | Your social security number

If a joint return, spouse's first name and initial | Last name | Spouse's social security number

Home address (number and street). If you have a P.O. box, see page 18. | Apt. no.

City, town or post office, state, and ZIP code. If you have a foreign address, see page 18.

▲ **IMPORTANT!** ▲
You must enter your SSN(s) above.

Presidential Election Campaign (See page 18.)

| | | Yes | No |
Do you want $3 to go to this fund? . . . . |
If a joint return, does your spouse want $3 to go to this fund? . . . . |

Note. Checking "Yes" will not change your tax or reduce your refund.

Filing Status

Check only one box.

1 ☐ Single
2 ☐ Married filing joint return (even if only one had income)
3 ☐ Married filing separate return. Enter spouse's social security no. above and full name here. ▶ _____
4 ☐ Head of household (with qualifying person). (See page 18.) If the qualifying person is a child but not your dependent, enter this child's name here. ▶ _____
5 ☐ Qualifying widow(er) with dependent child (year spouse died ▶ 19). (See page 18.)

Exemptions

6a ☐ **Yourself.** If your parent (or someone else) can claim you as a dependent on his or her tax return, **do not** check box 6a. . . . .

b ☐ **Spouse** . . . .

c **Dependents:**

(1) First name Last name	(2) Dependent's social security number	(3) Dependent's relationship to you	(4)✔ if qualifying child for child tax credit (see page 19)
			☐
			☐
			☐
			☐
			☐
			☐

If more than six dependents, see page 19.

No. of boxes checked on 6a and 6b ____

No. of your children on 6c who:
• lived with you ____
• did not live with you due to divorce or separation (see page 19) ____

Dependents on 6c not entered above ____

Add numbers entered on lines above ▶ ☐

d Total number of exemptions claimed . . . .

Income

Attach Copy B of your Forms W-2 and W-2G here. Also attach Form(s) 1099-R if tax was withheld.

If you did not get a W-2, see page 20.

Enclose, but do not staple, any payment. Also, please use Form 1040-V.

7 Wages, salaries, tips, etc. Attach Form(s) W-2 . . . . | 7 |
8a **Taxable** interest. Attach Schedule B if required . . . . | 8a |
b Tax-exempt interest. DO NOT include on line 8a . . . | 8b | |
9 Ordinary dividends. Attach Schedule B if required . . . . | 9 |
10 Taxable refunds, credits, or offsets of state and local income taxes (see page 21) . . | 10 |
11 Alimony received . . . . | 11 |
12 Business income or (loss). Attach Schedule C or C-EZ . . . . | 12 |
13 Capital gain or (loss). Attach Schedule D if required. If not required, check here ▶ ☐ | 13 |
14 Other gains or (losses). Attach Form 4797 . . . . | 14 |
15a Total IRA distributions . | 15a | | b Taxable amount (see page 22) | 15b |
16a Total pensions and annuities | 16a | | b Taxable amount (see page 22) | 16b |
17 Rental real estate, royalties, partnerships, S corporations, trusts, etc. Attach Schedule E | 17 |
18 Farm income or (loss). Attach Schedule F . . . . | 18 |
19 Unemployment compensation . . . . | 19 |
20a Social security benefits . | 20a | | b Taxable amount (see page 24) | 20b |
21 Other income. List type and amount (see page 24) . . . . | 21 |
22 Add the amounts in the far right column for lines 7 through 21. This is your **total income** ▶ | 22 |

Adjusted Gross Income

23 IRA deduction (see page 26) . . . . | 23 |
24 Student loan interest deduction (see page 26) . . . | 24 |
25 Medical savings account deduction. Attach Form 8853 . | 25 |
26 Moving expenses. Attach Form 3903 . . . . . | 26 |
27 One-half of self-employment tax. Attach Schedule SE . | 27 |
28 Self-employed health insurance deduction (see page 28) | 28 |
29 Keogh and self-employed SEP and SIMPLE plans . . | 29 |
30 Penalty on early withdrawal of savings . . . . . | 30 |
31a Alimony paid   b Recipient's SSN ▶ _____ | 31a |
32 Add lines 23 through 31a . . . . ▶ | 32 |
33 Subtract line 32 from line 22. This is your **adjusted gross income** . . . . . ▶ | 33 |

For Disclosure, Privacy Act, and Paperwork Reduction Act Notice, see page 54.   Cat. No. 11320B   Form **1040** (1999)

FIGURE A.12 U.S. Individual Income Tax Return

Tax and Credits

34 Amount from line 33 (adjusted gross income) **34**

35a Check if: ☐ **You** were 65 or older, ☐ Blind; ☐ **Spouse** was 65 or older, ☐ Blind. Add the number of boxes checked above and enter the total here . . . . ▶ **35a**

   b If you are married filing separately and your spouse itemizes deductions or you were a dual-status alien, see page 30 and check here . . . . . . ▶ **35b** ☐

| **Standard Deduction for Most People** |
| Single: $4,300 |
| Head of household: $6,350 |
| Married filing jointly or Qualifying widow(er): $7,200 |
| Married filing separately: $3,600 |

36 Enter your **itemized deductions** from Schedule A, line 28, **OR standard deduction** shown on the left. **But** see page 30 to find your standard deduction if you checked any box on line 35a or 35b **or** if someone can claim you as a dependent **36**

37 Subtract line 36 from line 34 . . . . **37**

38 If line 34 is $94,975 or less, multiply $2,750 by the total number of exemptions claimed on line 6d. If line 34 is over $94,975, see the worksheet on page 31 for the amount to enter . **38**

39 **Taxable income.** Subtract line 38 from line 37. If line 38 is more than line 37, enter -0- . **39**

40 **Tax** (see page 31). Check if any tax is from **a** ☐ Form(s) 8814   **b** ☐ Form 4972 . . ▶ **40**

41 Credit for child and dependent care expenses. Attach Form 2441   **41**

42 Credit for the elderly or the disabled. Attach Schedule R . .   **42**

43 Child tax credit (see page 33) **43**

44 Education credits. Attach Form 8863 . . . . . .   **44**

45 Adoption credit. Attach Form 8839 . . . .   **45**

46 Foreign tax credit. Attach Form 1116 if required . . .   **46**

47 Other. Check if from **a** ☐ Form 3800   **b** ☐ Form 8396   **c** ☐ Form 8801   **d** ☐ Form (specify) _____   **47**

48 Add lines 41 through 47. These are your **total credits** **48**

49 Subtract line 48 from line 40. If line 48 is more than line 40, enter -0- . . . . . . ▶ **49**

Other Taxes

50 Self-employment tax. Attach Schedule SE **50**

51 Alternative minimum tax. Attach Form 6251 . . . . **51**

52 Social security and Medicare tax on tip income not reported to employer. Attach Form 4137 **52**

53 Tax on IRAs, other retirement plans, and MSAs. Attach Form 5329 if required **53**

54 Advance earned income credit payments from Form(s) W-2 . . . . **54**

55 Household employment taxes. Attach Schedule H **55**

56 Add lines 49 through 55. This is your **total tax** . . . . ▶ **56**

Payments

57 Federal income tax withheld from Forms W-2 and 1099 . .   **57**

58 1999 estimated tax payments and amount applied from 1998 return .   **58**

59a **Earned income credit.** Attach Sch. EIC if you have a qualifying child

   b Nontaxable earned income: amount . . ▶ _____ and type ▶ **59a**

60 Additional child tax credit. Attach Form 8812 . . . . .   **60**

61 Amount paid with request for extension to file (see page 48)   **61**

62 Excess social security and RRTA tax withheld (see page 48)   **62**

63 Other payments. Check if from **a** ☐ Form 2439 **b** ☐ Form 4136   **63**

64 Add lines 57, 58, 59a, and 60 through 63. These are your **total payments** . . . . ▶ **64**

Refund

Have it directly deposited! See page 48 and fill in 66b, 66c, and 66d.

65 If line 64 is more than line 56, subtract line 56 from line 64. This is the amount you **OVERPAID** **65**

66a Amount of line 65 you want **REFUNDED TO YOU**. . . . . ▶ **66a**

▶ **b** Routing number [ ][ ][ ][ ][ ][ ][ ][ ][ ] ▶ **c** Type: ☐ Checking ☐ Savings

▶ **d** Account number [ ][ ][ ][ ][ ][ ][ ][ ][ ][ ][ ][ ][ ][ ][ ][ ][ ]

67 Amount of line 65 you want **APPLIED TO YOUR 2000 ESTIMATED TAX** ▶ **67**

Amount You Owe

68 If line 56 is more than line 64, subtract line 64 from line 56. This is the **AMOUNT YOU OWE**. For details on how to pay, see page 49 . . . . ▶ **68**

69 Estimated tax penalty. Also include on line 68 . . . . . **69**

Sign Here

Under penalties of perjury, I declare that I have examined this return and accompanying schedules and statements, and to the best of my knowledge and belief, they are true, correct, and complete. Declaration of preparer (other than taxpayer) is based on all information of which preparer has any knowledge.

Joint return? See page 18.

Keep a copy for your records.

| Your signature | Date | Your occupation | Daytime telephone number (optional) ( ) |
| Spouse's signature. If a joint return, BOTH must sign. | Date | Spouse's occupation | |

Paid Preparer's Use Only

Preparer's signature		Date		Check if self-employed ☐	Preparer's SSN or PTIN
Firm's name (or yours if self-employed) and address					EIN
					ZIP code

Form **1040** (1999)

FIGURE A.12 *Continued*

SCHEDULE C (Form 1040)	**Profit or Loss From Business** (Sole Proprietorship)	OMB No. 1545-0074
Department of the Treasury Internal Revenue Service (99)	▶ Partnerships, joint ventures, etc., must file Form 1065 or Form 1065-B. ▶ Attach to Form 1040 or Form 1041. ▶ See Instructions for Schedule C (Form 1040).	**1999** Attachment Sequence No. **09**

Name of proprietor	Social security number (SSN)

A Principal business or profession, including product or service (see page C-1) | **B** Enter code from pages C-8 & 9 ▶

C Business name. If no separate business name, leave blank. | **D** Employer ID number (EIN), if any

E Business address (including suite or room no.) ▶ ....
City, town or post office, state, and ZIP code

F Accounting method: **(1)** ☐ Cash **(2)** ☐ Accrual **(3)** ☐ Other (specify) ▶ ....

G Did you "materially participate" in the operation of this business during 1999? If "No," see page C-2 for limit on losses . ☐ Yes ☐ No

H If you started or acquired this business during 1999, check here . . . . ▶ ☐

Part I   Income

1	Gross receipts or sales. **Caution:** *If this income was reported to you on Form W-2 and the "Statutory employee" box on that form was checked, see page C-2 and check here* . . . . . . ▶ ☐	1	
2	Returns and allowances	2	
3	Subtract line 2 from line 1	3	
4	Cost of goods sold (from line 42 on page 2)	4	
5	**Gross profit.** Subtract line 4 from line 3	5	
6	Other income, including Federal and state gasoline or fuel tax credit or refund (see page C-3) . . .	6	
7	**Gross income.** Add lines 5 and 6 . . . . ▶	7	

Part II   Expenses. Enter expenses for business use of your home **only** on line 30.

8	Advertising	8			19	Pension and profit-sharing plans	19	
9	Bad debts from sales or services (see page C-3) . .	9			20	Rent or lease (see page C-4):		
					a	Vehicles, machinery, and equipment .	20a	
10	Car and truck expenses (see page C-3)	10			b	Other business property . .	20b	
11	Commissions and fees . .	11			21	Repairs and maintenance . .	21	
12	Depletion	12			22	Supplies (not included in Part III) .	22	
13	Depreciation and section 179 expense deduction (not included in Part III) (see page C-3) .	13			23	Taxes and licenses	23	
					24	Travel, meals, and entertainment:		
					a	Travel	24a	
14	Employee benefit programs (other than on line 19) . . .	14			b	Meals and entertainment .		
15	Insurance (other than health) .	15			c	Enter nondeductible amount included on line 24b (see page C-5) .		
16	Interest:							
a	Mortgage (paid to banks, etc.) .	16a			d	Subtract line 24c from line 24b	24d	
b	Other	16b			25	Utilities	25	
17	Legal and professional services	17			26	Wages (less employment credits) .	26	
18	Office expense	18			27	Other expenses (from line 48 on page 2)	27	

28	**Total expenses** before expenses for business use of home. Add lines 8 through 27 in columns . ▶	28	
29	Tentative profit (loss). Subtract line 28 from line 7	29	
30	Expenses for business use of your home. Attach **Form 8829**	30	
31	**Net profit or (loss).** Subtract line 30 from line 29.		
	• If a profit, enter on **Form 1040, line 12,** and ALSO on **Schedule SE, line 2** (statutory employees, see page C-6). Estates and trusts, enter on Form 1041, line 3. }	31	
	• If a loss, you MUST go on to line 32.		
32	If you have a loss, check the box that describes your investment in this activity (see page C-6).		
	• If you checked 32a, enter the loss on **Form 1040, line 12,** and ALSO on **Schedule SE, line 2** (statutory employees, see page C-6). Estates and trusts, enter on Form 1041, line 3. }	32a ☐ All investment is at risk. 32b ☐ Some investment is not at risk.	
	• If you checked 32b, you MUST attach **Form 6198.**		

For Paperwork Reduction Act Notice, see Form 1040 instructions.   Cat. No. 11334P   Schedule C (Form 1040) 1999

FIGURE A.12 *Continued*

Part III   **Cost of Goods Sold** (see page C-6)

33   Method(s) used to value closing inventory: **a** ☐ Cost   **b** ☐ Lower of cost or market   **c** ☐ Other (attach explanation)

34   Was there any change in determining quantities, costs, or valuations between opening and closing inventory? If "Yes," attach explanation . . . . ☐ Yes   ☐ No

35 Inventory at beginning of year. If different from last year's closing inventory, attach explanation . .	35	
36 Purchases less cost of items withdrawn for personal use	36	
37 Cost of labor. Do not include any amounts paid to yourself	37	
38 Materials and supplies	38	
39 Other costs	39	
40 Add lines 35 through 39	40	
41 Inventory at end of year	41	
42 **Cost of goods sold.** Subtract line 41 from line 40. Enter the result here and on page 1, line 4 . .	42	

Part IV   **Information on Your Vehicle.** Complete this part **ONLY** if you are claiming car or truck expenses on line 10 and are not required to file Form 4562 for this business. See the instructions for line 13 on page C-3 to find out if you must file.

43   When did you place your vehicle in service for business purposes? (month, day, year) ▶ ..../........../......

44   Of the total number of miles you drove your vehicle during 1999, enter the number of miles you used your vehicle for:

a Business .... **b** Commuting .... **c** Other ....

45   Do you (or your spouse) have another vehicle available for personal use? . . . . ☐ Yes   ☐ No

46   Was your vehicle available for use during off-duty hours? . . . . ☐ Yes   ☐ No

47a   Do you have evidence to support your deduction? . . . . ☐ Yes   ☐ No

  b If "Yes," is the evidence written? . . . . ☐ Yes   ☐ No

Part V   **Other Expenses.** List below business expenses not included on lines 8–26 or line 30.

--		
--		
--		
--		
--		
--		
--		
--		
--		
48 **Total other expenses.** Enter here and on page 1, line 27	48	

Schedule C (Form 1040) 1999

FIGURE A.12 *Continued*

Form **1040-C**	**U.S. Departing Alien Income Tax Return**	OMB No. 1545-0086
Department of the Treasury Internal Revenue Service	For tax period or year beginning _____, 2000, and ending _____, _____ ▶ See separate instructions. ▶ File original and one copy.	**2000**

Please print or type

Your first name and initial	Last name	Your identifying number (see page 2)
If a joint return, spouse's first name and initial (see instructions)	Last name	Spouse's identifying number
U.S. address (number, street, and apt. no. or rural route)	Passport or alien registration card number	Original date of your entry into the U.S.
	Your number	Spouse's number	
City, state, and ZIP code		Date of departure

Complete foreign address	Date on which you last arrived in the U.S.

Of what country are you a citizen or subject?	Of what country are you a resident?

A Is your employer willing to furnish a letter guaranteeing that the tax will be paid?. . . . . ☐ **Yes** ☐ **No**
If "Yes," please attach **the letter** and leave the remainder of this form blank except for the signature area on page 2.

Caution: *Form 1040-C is* **not** *a final income tax return. You* **must** *file a final return on the correct form after your tax year ends. See* ***Final Return Required*** *on page 1 of the instructions.*

Part I   Explanation of Status—Resident or Nonresident Alien

1 Check the applicable box or boxes below:

Note: *A nonresident alien who has income from real property may elect to treat this income as effectively connected income. Gain or loss on the disposition of a U.S. real property interest by a nonresident alien is effectively connected income or loss. For details, see the* ***1999 Form 1040NR instructions*** *or* **Pub. 519,** *U.S. Tax Guide for Aliens.*

☐ **Group I**—Resident alien.
☐ **Group II**—Nonresident alien with income effectively connected with a U.S. trade or business.
☐ **Group III**—Nonresident alien with income not effectively connected with a U.S. trade or business.

2 Kind of trade or business or occupation in the United States ▶ ....

3 Visa number and class under which you were last admitted to the United States ▶ ....

4 Do you have a permit to reenter the United States?. . . . . ☐ **Yes** ☐ **No**
If "Yes," enter the expiration date ▶ ....

5 Have you signed a waiver of rights, privileges, exemptions, and immunities as described under **Exceptions** on page 2 of the instructions?. . . . . ☐ **Yes** ☐ **No**
If "Yes," enter the date signed ▶ ....

6 If you were employed in the United States, did you file **Form 1078,** Certificate of Alien Claiming Residence in the United States? . . . . ☐ **Yes** ☐ **No**

7 Have you applied for U.S. citizenship? . . . . ☐ **Yes** ☐ **No**

8 If you filed income tax returns in the United States, give the following information for 1999:

a Your U.S. address shown on return ▶ ....

b Taxable income reported $ .... **c** Tax paid $ .... **d** Balance due $ ....

9 Do you know of any current charges against you concerning your U.S. taxes for any tax period? . . . ☐ **Yes** ☐ **No**

10 Do you plan to return to the United States? . . . . ☐ **Yes** ☐ **No**
If "Yes," complete lines 11 through 13 below.

11 Are your spouse and any children remaining in the United States?. . . . . ☐ **Yes** ☐ **No**

12 Show the approximate value and location in the United States of any property held by you:

	Value	Location
a Real property { · · · · · · · ·	$_____ ;	....
· · · · · · · ·	$_____ ;	....
b Stocks and bonds · · · · · · ·	$_____ ;	....
c Cash · · · · · · ·	$_____ ;	....
d Other (specify) ▶	$_____ ;	....

13 If you will not return before **(a)** the due date for filing a final U.S. income tax return for the current year, or **(b)** the due date for filing a final U.S. income tax return for the preceding year, what arrangements have you made to file the final income tax return(s) and pay the tax(es)? ▶ ....
....
....

For **Privacy Act and Paperwork Reduction Act Notice, see page 5 of instructions.**   Cat. No. 11310F   Form **1040-C** (2000)

FIGURE A.13 U.S. Departing Alien Income Tax Return

Part II	**Exemptions**

Group I—If you are a resident alien, you may claim the same exemptions allowed U.S. citizens on Form 1040.

Group II—If you are a nonresident alien with income effectively connected with a U.S. business, you may claim one exemption. Residents of Canada, India, Mexico, Japan, the Republic of Korea, or U.S. nationals (American Samoans), see page 3 of the instructions.

Group III—If you are a nonresident alien with income not effectively connected with a U.S. business, do not claim any exemptions from that income.

14a ☐ Yourself   **b** ☐ Spouse

> **Caution:** *If your parent (or someone else) can claim you as a dependent on his or her 2000 tax return, do not check box 14a.*

No. of boxes checked on 14a and 14b . . . . _____

c **Dependents:**		(2) Dependent's SSN or ITIN	(3) Dependent's relationship to you	(4) ✓ if qualifying child for child tax credit
(1) First name	Last name			

No. of your children on 14c who:
● lived with you. . _____
● did not live with you due to divorce or separation . . _____
Dependents on 14c not entered above _____

d Total number of exemptions claimed . . . .

Add numbers entered on lines above ▶ ☐

Part III	**Figuring Your Income Tax**

Groups I and II

15 Total income (from page 3, Schedule A, line 4, column (d) or (e)). **15**
16 Adjustments. See page 3 of the instructions and attach appropriate form or statement . . **16**
17 Adjusted gross income. Subtract line 16 from line 15 . . . . **17**
18 Tax (from page 4, Schedule D, line 6 or 12, whichever applies) **18**
19 Credits. See page 3 of the instructions and attach appropriate form or statement **19**
20 Subtract line 19 from line 18. If zero or less, enter -0- **20**
21 Other taxes. See page 3 of the instructions and attach appropriate form **21**
22 Tax for Group I or II. Add lines 20 and 21 . . . . **22**

Group III

23 Total income (from page 3, Schedule A, line 4, column (f)) **23**
24 Tax (30% of line 23). If less than 30%, attach statement showing computation **24**
25 **Total tax.** Add lines 22 and 24 . . . . ▶ **25**

Tax Summary

26 U.S. income tax paid or withheld at source (from page 3, Schedule A, line 4, column (c), or withheld from Forms W-2, W-2G, 1099-R, etc.) **26**
27 Estimated U.S. income tax paid **27**
28 Other payments (specify) ▶_____ **28**
29 **Total payments.** Add lines 26 through 28 . . . . ▶ **29**
30 If line 25 is more than line 29, subtract line 29 from line 25. This is the **Amount You Owe** . **30**
31 If line 29 is more than line 25, subtract line 25 from line 29. This is the amount you **Overpaid.** Any overpayment of tax will be refunded only when you file your final return for the tax year **31**

Note: *Your tax liability on your final return may be different from the figure you entered on line 25 above.*

Sign Here
Keep a copy of this return for your records.

Under penalties of perjury, I declare that I have examined this return and accompanying schedules and statements, and to the best of my knowledge and belief, they are true, correct, and complete. Declaration of preparer (other than taxpayer) is based on all information of which preparer has any knowledge.

▶ Your signature   Date   ▶ Spouse's signature   Date
(A return made by an agent must be accompanied by a power of attorney.)   (If filing jointly, BOTH must sign even if only one had income.)

Paid Preparer's Use Only

Preparer's signature ▶	Date	Check if self-employed ☐	Preparer's SSN or PTIN
Firm's name (or yours if self-employed) and address ▶			EIN
			ZIP code

Certificate of Compliance

This certifies that the above individual(s) has satisfied all the requirements of the Internal Revenue Code and the Internal Revenue Regulations relating to departing aliens according to all information available to me at this date. This certificate is effective for the tax period

beginning .... , 2000, and ending .... , ... or the tax year ended .... , ...

....
(District Director of Internal Revenue)

Date .... , ... By ....
(Name)   (Title)

Form **1040-C** (2000)

FIGURE A.13 *Continued*

Schedule A   **Income** (Do not include exempt income on lines 1 through 4.)

1 (a) Payer of income	(b) Type of income (such as salary, wages, taxable interest, dividends, rents, alimony received, etc.)	(c) Amount of U.S. income tax paid or withheld at source	(d) Resident alien income	Nonresident alien income	
				(e) Effectively connected with a U.S. trade or business*	(f) Not effectively connected with a U.S. trade or business**
2 Net gain, if any, from Schedule D (Form 1040)	**2**				
3 Net gain, if any, from Schedule B, line 2 . .	**3**				
4 Totals	**4**				
5 Tax-exempt interest income. Do not include on line 4 .	**5**				

* Enter in column (e): (1) salary and wages as shown on Form W-2; (2) net income from the operation of a business from separate **Schedule C (Form 1040)**, **Schedule C-EZ (Form 1040)**, or other appropriate business schedule; and (3) any other income effectively connected with a U.S. trade or business.

** Including alimony received.

Include any U.S. income tax that was paid or withheld on income in column (c), lines 1 through 3.

Schedule B   **Gains and Losses From Sales or Exchanges of Nonresidents' Property Not Effectively Connected With a U.S. Trade or Business** (Capital gains and income other than capital gains)

You must complete this schedule if you are a nonresident alien with gains from the sale or exchange of property (except U.S. real property interests) from sources in the United States that are not effectively connected with a U.S. trade or business. **Include any U.S. income tax that was paid or withheld on these gains on Schedule A, column (c), line 3.**

1 (a) Description of property (If necessary, attach statement of descriptive details not shown below.)	(b) Date acquired (mo., day, yr.)	(c) Date sold (mo., day, yr.)	(d) Sales price	(e) Cost or other basis	(f) Gain or (loss) subtract (e) from (d)
2 Net gain. Enter on Schedule A, line 3, column (f).				**2**	

Schedule C   **Itemized Deductions**

- If you are a resident alien reporting income on Schedule A, column (d), you may claim the same deductions allowable on **Schedule A (Form 1040).**
- If you are a nonresident alien reporting income on Schedule A, column (e), you may claim only deductions that are connected to U.S. trade or business income and not deducted elsewhere. See **Schedule A (Form 1040NR).** However, casualty or theft losses and charitable contributions do not have to be related to U.S. trade or business income. You should file **Form 4684,** Casualties and Thefts, to support casualty or theft loses shown below.
- If you are a nonresident alien reporting income on Schedule A, column (f), do not claim any deductions related to that income.

1 (a) Type of deduction (such as interest, taxes, contributions, etc.)	(b) Amount of deduction	(c) Type of deduction (such as interest, taxes, contributions, etc.)	(d) Amount of deduction

2 **Total itemized deductions.** Add the amounts in columns (b) and (d) of line 1. Enter the total here and on Schedule D, line 2 or line 8, whichever applies. **Exception.** If the amount on Form 1040-C, line 17, is over $128,950 ($64,475 if married filing separately), see page 5 of the instructions for the amount to enter	**2**

Form **1040-C** (2000)

FIGURE A.13 *Continued*

Schedule D   **Tax Computation**

Tax for Resident Alien—Group I Only (For description of groups, see Form 1040-C, line 1.)

1   Enter amount from Form 1040-C, line 17 . . . . **1**

2   If you itemize deductions, enter amount from page 3, Schedule C, line 2 (to the extent they are allowable on **Schedule A (Form 1040)**). If you do not plan to itemize deductions, enter your standard deduction. See **Standard Deduction** on page 5 of the instructions **2**

3   Subtract line 2 from line 1 . . . .   **3**

4   Exemptions. If line 1 above is $96,700 or less, multiply $2,800 by the total number of exemptions claimed on Form 1040-C, line 14d. If line 1 above is over $96,700, see the worksheet on page 6 of the instructions **4**

5   **Taxable income.** Subtract line 4 from line 3 . . . .   **5**

6   **Tax.** Figure your tax on the amount on line 5 by using the 2000 Tax Rate Schedules on page 6 of the instructions. Include in the total any tax from **Form 4972, Form 6251,** and **Form 8814.** Enter the tax here and on Form 1040-C, line 18 . . . . ▶   **6**

Tax for Nonresident Alien With Income Effectively Connected With a U.S. Trade or Business—Group II Only

7   Enter amount from Form 1040-C, line 17 . . . . **7**

8   Enter itemized deductions from page 3, Schedule C, line 2 (to the extent they are allowable on **Schedule A (Form 1040NR)**) **8**

9   Subtract line 8 from line 7 . . . .   **9**

10 Exemptions. If line 7 above is $96,700 or less, multiply $2,800 by the total number of exemptions claimed on Form 1040-C, line 14d. If line 7 above is over $96,700, see the worksheet on page 6 of the instructions **10**

11 **Taxable income.** Subtract line 10 from line 9 . . . .   **11**

12 **Tax.** Figure your tax on the amount on line 11 by using the 2000 Tax Rate Schedules on page 6 of the instructions. Include in the total any tax from **Form 4972, Form 6251,** and **Form 8814.** Enter the tax here and on Form 1040-C, line 18 . . . . ▶   **12**

Form **1040-C** (2000)

FIGURE A.13   *Continued*

1041 U.S. Income Tax Return for Estates and Trusts

Department of the Treasury—Internal Revenue Service

1999

	OMB No. 1545-0092

For calendar year 1999 or fiscal year beginning _____ 1999, and ending _____ .

A	Type of entity:	Name of estate or trust (If a grantor type trust, see page 8 of the instructions.)	C	Employer identification number
	☐ Decedent's estate			
	☐ Simple trust		D	Date entity created
	☐ Complex trust			
	☐ Grantor type trust	Name and title of fiduciary	E	Nonexempt charitable and split-interest trusts, check applicable boxes (see page 10 of the instructions):
	☐ Bankruptcy estate–Ch. 7			
	☐ Bankruptcy estate–Ch. 11	Number, street, and room or suite no. (If a P.O. box, see page 8 of the instructions.)		
	☐ Pooled income fund			☐ Described in section 4947(a)(1)
B	Number of Schedules K-1 attached (see instructions) ▶	City or town, state, and ZIP code		☐ Not a private foundation
				☐ Described in section 4947(a)(2)

F	Check applicable boxes:	☐ Initial return ☐ Final return ☐ Amended return	G Pooled mortgage account (see page 10 of the instructions):
		☐ Change in fiduciary's name ☐ Change in fiduciary's address	☐ Bought ☐ Sold Date:

Income

1	Interest income	1	
2	Ordinary dividends	2	
3	Business income or (loss) (attach Schedule C or C-EZ (Form 1040))	3	
4	Capital gain or (loss) (attach Schedule D (Form 1041))	4	
5	Rents, royalties, partnerships, other estates and trusts, etc. (attach Schedule E (Form 1040))	5	
6	Farm income or (loss) (attach Schedule F (Form 1040))	6	
7	Ordinary gain or (loss) (attach Form 4797)	7	
8	Other income. List type and amount	8	
9	**Total income.** Combine lines 1 through 8 . . . . ▶	9	

Deductions

10	Interest. Check if Form 4952 is attached ▶ ☐	10	
11	Taxes	11	
12	Fiduciary fees	12	
13	Charitable deduction (from Schedule A, line 7)	13	
14	Attorney, accountant, and return preparer fees	14	
15a	Other deductions NOT subject to the 2% floor (attach schedule)	15a	
b	Allowable miscellaneous itemized deductions subject to the 2% floor	15b	
16	**Total.** Add lines 10 through 15b	16	
17	Adjusted total income or (loss). Subtract line 16 from line 9. Enter here and on Schedule B, line 1 ▶	17	
18	Income distribution deduction (from Schedule B, line 15) (attach Schedules K-1 (Form 1041))	18	
19	Estate tax deduction (including certain generation-skipping taxes) (attach computation) . .	19	
20	Exemption	20	
21	**Total deductions.** Add lines 18 through 20 . . . . ▶	21	

Tax and Payments

22	Taxable income. Subtract line 21 from line 17. If a loss, see page 14 of the instructions	22	
23	**Total tax** (from Schedule G, line 8)	23	
24	**Payments: a** 1999 estimated tax payments and amount applied from 1998 return . . .	24a	
b	Estimated tax payments allocated to beneficiaries (from Form 1041-T)	24b	
c	Subtract line 24b from line 24a	24c	
d	Tax paid with extension of time to file: ☐ Form 2758 ☐ Form 8736 ☐ Form 8800	24d	
e	Federal income tax withheld. If any is from Form(s) 1099, check ▶ ☐	24e	
	Other payments: **f** Form 2439 .... ; **g** Form 4136 .... ; Total ▶	24h	
25	**Total payments.** Add lines 24c through 24e, and 24h . . . . ▶	25	
26	Estimated tax penalty (see page 15 of the instructions)	26	
27	**Tax due.** If line 25 is smaller than the total of lines 23 and 26, enter amount owed . . .	27	
28	**Overpayment.** If line 25 is larger than the total of lines 23 and 26, enter amount overpaid	28	
29	Amount of line 28 to be: **a Credited to 2000 estimated tax** ▶ _____ **b Refunded** ▶	29	

Please Sign Here

Under penalties of perjury, I declare that I have examined this return, including accompanying schedules and statements, and to the best of my knowledge and belief, it is true, correct, and complete. Declaration of preparer (other than fiduciary) is based on all information of which preparer has any knowledge.

▶ _____		▶ _____	
Signature of fiduciary or officer representing fiduciary	Date	EIN of fiduciary if a financial institution (see page 5 of the instructions)	

Paid Preparer's Use Only

Preparer's signature ▶	Date	Check if self-employed ▶ ☐	Preparer's SSN or PTIN
Firm's name (or yours if self-employed) and address		EIN ▶	
		ZIP code ▶	

For Paperwork Reduction Act Notice, see the separate instructions.   Cat. No. 11370H   Form **1041** (1999)

FIGURE A.14 U.S. Income Tax Return for Estates and Trusts

Schedule A	**Charitable Deduction.** Do not complete for a simple trust or a pooled income fund.		
1	Amounts paid or permanently set aside for charitable purposes from gross income (see page 15)	1	
2	Tax-exempt income allocable to charitable contributions (see page 16 of the instructions) . .	2	
3	Subtract line 2 from line 1	3	
4	Capital gains for the tax year allocated to corpus and paid or permanently set aside for charitable purposes	4	
5	Add lines 3 and 4	5	
6	Section 1202 exclusion allocable to capital gains paid or permanently set aside for charitable purposes (see page 16 of the instructions)	6	
7	**Charitable deduction.** Subtract line 6 from 5. Enter here and on page 1, line 13	7	

Schedule B	**Income Distribution Deduction**		
1	Adjusted total income (from page 1, line 17) (see page 16 of the instructions)	1	
2	Adjusted tax-exempt interest	2	
3	Total net gain from Schedule D (Form 1041), line 16, column (1) (see page 16 of the instructions)	3	
4	Enter amount from Schedule A, line 4 (reduced by any allocable section 1202 exclusion). . .	4	
5	Capital gains for the tax year included on Schedule A, line 1 (see page 16 of the instructions)	5	
6	Enter any gain from page 1, line 4, as a negative number. If page 1, line 4, is a loss, enter the loss as a positive number	6	
7	**Distributable net income (DNI).** Combine lines 1 through 6. If zero or less, enter -0-. . . .	7	
8	If a complex trust, enter accounting income for the tax year as determined under the governing instrument and applicable local law	8		
9	Income required to be distributed currently	9	
10	Other amounts paid, credited, or otherwise required to be distributed	10	
11	Total distributions. Add lines 9 and 10. If greater than line 8, see page 17 of the instructions	11	
12	Enter the amount of tax-exempt income included on line 11	12	
13	Tentative income distribution deduction. Subtract line 12 from line 11	13	
14	Tentative income distribution deduction. Subtract line 2 from line 7. If zero or less, enter -0-	14	
15	**Income distribution deduction.** Enter the smaller of line 13 or line 14 here and on page 1, line 18	15	

Schedule G	**Tax Computation** (see page 17 of the instructions)			
1	**Tax: a** ☐ Tax rate schedule or ☐ Schedule D (Form 1041) . .	1a		
	b Tax on lump-sum distributions (attach Form 4972). . . .	1b		
	c Total. Add lines 1a and 1b. . . . . ▶	1c		
2a	Foreign tax credit (attach Form 1116)	2a		
b	Check: ☐ Nonconventional source fuel credit ☐ Form 8834 . . .	2b		
c	General business credit. Enter here and check which forms are attached: ☐ Form 3800 or ☐ Forms (specify) ▶.............................	2c		
d	Credit for prior year minimum tax (attach Form 8801)	2d		
3	**Total credits.** Add lines 2a through 2d . . . . ▶	3		
4	Subtract line 3 from line 1c	4		
5	Recapture taxes. Check if from: ☐ Form 4255 ☐ Form 8611.	5		
6	Alternative minimum tax (from Schedule I, line 39).	6		
7	Household employment taxes. Attach Schedule H (Form 1040)	7		
8	**Total tax.** Add lines 4 through 7. Enter here and on page 1, line 23 . . . . ▶	8		

	Other Information	Yes	No
1	Did the estate or trust receive tax-exempt income? If "Yes," attach a computation of the allocation of expenses. Enter the amount of tax-exempt interest income and exempt-interest dividends ▶ $		
2	Did the estate or trust receive all or any part of the earnings (salary, wages, and other compensation) of any individual by reason of a contract assignment or similar arrangement?.		
3	At any time during calendar year 1999, did the estate or trust have an interest in or a signature or other authority over a bank, securities, or other financial account in a foreign country? See page 18 of the instructions for exceptions and filing requirements for Form TD F 90-22.1. If "Yes," enter the name of the foreign country ▶		
4	During the tax year, did the estate or trust receive a distribution from, or was it the grantor of, or transferor to, a foreign trust? If "Yes," the estate or trust may have to file Form 3520. See page 19 of the instructions . .		
5	Did the estate or trust receive, or pay, any qualified residence interest on seller-provided financing? If "Yes," see page 19 for required attachment		
6	If this is an estate or a complex trust making the section 663(b) election, check here (see page 19) . . ▶ ☐		
7	To make a section 643(e)(3) election, attach Schedule D (Form 1041), and check here (see page 19). . . ▶ ☐		
8	If the decedent's estate has been open for more than 2 years, attach an explanation for the delay in closing the estate, and check here ▶ ☐		
9	Are any present or future trust beneficiaries skip persons? See page 19 of the instructions		

Form **1041** (1999)

FIGURE A.14 *Continued*

Schedule I	Alternative Minimum Tax (see pages 19 through 24 of the instructions)

Part I—Estate's or Trust's Share of Alternative Minimum Taxable Income

1	Adjusted total income or (loss) (from page 1, line 17)	**1**	
2	Net operating loss deduction. Enter as a positive amount	**2**	
3	Add lines 1 and 2	**3**	
4	**Adjustments and tax preference items:**		
a	Interest	**4a**	
b	Taxes	**4b**	
c	Miscellaneous itemized deductions (from page 1, line 15b)	**4c**	
d	Refund of taxes	**4d** ( )	
e	Depreciation of property placed in service after 1986	**4e**	
f	Circulation and research and experimental expenditures	**4f**	
g	Mining exploration and development costs	**4g**	
h	Long-term contracts entered into after February 28, 1986	**4h**	
i	Amortization of pollution control facilities	**4i**	
j	Installment sales of certain property	**4j**	
k	Adjusted gain or loss (including incentive stock options)	**4k**	
l	Certain loss limitations	**4l**	
m	Tax shelter farm activities	**4m**	
n	Passive activities	**4n**	
o	Beneficiaries of other trusts or decedent's estates	**4o**	
p	Tax-exempt interest from specified private activity bonds	**4p**	
q	Depletion	**4q**	
r	Accelerated depreciation of real property placed in service before 1987	**4r**	
s	Accelerated depreciation of leased personal property placed in service before 1987	**4s**	
t	Intangible drilling costs	**4t**	
u	Other adjustments	**4u**	
5	Combine lines 4a through 4u	**5**	
6	Add lines 3 and 5	**6**	
7	Alternative tax net operating loss deduction (see page 22 of the instructions for limitations) . .	**7**	
8	Adjusted alternative minimum taxable income. Subtract line 7 from line 6. Enter here and on line 13	**8**	
	Note: *Complete Part II below before going to line 9.*		
9	Income distribution deduction from line 27 below	**9**	
10	Estate tax deduction (from page 1, line 19)	**10**	
11	Add lines 9 and 10	**11**	
12	Estate's or trust's share of alternative minimum taxable income. Subtract line 11 from line 8 .	**12**	
	If line 12 is:		
	• $22,500 or less, stop here and enter -0- on Schedule G, line 6. The estate or trust is not liable for the alternative minimum tax.		
	• Over $22,500, but less than $165,000, go to line 28.		
	• $165,000 or more, enter the amount from line 12 on line 34 and go to line 35.		

Part II—Income Distribution Deduction on a Minimum Tax Basis

13	Adjusted alternative minimum taxable income (from line 8)	**13**	
14	Adjusted tax-exempt interest (other than amounts included on line 4p)	**14**	
15	Total net gain from Schedule D (Form 1041), line 16, column (1). If a loss, enter -0-	**15**	
16	Capital gains for the tax year allocated to corpus and paid or permanently set aside for charitable purposes (from Schedule A, line 4) .	**16**	
17	Capital gains paid or permanently set aside for charitable purposes from gross income (see page 23 of the instructions) .	**17**	
18	Capital gains computed on a minimum tax basis included on line 8	**18** (	
19	Capital losses computed on a minimum tax basis included on line 8. Enter as a positive amount	**19**	
20	Distributable net alternative minimum taxable income (DNAMTI). Combine lines 13 through 19. If zero or less, enter -0- .	**20**	
21	Income required to be distributed currently (from Schedule B, line 9)	**21**	
22	Other amounts paid, credited, or otherwise required to be distributed (from Schedule B, line 10)	**22**	
23	Total distributions. Add lines 21 and 22	**23**	
24	Tax-exempt income included on line 23 (other than amounts included on line 4p)	**24**	
25	Tentative income distribution deduction on a minimum tax basis. Subtract line 24 from line 23 .	**25**	
26	Tentative income distribution deduction on a minimum tax basis. Subtract line 14 from line 20. If zero or less, enter -0- .	**26**	
27	**Income distribution deduction on a minimum tax basis.** Enter the smaller of line 25 or line 26. Enter here and on line 9	**27**	

Form **1041** (1999)

FIGURE A.14 *Continued*

207

Part III—Alternative Minimum Tax

28	Exemption amount		28	$22,500 00
29	Enter the amount from line 12	29		
30	Phase-out of exemption amount	30	$75,000 00	
31	Subtract line 30 from line 29. If zero or less, enter -0-	31		
32	Multiply line 31 by 25% (.25)		32	
33	Subtract line 32 from line 28. If zero or less, enter -0-		33	
34	Subtract line 33 from line 29		34	

35 If the estate or trust completed Schedule D (Form 1041) and has an amount on line 24 or 26 (or would have had an amount on either line if Part V had been completed) (as refigured for the AMT, if necessary), go to Part IV below to figure line 35. **All others:** If line 34 is—
- $175,000 or less, multiply line 34 by 26% (.26).
- Over $175,000, multiply line 34 by 28% (.28) and subtract $3,500 from the result . . . . | 35 |

36	Alternative minimum foreign tax credit (see page 23 of instructions)	36
37	Tentative minimum tax. Subtract line 36 from line 35	37
38	Enter the tax from Schedule G, line 1a (minus any foreign tax credit from Schedule G, line 2a).	38
39	**Alternative minimum tax.** Subtract line 38 from line 37. If zero or less, enter -0-. Enter here and on Schedule G, line 6	39

Part IV—Line 35 Computation Using Maximum Capital Gains Rates

Caution: *If the estate or trust did not complete Part V of Schedule D (Form 1041), complete lines 19 through 26 of Schedule D (as refigured for the AMT, if necessary) before completing this part.*

40	Enter the amount from line 34		40	
41	Enter the amount from Schedule D (Form 1041), line 26 (as refigured for AMT, if necessary)	41		
42	Enter the amount from Schedule D (Form 1041), line 24 (as refigured for AMT, if necessary)	42		
43	Add lines 41 and 42. If zero or less, enter -0-	43		
44	Enter the amount from Schedule D (Form 1041), line 21 (as refigured for AMT, if necessary)	44		
45	Enter the **smaller** of line 43 or line 44		45	
46	Subtract line 45 from line 40. If zero or less, enter -0-		46	
47	If line 46 is $175,000 or less, multiply line 46 by 26% (.26). Otherwise, multiply line 46 by 28% (.28) and subtract $3,500 from the result . . . . . ▶		47	
48	Enter the amount from Schedule D (Form 1041), line 35 (as figured for the regular tax)		48	
49	Enter the **smallest** of line 40, line 41, or line 48		49	
50	Multiply line 49 by 10% (.10) . . . . ▶		50	
51	Enter the **smaller** of line 40 or line 41		51	
52	Enter the amount from line 49		52	
53	Subtract line 52 from line 51. If zero or less, enter -0-		53	
54	Multiply line 53 by 20% (.20) . . . . ▶		54	
55	Enter the amount from line 40		55	
56	Add lines 46, 49, and 53		56	
57	Subtract line 56 from line 55		57	
58	Multiply line 57 by 25% (.25) . . . . ▶		58	
59	Add lines 47, 50, 54, and 58		59	
60	If line 40 is $175,000 or less, multiply line 40 by 26% (.26). Otherwise, multiply line 40 by 28% (.28) and subtract $3,500 from the result		60	
61	Enter the **smaller** of line 59 or line 60 here and on line 35 . . . . ▶		61	

Form **1041** (1999)

FIGURE A.14 *Continued*

208

Form **2848**
(Rev. December 1997)
Department of the Treasury
Internal Revenue Service

Power of Attorney
and Declaration of Representative

▶ **See the separate instructions.**

OMB No. 1545-0150

For IRS Use Only

Received by:

Name _____

Telephone _____

Function _____

Date ___ / ___ / ___

Part I **Power of Attorney** (Please type or print.)

1 **Taxpayer information** (Taxpayer(s) must sign and date this form on page 2, line 9.)

Taxpayer name(s) and address	Social security number(s)	Employer identification number
	Daytime telephone number	Plan number (if applicable)

hereby appoint(s) the following representative(s) as attorney(s)-in-fact:

2 **Representative(s)** (Representative(s) must sign and date this form on page 2, Part II.)

Name and address	CAF No. .... Telephone No. .... Fax No. .... Check if new: Address ☐ Telephone No. ☐
Name and address	CAF No. .... Telephone No. .... Fax No. .... Check if new: Address ☐ Telephone No. ☐
Name and address	CAF No. .... Telephone No. .... Fax No. .... Check if new: Address ☐ Telephone No. ☐

to represent the taxpayer(s) before the Internal Revenue Service for the following tax matters:

3 **Tax matters**

Type of Tax (Income, Employment, Excise, etc.)	Tax Form Number (1040, 941, 720, etc.)	Year(s) or Period(s)

4 **Specific use not recorded on Centralized Authorization File (CAF).** If the power of attorney is for a specific use not recorded on CAF, check this box. (See instruction for **Line 4—Specific uses not recorded on CAF.**) . . . . ▶ ☐

5 **Acts authorized.** The representatives are authorized to receive and inspect confidential tax information and to perform any and all acts that I (we) can perform with respect to the tax matters described on line 3, for example, the authority to sign any agreements, consents, or other documents. The authority does not include the power to receive refund checks (see line 6 below), the power to substitute another representative unless specifically added below, or the power to sign certain returns (see instruction for **Line 5—Acts authorized**).

List any specific additions or deletions to the acts otherwise authorized in this power of attorney: ....

Note: *In general, an unenrolled preparer of tax returns cannot sign any document for a taxpayer. See Revenue Procedure 81-38, printed as Pub. 470, for more information.*

Note: *The tax matters partner of a partnership is not permitted to authorize representatives to perform certain acts. See the instructions for more information.*

6 **Receipt of refund checks.** If you want to authorize a representative named on line 2 to receive, **BUT NOT TO ENDORSE OR CASH,** refund checks, initial here _____ and list the name of that representative below.

Name of representative to receive refund check(s) ▶

For Paperwork Reduction and Privacy Act Notice, see the separate instructions.   Cat. No. 11980J   Form **2848** (Rev. 12-97)

FIGURE A.15 Power of Attorney and Declaration of Representative

7 **Notices and communications.** Original notices and other written communications will be sent to you and a copy to the first representative listed on line 2 unless you check one or more of the boxes below.

  a If you want the first representative listed on line 2 to receive the original, and yourself a copy, of such notices or communications, check this box . . . . ▶ ☐
  b If you also want the second representative listed to receive a copy of such notices and communications, check this box . . . . ▶ ☐
  c If you do not want any notices or communications sent to your representative(s), check this box . . . . ▶ ☐

8 **Retention/revocation of prior power(s) of attorney.** The filing of this power of attorney automatically revokes all earlier power(s) of attorney on file with the Internal Revenue Service for the same tax matters and years or periods covered by this document. If you **do not** want to revoke a prior power of attorney, check here. . . . . ▶ ☐
YOU MUST ATTACH A COPY OF ANY POWER OF ATTORNEY YOU WANT TO REMAIN IN EFFECT.

9 **Signature of taxpayer(s).** If a tax matter concerns a joint return, **both** husband and wife must sign if joint representation is requested, otherwise, see the instructions. If signed by a corporate officer, partner, guardian, tax matters partner, executor, receiver, administrator, or trustee on behalf of the taxpayer, I certify that I have the authority to execute this form on behalf of the taxpayer.

▶ **IF NOT SIGNED AND DATED, THIS POWER OF ATTORNEY WILL BE RETURNED.**

Signature	Date	Title (if applicable)

Print Name		

Signature	Date	Title (if applicable)

Print Name		

Part II **Declaration of Representative**

Under penalties of perjury, I declare that:
  • I am not currently under suspension or disbarment from practice before the Internal Revenue Service;
  • I am aware of regulations contained in Treasury Department Circular No. 230 (31 CFR, Part 10), as amended, concerning the practice of attorneys, certified public accountants, enrolled agents, enrolled actuaries, and others;
  • I am authorized to represent the taxpayer(s) identified in Part I for the tax matter(s) specified there; and
  • I am one of the following:
  a Attorney—a member in good standing of the bar of the highest court of the jurisdiction shown below.
  b Certified Public Accountant—duly qualified to practice as a certified public accountant in the jurisdiction shown below.
  c Enrolled Agent—enrolled as an agent under the requirements of Treasury Department Circular No. 230.
  d Officer—a bona fide officer of the taxpayer's organization.
  e Full-Time Employee—a full-time employee of the taxpayer.
  f Family Member—a member of the taxpayer's immediate family (i.e., spouse, parent, child, brother, or sister).
  g Enrolled Actuary—enrolled as an actuary by the Joint Board for the Enrollment of Actuaries under 29 U.S.C. 1242 (the authority to practice before the Service is limited by section 10.3(d)(1) of Treasury Department Circular No. 230).
  h Unenrolled Return Preparer—an unenrolled return preparer under section 10.7(c)(viii) of Treasury Department Circular No. 230.

▶ **IF THIS DECLARATION OF REPRESENTATIVE IS NOT SIGNED AND DATED, THE POWER OF ATTORNEY WILL BE RETURNED.**

Designation—Insert above letter **(a–h)**	Jurisdiction (state) or Enrollment Card No.	Signature	Date

FIGURE A.15 *Continued*

Request for Copy or Transcript of Tax Form

▶ **Read instructions before completing this form.**

▶ **Type or print clearly. Request may be rejected if the form is incomplete or illegible.**

OMB No. 1545-0429

Note: *Do not use this form to get tax account information.* Instead, see instructions below.

1a Name shown on tax form. If a joint return, enter the name shown first.	1b First social security number on tax form or employer identification number (see instructions)
2a If a joint return, spouse's name shown on tax form	2b Second social security number on tax form

3 Current name, address (including apt., room, or suite no.), city, state, and ZIP code

4 Address, (including apt., room, or suite no.), city, state, and ZIP code shown on the last return filed if different from line 3

5 If copy of form or a tax return transcript is to be mailed to someone else, enter the third party's name and address

6 If we cannot find a record of your tax form and you want the payment refunded to the third party, check here . . . . ▶ ☐

7 If name in third party's records differs from line 1a above, enter that name here (see instructions) ▶

8 Check only one box to show what you want. There is **no charge** for items 8a, b, and c:

  a ☐ Tax return transcript of Form 1040 series filed during the **current calendar year** and the **3 prior calendar years** (see instructions).

  b ☐ Verification of nonfiling.

  c ☐ Form(s) W-2 information (see instructions).

  d ☐ Copy of tax form and all attachments (including Form(s) W-2, schedules, or other forms). **The charge is $23 for each period requested.**
    Note: *If these copies must be certified for court or administrative proceedings, see instructions and check here* . . . . . ▶ ☐

9 If this request is to meet a requirement of one of the following, check all boxes that apply.
  ☐ Small Business Administration ☐ Department of Education ☐ Department of Veterans Affairs ☐ Financial institution

10 **Tax form number** (Form 1040, 1040A, 941, etc.)

11 **Tax period(s)** (year or period ended date). If more than four, see instructions.

12 Complete only if **line 8d** is checked.
Amount due:

  a Cost for each period . . . . $ **23.00**

  b Number of tax periods requested on line 11

  c Total cost. Multiply line 12a by line 12b. . $

Full payment must accompany your request. Make check or money order payable to "Internal Revenue Service."

Caution: *Before signing, make sure all items are complete and the form is dated.*

I declare that I am either the taxpayer whose name is shown on line 1a or 2a, or a person authorized to obtain the tax information requested. I am aware that based upon this form, the IRS will release the tax information requested to any party shown on line 5. The IRS has no control over what that party does with the information.

Telephone number of requester
( )

Please Sign Here

▶ Signature. See instructions. If other than taxpayer, attach authorization document. Date

Best time to call

▶ Title (if line 1a above is a corporation, partnership, estate, or trust)

TRY A TAX RETURN TRANSCRIPT (see line 8a instructions)

Spouse's signature Date

Instructions

Section references are to the Internal Revenue Code.

TIP: If you had your tax form filled in by a paid preparer, check first to see if you can get a copy from the preparer. This may save you both time and money.

Purpose of Form.—Use Form 4506 to get a tax return transcript, verification that you did not file a Federal tax return, Form W-2 information, or a copy of a tax form. Allow 6 weeks after you file a tax form before you request a copy of it or a transcript. For W-2

information, wait 13 months after the end of the year in which the wages were earned. For example, wait until Feb. 1999 to request W-2 information for wages earned in 1997.

Do not use this form to request Forms 1099 or tax account information. See this page for details on how to get these items.

Note: *Form 4506 must be received by the IRS within 60 calendar days after the date you signed and dated the request.*

How Long Will It Take?—You can get a tax return transcript or verification of nonfiling within 7 to 10 workdays after the IRS receives your request. It can take up to 60 calendar

days to get a copy of a tax form or W-2 information. To avoid any delay, be sure to furnish all the information asked for on Form 4506.

Forms 1099.—If you need a copy of a Form 1099, contact the payer. If the payer cannot help you, call or visit the IRS to get Form 1099 information.

Tax Account Information.—If you need a statement of your tax account showing any later changes that you or the IRS made to the original return, request tax account information. Tax account information lists

(Continued on back)

For Privacy Act and Paperwork Reduction Act Notice, see back of form.   Cat. No. 41721E   Form **4506** (Rev. 5-97)

FIGURE A.16 Request for Copy or Transcript of Tax Form

certain items from your return, including any later changes.

To request tax account information, write or visit an IRS office or call the IRS at the number listed in your telephone directory.

If you want your tax account information sent to a third party, complete **Form 8821,** Tax Information Authorization. You may get this form by phone (call 1-800-829-3676) or on the Internet (at http://www.irs.ustreas.gov).

Line 1b.—Enter your employer identification number (EIN) **only** if you are requesting a copy of a **business** tax form. Otherwise, enter the first social security number (SSN) shown on the tax form.

Line 2b.—If requesting a copy or transcript of a joint tax form, enter the second SSN shown on the tax form.

Note: *If you do not complete line 1b and, if applicable, line 2b, there may be a delay in processing your request.*

Line 5.—If you want someone else to receive the tax form or tax return transcript (such as a CPA, an enrolled agent, a scholarship board, or a mortgage lender), enter the name and address of the individual. If we cannot find a record of your tax form, we will notify the third party directly that we cannot fill the request.

Line 7.—Enter the name of the client, student, or applicant if it is different from the name shown on line 1a. For example, the name on line 1a may be the parent of a student applying for financial aid. In this case, you would enter the student's name on line 7 so the scholarship board can associate the tax form or tax return transcript with their file.

Line 8a.—If you want a tax return transcript, check this box. Also, on line 10 enter the tax form number and on line 11 enter the tax period for which you want the transcript.

A tax return transcript is available only for returns in the 1040 series (Form 1040, Form 1040A, 1040EZ, etc.). It shows most line items from the original return, including accompanying forms and schedules. In many cases, a transcript will meet the requirement of any lending institution such as a financial institution, the Department of Education, or the Small Business Administration. It may also be used to verify that you did not claim any itemized deductions for a residence.

Note: *A tax return transcript does not reflect any changes you or the IRS made to the original return. If you want a statement of your tax account with the changes, see Tax Account Information on page 1.*

Line 8b.—Check this box only if you want proof from the IRS that you did not file a return for the year. Also, on line 11 enter the tax period for which you want verification of nonfiling.

Line 8c.—If you want only Form(s) W-2 information, check this box. Also, on line 10 enter "Form(s) W-2 only" and on line 11 enter the tax period for which you want the information.

You may receive a copy of your actual Form W-2 or a transcript of the information, depending on how your employer filed the form. However, state withholding information is not shown on a transcript. If you have filed your tax return for the year the wages were earned, you can get a copy of the actual Form W-2 by requesting a complete copy of your return and paying the required fee.

Contact your employer if you have lost your current year's Form W-2 or have not received it by the time you are ready to prepare your tax return.

Note: *If you are requesting information about your spouse's Form W-2, your spouse must sign Form 4506.*

Line 8d.—If you want a certified copy of a tax form for court or administrative proceedings, check the box to the right of line 8d. It will take at least 60 days to process your request.

Line 11.—Enter the year(s) of the tax form or tax return transcript you want. For fiscal-year filers or requests for quarterly tax forms, enter the date the period ended; for example, 3/31/96, 6/30/96, etc. If you need more than four different tax periods, use additional Forms 4506. Tax forms filed 6 or more years ago may not be available for making copies. However, tax account information is generally still available for these periods.

Line 12c.—Write your SSN or EIN **and** "Form 4506 Request" on your check or money order. If we cannot fill your request, we will refund your payment.

Signature.—Requests for copies of tax forms or tax return transcripts to be sent to a third party must be signed by the person whose name is shown on line 1a or by a person authorized to receive the requested information.

Copies of tax forms or tax return transcripts for a jointly filed return may be furnished to either the husband or the wife. Only one signature is required. However, see the line 8c instructions. Sign Form 4506 exactly as your name appeared on the original tax form. If you changed your name, **also** sign your current name.

For a corporation, the signature of the president of the corporation, or any principal officer and the secretary, or the principal officer and another officer are generally required. For more details on who may obtain tax information on corporations, partnerships, estates, and trusts, see section 6103.

If you are **not** the taxpayer shown on line 1a, you must attach your authorization to receive a copy of the requested tax form or tax return transcript. You may **attach a copy of the authorization document** if the original has already been filed with the IRS. This will generally be a **power of attorney** (Form 2848), or **other authorization,** such as Form 8821, or evidence of entitlement (for Title 11 Bankruptcy or Receivership Proceedings). If the taxpayer is deceased, you must send Letters Testamentary or other evidence to establish that you are authorized to act for the taxpayer's estate.

Where To File.—Mail Form 4506 with the correct total payment attached, if required, to the **Internal Revenue Service Center** for the place where you lived when the requested tax form was filed.

Note: *You must use a separate form for each service center from which you are requesting a copy of your tax form or tax return transcript.*

If you lived in:	Use this address:
New Jersey, New York (New York City and counties of Nassau, Rockland, Suffolk, and Westchester)	1040 Waverly Ave. Photocopy Unit Stop 532 Holtsville, NY 11742
New York (all other counties), Connecticut, Maine, Massachusetts, New Hampshire, Rhode Island, Vermont	310 Lowell St. Photocopy Unit Stop 679 Andover, MA 01810
Florida, Georgia, South Carolina	4800 Buford Hwy. Photocopy Unit Stop 91 Doraville, GA 30362
Indiana, Kentucky, Michigan, Ohio, West Virginia	P.O. Box 145500 Photocopy Unit Stop 521 Cincinnati, OH 45250
Kansas, New Mexico, Oklahoma, Texas	3651 South Interregional Hwy. Photocopy Unit Stop 6716 Austin, TX 73301
Alaska, Arizona, California (counties of Alpine, Amador, Butte, Calaveras, Colusa, Contra Costa, Del Norte, El Dorado, Glenn, Humboldt, Lake, Lassen, Marin, Mendocino, Modoc, Napa, Nevada, Placer, Plumas, Sacramento, San Joaquin, Shasta, Sierra, Siskiyou, Solano, Sonoma, Sutter, Tehama, Trinity, Yolo, and Yuba), Colorado, Idaho, Montana, Nebraska, Nevada, North Dakota, Oregon, South Dakota, Utah, Washington, Wyoming	P.O. Box 9941 Photocopy Unit Ogden, UT 84409
California (all other counties), Hawaii	5045 E. Butler Avenue Photocopy Unit Stop 52180 Fresno, CA 93888
Illinois, Iowa, Minnesota, Missouri, Wisconsin	2306 E. Bannister Road Photocopy Unit Stop 6700, Annex 1 Kansas City, MO 64999
Alabama, Arkansas, Louisiana, Mississippi, North Carolina, Tennessee	P.O. Box 30309 Photocopy Unit Stop 46 Memphis, TN 38130
Delaware, District of Columbia, Maryland, Pennsylvania, Virginia, a foreign country, or A.P.O. or F.P.O address	11601 Roosevelt Blvd. Photocopy Unit DP 536 Philadelphia, PA 19255

Privacy Act and Paperwork Reduction Act Notice.—We ask for the information on this form to establish your right to gain access to your tax form or transcript under the Internal Revenue Code, including sections 6103 and 6109. We need it to gain access to your tax form or transcript in our files and properly respond to your request. If you do not furnish the information, we will not be able to fill your request. We may give the information to the Department of Justice or other appropriate law enforcement official, as provided by law.

You are not required to provide the information requested on a form that is subject to the Paperwork Reduction Act unless the form displays a valid OMB control number. Books or records relating to a form or its instructions must be retained as long as their contents may become material in the administration of any Internal Revenue law. Generally, tax returns and return information are confidential, as required by section 6103.

The time needed to complete and file this form will vary depending on individual circumstances. The estimated average time is: **Recordkeeping,** 13 min.; **Learning about the law or the form,** 7 min.; **Preparing the form,** 26 min.; and **Copying, assembling, and sending the form to the IRS,** 17 min.

If you have comments concerning the accuracy of these time estimates or suggestions for making this form simpler, we would be happy to hear from you. You can write to the Tax Forms Committee, Western Area Distribution Center, Rancho Cordova, CA 95743-0001. **DO NOT** send the form to this address. Instead, see **Where To File** on this page.

FIGURE A.16 *Continued*

Form **4768**

(Rev. January 2000)

Department of the Treasury
Internal Revenue Service

**Application for Extension of Time To File a Return
and/or Pay U.S. Estate
(and Generation-Skipping Transfer) Taxes**

For filers of Form 706, 706-A, 706-D, or 706-NA (circle only one)

OMB No. 1545-0181

Note: *Use Form 2758 to request an extension for Forms 706-GS(D) and 706-GS(T).*

Part I   Identification

Decedent's first name and middle initial	Decedent's last name	Date of death

Name of executor	Name of application filer (if other than the executor)	Decedent's social security number

Address of executor (Number, street, and room or suite no.)		Estate tax return due date

City, state, and ZIP code

Part II   Extension of Time To File (Sec. 6081)

You must attach your written statement to explain in detail why it is impossible or impractical to file a reasonably complete return within 9 months after the date of the decedent's death.

Extension date requested

Part III   Extension of Time To Pay (Sec. 6161)

You must attach your written statement to explain in detail why it is impossible or impractical to pay the full amount of the estate (or GST) tax by the return due date. If the taxes cannot be determined because the size of the gross estate is unascertainable, check here ▶ ☐ and enter "-0-" or other appropriate amount on Part IV, line 3. You must attach an explanation.

Extension date requested

Part IV   Payment To Accompany Extension Request

1	Amount of estate and GST taxes estimated to be due	1	
2	Amount of cash shortage (complete Part III)	2	
3	Balance due (subtract line 2 from line 1) (Pay with this application.)	3	

Signature and Verification

If filed by executor—Under penalties of perjury, I declare that I am an executor of the estate of the above-named decedent and that to the best of my knowledge and belief, the statements made herein and attached are true and correct.

_____   _____   _____
Executor's signature   Title   Date

If filed by someone other than the executor—Under penalties of perjury, I declare that to the best of my knowledge and belief, the statements made herein and attached are true and correct, that I am authorized by the executor to file this application, and that I am (check box(es) that applies):

☐ A member in good standing of the bar of the highest court of (specify jurisdiction) ▶ ....
☐ A certified public accountant duly qualified to practice in (specify jurisdiction) ▶ ....
☐ A person enrolled to practice before the Internal Revenue Service.
☐ A duly authorized agent holding a power of attorney. (The power of attorney need not be submitted unless requested.)

_____   _____
Filer's signature (other than the executor)   Date

Part V   Notice to Applicant—To be completed by the Internal Revenue Service

1 The application for extension of time to file (Part II) is:	2 The application for extension of time to pay (Part III) is:
☐ Approved	☐ Approved
☐ Not approved because	☐ Not approved because ....
☐ Other	☐ Other ....

Internal Revenue Service official	Date	Internal Revenue Service official	Date

For Paperwork Reduction Act Notice, see instructions on the back of this form.   Cat. No. 41984P   Form **4768** (Rev. 1-2000)

FIGURE A.17   Application for Extension of Time to File a Return and/or Pay U.S. Estate (and Generation-Skipping Transfer) Taxes

General Instructions

Section references are to the Internal Revenue Code unless otherwise noted.

Who May File. An executor filing **Form 706,** United States Estate (and Generation-Skipping Transfer) Tax Return, or **Form 706-NA,** United States Estate (and Generation-Skipping Transfer) Tax Return, Estate of nonresident not a citizen of the United States, for a decedent's estate may file Form 4768 to apply for an extension of time to file under section 6081 and/or an extension of time to pay the estate tax under section 6161. See the instructions for Form 706 or 706-NA for a definition of "executor." Also, an authorized attorney, certified public accountant, enrolled agent, or agent holding power of attorney may use this form to apply for an extension of time on behalf of the executor.

A qualified heir who is filing **Form 706-A,** United States Additional Estate Tax Return, or **Form 706-D,** United States Additional Estate Tax Return Under Code Section 2057, may use Form 4768 to request an extension of time to file the return and/or pay the additional tax.

The form must be signed by the person filing the application. If filed by an attorney, certified public accountant, enrolled agent, or agent holding a power of attorney, check the appropriate box.

See the instructions for **Form 706-QDT,** U.S. Estate Tax Return for Qualified Domestic Trusts, for information on how to request an extension for that form.

When To File. File Form 4768 early enough to permit the IRS to consider the application and reply before the estate tax due date. Except for certain section 6166 elections (closely held business), an application for an extension of time to pay estate tax received after the estate tax due date will not be considered by the IRS.

How and Where To File. If only Part II or only Part III is completed, file Form 4768 in duplicate; if both Part II and Part III are completed, file Form 4768 in quadruplicate with the IRS office where the estate tax return will be filed. All applications relating to Form 706-NA must be filed with the Internal Revenue Service Center, Philadelphia, PA 19255.

Interest. Interest from the estate (and GST) tax due date must be paid on the estate (and GST) tax for which an extension of time to pay is approved.

Penalties. Penalties may be imposed for failure to file the estate (and GST) tax return within the extension period granted, or failure to pay the balance of the estate (and GST) tax due within the extension period granted.

Bond. If an extension of time to pay is granted, the executor may be required to furnish a bond.

File a separate Form 4768 for each form for which you are requesting an extension. Circle the appropriate form number in the heading of Form 4768.

If you are applying for an extension for Form 706-A or 706-D, substitute "qualified heir" for "executor" wherever "executor" appears in Form 4768 and its instructions.

Specific Instructions

Due Dates. The due date for Form 706 and 706-NA is 9 months after the date of the decedent's death. If there is no numerically corresponding number in the 9th month, the due date is the last date of the 9th month. If the due date falls on a Saturday, Sunday, or a legal holiday, the return is due on the next business day.

Form 706-A is due 6 months after the taxable disposition or cessation of qualified use.

Form 706-D is due 6 months after the taxable disposition, cessation of qualified use of the family-owned business interest, or disqualifying act.

Part II, Extension of Time To File (Sec. 6081). The time to file an extension may not exceed 6 months unless the executor is out of the country.

The application must establish sufficient cause why it is impossible or impractical for the executor to file a reasonably complete return by the estate (and GST) tax return due date.

If the application is for an extension of time to file only, you must include the amount of the estate (and GST) tax estimated to be due on the "Balance due" line in Part IV and a check or money order payable to the United States Treasury. Write the decedent's social security number on the check or money order and the type of return; e.g., Form 706-A.

The IRS will complete Part V and return a copy to the executor. If the application is approved, attach the copy to the estate (and GST) tax return that is filed. The estate (and GST) tax return must be filed before the extension of time is up. It may not be amended after this time, although supplemental information may later be filed which may result in a different amount of tax.

Note: *An extension of time to file does NOT extend the time to pay.*

Part III, Extension of Time To Pay (Sec. 6161). An extension of time to pay under section 6161(a)(1) may not exceed 12 months. A discretionary extension of time to pay for reasonable cause under section 6161(a)(2) may not exceed 10 years. Different extension periods may apply to extensions of time granted for a deficiency, a section 6163 election (reversionary or remainder interest), or a section 6166 election (closely held business).

The application must establish why it is impossible or impractical for the executor to pay the full amount of the estate tax by the estate tax return due date. Examples of reasonable cause provided in section 20.6161-1 of the regulations include the following:

1. An estate includes sufficient liquid assets to pay the estate (and GST) tax when otherwise due. The liquid assets, however, are located in several jurisdictions and are not immediately subject to the control of the executor. Consequently, such assets cannot readily be collected by the executor even with reasonable effort.

2. An estate is comprised in substantial part of assets consisting of rights to receive payments in the future (e.g., annuities, copyright royalties, contingent fees, or accounts receivable). These assets provide insufficient present cash with which to pay the estate (and GST) tax when otherwise due and the estate cannot borrow against these assets except upon terms that would cause a loss to the estate.

3. An estate includes a claim to substantial assets which cannot be collected without litigation. Consequently, the size of the gross estate is unascertainable at the time the tax is otherwise due.

4. An estate does not have sufficient funds (without borrowing at a rate of interest higher than that generally available) with which to pay the entire estate (and GST) tax when otherwise due, to provide a reasonable allowance during

---

the remaining period of administration of the estate for the decedent's surviving spouse and dependent children, and to satisfy claims against the estate that are due and payable. In addition, the executor has made a reasonable effort to convert assets in the executor's possession (other than an interest in a closely held business to which section 6166 applies) into cash.

In general, an extension of time to pay will be granted only for the amount of the cash shortage. You must show on Part IV the amount of the estate (and GST) tax (attach a copy of the return if it has already been filed; otherwise estimate the tax), the amount of the cash shortage, including a statement of the current assets in the estate and the assets already distributed, a plan for partial payments during the extension period, and the balance due. You must attach a check or money order payable to the United States Treasury for the balance due. Please write the decedent's social security number on the check or money order, and the type of return; e.g., Form 706-A.

The IRS will complete Part V and return a copy to the executor. If an approved application has different extension dates in Parts II and III, the IRS will return two copies to the executor. Attach one of the copies to the estate tax return that is filed. Submit the other copy with the separate payment. The part of the estate tax for which the extension is granted must be paid with interest from the estate tax due date before the expiration of the extension period.

Note: *An extension of time to pay does NOT extend the time to file.*

If an application for extension of time to pay is denied, a written appeal may be made to the regional commissioner within 10 days from the time the denial is mailed. For more details, see section 20.6161-1(b) of the regulations.

Paperwork Reduction Act Notice. We ask for the information on this form to carry out the Internal Revenue laws of the United States. You are required to give us the information. We need it to ensure that taxpayers are complying with these laws and to allow us to figure and collect the right amount of tax.

You are not required to provide the information requested on a form that is subject to the Paperwork Reduction Act unless the form displays a valid OMB control number. Books or records relating to a form or its instructions must be retained as long as their contents may become material in the administration of any Internal Revenue law. Generally, tax returns and return information are confidential, as required by section 6103.

The time needed to complete and file this form will vary depending on individual circumstances. The estimated average time is:

Recordkeeping	13 min.
Learning about the law or the form	16 min.
Preparing the form	22 min.
Copying, assembling, and sending the form to the IRS	20 min.

If you have comments concerning the accuracy of these time estimates or suggestions for making this form simpler, we would be happy to hear from you. You can write to the Tax Forms Committee, Western Area Distribution Center, Rancho Cordova, CA 95743-0001.

DO NOT send this extension form to this office. Instead, see **How and Where To File.**

FIGURE A.17 *Continued*

214

Wills

1. Will of _____

   I _____ a resident of _____ state
   and declare that this is my will.

2. I revoke any prior wills.

3. My marital status is _____.

4. I have the following children:

   Name _____ Age and date of birth _____

   Name _____ Age and date of birth _____

   If I leave nothing to any of my children or grandchildren, that is
   my true intention.

5. I make the following specific bequests of property.

   I leave _____ to _____. If this bene-

   ficiary does not survive me, to _____.

6. I leave the remainder of my property to _____.

7. I name _____ as executor of my will. If this person
   does not outlive me, I name _____.

   Continued

FIGURE B.1 General Will

8. I grant the following powers to my executor:

To receive and administer my property and any sale or lease of it as a portion of my estate.

To have full power to make stock and other security transactions deemed necessary on behalf of my estate.

To repay any liabilities and debts incurred by my estate.

9. If at the time of my death I have minor children, I name _____ _____ as personal guardian. If that person is unable to do so, I name _____.

I name _____ to act as my property guardian for the children. If that person is unable to do so, I name _____.

10. I subscribe my name to this will _____ (day) of _____ (year) in the state of _____ . I declare it is my will, and I am signing it willingly and voluntarily. I am at the age of which I am legally able to write this will, am of sound mind, and am under no undue influence.

_____ Signature

Witnesses:

On this day of _____. The testator, _____, declared to us that this will is his or hers and asked us to witness it. The will was signed in our presence. We declare that we are in fact witnesses and are of competent mind to witness this will. The testator by all accounts is of sound mind to execute this will with no undue influence.

We declare under the penalty of perjury that all of this is true and accurate this day _____ at _____ (city and state).

Witness signature _____ Print name _____

Street address, city, and state _____

Witness signature _____ Print name _____

Street address, city, and state _____

FIGURE B.1 *Continued*

SAMPLE LIVING WILL DECLARATION

I, _____ , being of sound mind, willfully and voluntarily make this declaration to be followed if I become incompetent.

This declaration reflects my firm and settled commitment to refuse life-sustaining treatment under the circumstances indicated below.

I direct my attending physician to withhold or withdraw life-sustaining treatment that serves only to prolong the process of my dying if I should be in a terminal condition or in a state of permanent unconsciousness.

I direct that treatment be limited to measures to keep me comfortable and to relieve pain, including any pain that might occur by withholding or withdrawing life-sustaining treatment.

In addition, if I am in the condition described above, I feel especially strongly about the following forms of treatment:

I ☐ do ☐ do not want cardiac resuscitation.
I ☐ do ☐ do not want mechanical respiration.
I ☐ do ☐ do not want tube feeding or any other artificial or invasive form of
                     nutrition (food) or hydration (water).
I ☐ do ☐ do not want blood or blood products.
I ☐ do ☐ do not want kidney dialysis.
I ☐ do ☐ do not want antibiotics.

I realize that if I do not specifically indicate my preferences regarding any forms of treatment listed above, I may receive that form of treatment.

Other instructions:

I ☐ do ☐ do not want to designate another person as my surrogate to make medical treatment decisions for me if I should be incompetent and in a terminal condition or in a state of permanent unconsciousness.

Surrogate:

Name _____

Address _____

Substitute surrogate (if the above is unable to serve):

Name _____

Address _____

I made this declaration on the _____ day of _____

Name _____

Address _____

The declarant or the person on behalf of and at the direction of the declarant knowingly and voluntarily signed this writing by signature or mark in my presence.

Witness Signature _____

Witness Address _____

Witness Signature _____

Witness Address _____

FIGURE B.2   Sample Living Will Declaration
Source: Ceridian Performance Partners (CPP)

Resources

1. Request two dozen copies of the death certificate from the funeral director or coroner's office. _____
2. Make sure any organ donations have been executed as requested in the will. _____
3. Meet with decedent's close family to obtain any necessary information and keep the lines of communication open. _____
4. Help with cemetery and funeral arrangements. _____
5. Make sure the immediate survivors have enough cash to meet their living expenses until the estate is settled. _____
6. Collect all funeral expense receipts. _____
7. Make sure the decedent's bank knows of the death, and make necessary arrangements with the accounts. _____
8. Find the will. _____
9. Figure out assets and liabilities. _____
10. Hire an attorney if need be. _____
11. File the will with the probate court register of wills. _____
12. Review all insurance policies (life, property, health). _____
13. Get claim forms from insurer. _____
14. Go over wills for any survivors and redo as need be. _____
15. Get permission to open safe-deposit box at the bank. _____
16. Contact Social Security Administration to get forms to apply for survivor's benefits. _____
17. Get appraisals of any property owned. _____

FIGURE C.1   The Executor's To-Do Checklist

18. Review any investment accounts and notify brokerages of the death. _____
19. Talk to the deceased's employer about any death benefits or unpaid salary. _____
20. Set up an account at a local bank in the estate's name and get an identification number from the IRS. _____
21. Open a separate safe-deposit box for any estate items that are valuable. _____
22. Contact brokerages and close any accounts if that is necessary. _____
23. File income tax returns for state and federal and pay any due tax. _____
24. Make sure to pay any bills outstanding if the estate can afford it. _____
25. Be sure to cover any appraisal, attorney, or accountant fees from the estate assets. _____

FIGURE C.1 *Continued*

1. Locate the will and probate the will.
2. Take an inventory of the safe-deposit box.
3. Get a solid accounting of any securities accounts.
4. Get appraisals of property owned.
5. Get copies of the past five years of tax returns.
6. Get copies of any records of tax returns for gifts over the past five years.
7. Track down any debts owed.
8. File for pension money owed by an employer.
9. Get a tax identification number from the Internal Revenue Service if necessary.
10. Figure out what medical expenses were incurred before the death.
11. File tax return by April 15 after the year in which the death happened.
12. Decide whether to extend tax return filing.
13. Look into the possibility of an inheritance due.
14. File inheritance and federal tax returns within nine months of death or request an extension.

FIGURE C.2 The Executor's Bottom Line Duties

219

State of _____)   _____
                                        Account Number
City   ) SS.
County of_____)

_____, being duly sworn, deposes and says that (he), (she), (they) reside at _____, city of _____, State of _____, and is the Execut_____). (Administrat_____), (Survivor of) of the Estate of _____, deceased, who died on the _____ day of _____, 19___. At the time of death the domicile (Legal Residence) of said decedent was at _____, State of _____, and was not a resident of the State of New York (or of the State of _____) for at least 2 years previous to date of death and that the decedent executed no will or other instrument within two years prior to death stating that the decedent was a resident of the State of _____. The decedent's last Federal Income Tax Return was filed from the City of _____, State of _____, that the (certificates of stock), (bonds) enclosed herein were physically located in the City of _____, State of _____, at the time of death, that this affidavit is made for the purpose of securing the transfer or delivery of the enclosed (certificates of stock), (bonds), owned by said decedent at time of death.

Sworn to or affirmed before me this _____

day of _____, 19___

_____   _____

                                    Execut_____
                                    Administrat_____
                                    Survivor

My Commission Expires_____.   Estate of _____
                                    SIGNATURE(s) GUARANTEED
                                    LEGG MASON WOOD WALKER, INC.

                                    By_____
                                    Authorized Signature

FIGURE C.3 Affidavit of Domicile

Glossary

adjusted gross income (AGI) this is your taxable income minus any deductions for IRAs, Keogh plans, alimony payments and other deductions.

administrator a person picked by the local court to handle your estate when you die without a will.

alternative value date lets you figure the value of an estate six months after the date of death for federal estate tax purposes, unless the property has already been sold or passed along.

annual gift tax exclusion allows you to give tax-free gifts of up to $10,000 per person each calendar year.

applicable exclusion this is commonly called the Unified Credit to exclude from estate and gift tax up to $675,000 in 2000 and increasing to $1 million in 2006.

assets the things that make up your estate. They include everything from your car to your home, stocks, bonds, mutual funds, jewelry, land, and so on.

beneficiary person or institution designated through your will that will receive the benefits of your estate at your death.

bypass or credit shelter trust a trust that allows you and your spouse to leave $1.35 million to your heirs totally exempt from estate tax.

cash-value life insurance type of life insurance which blends a death benefit with a tax-deferred investment fund.

Certified Financial Planner (CFP) a finance professional who has completed a series of courses and exams.

charitable lease trust a trust that pays a charity a set amount over a certain time period, after which the principal passes to the beneficiaries.

charitable remainder annuity trust remainder trust in which the charity is required to pay you a certain sum annually.

charitable remainder trust a trust used to make a charitable contribution and avoid a large capital gains tax bill.

community property property held jointly by a husband and wife.

Crummey Trust allows you to give $10,000 a year tax-free but limits access to the funds for beneficiaries.

custodial account an account under the Uniform Gifts to Minors Act (UGMA) or Uniform Transfers to Minors Act (UTMA) that has a custodian selected by the executor of your will.

domicile a person's fixed, permanent, and principal residence for legal purposes.

durable power of attorney a written legal document that lets you designate another person to act on your behalf in the event you are disabled or incapacitated.

durable power of attorney for health care a written legal document that lets you designate another person to act on your behalf regarding health-care decisions.

education individual retirement accounts (IRA) lets you set aside up to $500 each year to pay for certain educational expenses.

election against the will by the surviving spouse lets the surviving spouse receive at least the amount of property determined by state statute.

estate tax tax due on the entire estate.

executor person named in your will to manage your estate.

family business legal designation of a business that must be owned at least 50 percent by one family, 70 percent by two families, or 90 percent by three families.

financial adviser professional who can help you get your estate plan in shape.

generation-skipping transfer tax (GSTT) there is a 55 percent tax applied to transfers to grandchildren or following generations.

generation-skipping trust allows married couples to save up to $2 million for their grandchildren and other generations, tax-free. For single people, the cut-off is $1 million. These savings are free of the 55% generation-skipping tax normally paid on gifts to grandchildren.

grantor retained income trust (GRIT) a trust that allows you to transfer assets to your heirs while you are still alive.

guardian person legally entrusted to care for minor child(ren).

handwritten will must be witnessed by at least two people to be valid in most states.

homestead exemption when house and land have been designated as a homestead, the surviving spouse and children are exempt from state taxes and claims by creditors on the property itself.

HOPE credit allows you to claim a tax credit of up to $1,500 each tax year for a student's tuition and other educational costs.

222

individual retirement account (IRA) a tax-deferred pension plan that allows you to invest in an account that is tax-free until you withdraw the money at retirement.

inheritance tax tax owed on the portion each beneficiary receives, not the entire estate.

intestate term applied when you die without a will.

irrevocable life insurance trust a trust that makes sure payouts from an insurance policy are exempt from estate taxes.

irrevocable trust a trust that cannot be changed materially after it has been legally put in writing.

joint tenancy with right of survivorship type of title placed on property that is co-owned. At the death of a co-owner, the other will become the sole property owner.

land trust allows you to transfer land into a trust that will protect the land from future development.

liabilities your debts.

lifetime gift and estate exclusion you have a $675,000 exclusion from estate tax on your property in 2000 rising to $1 million in 2006.

lifetime learning credit allows you to deduct up to 20 percent of the first $5,000 that you spend on tuition and related expenses.

living trust a trust that is active while you are alive and isn't considered to be a part of your will.

living will legal document that allows you to lay out the type of medical treatment you would want if you have been critically injured and can no longer make the decision.

marital deduction allows for the unlimited transfer of property from one spouse to another, generally free of estate or gift tax.

minor children children under the age of 16 or 18, depending on the state's laws.

oral will most states do not accept oral wills.

pour-over will in a living trust, this document lets you leave certain property to specific individuals and name a child's guardian.

probate the review or testing of a will before a court of law to ensure it is authentic.

qualified personal residence trust a trust where you place your home in an irrevocable trust. At the end of a specified time period the ownership passes to the named beneficiaries.

qualified terminable interest property (QTIP) trust this trust ensures that assets are passed on to named heirs without the surviving spouse making changes.

revocable trust a trust that can be changed over time.

Roth IRA individual retirement account in which your contributions are not deductible, but are tax-free when withdrawn at retirement.

second-to-die life insurance a life insurance policy that makes sure there is enough cash available to pay estate taxes.

settling an estate ensuring the legal transfer of assets after someone's death, according to their wishes.

shrinkage the sum of assets or property that will be whittled away due to the costs of the estate's settlement.

taxable property this includes real property (a house, commercial real estate, or raw land), tangible property (autos, art, jewels), and intangible property (securities such as stocks, bonds, and mutual funds, and bank or brokerage accounts).

testamentary trust a trust created in your will and activated only upon your death.

trust a legal document created during your lifetime that allows you to pass assets on to another person or persons through a legal entity. The assets are then managed for you or someone else.

trustee the person who will manage any property that is owned by a trust.

Unified Credit also referred to as an applicable exclusion, this credit allows taxpayers an exemption from gift and estate taxes.

Uniform Gifts to Minors Act (UGMA) this act allows certain types of property to be gifted to minors without creating a trust. Legally the child is the sole owner of the property although the adult is the custodian.

Uniform Transfers to Minors Act (UTMA) same theory as UGMA, but allows any kind of property to be transferred—personal, tangible and intangible.

unlimited marital deduction a deduction allowing for the unlimited transfer of any or all property from one spouse to another. It is generally free of estate and gift tax.

will a legal document directing the disposal of your property after your death.

Index

Accountant, functions of, 13, 47, 66, 78, 105, 111

Adjusted gross income (AGI), 72–73, 95

Administrator, defined, 120. *See also* Executor

Alternative value date, 86–87

A. M. Best, 104

American Academy of Estate Planning Attorneys, 41

American Bar Association, 41, 106

American College of Trust and Estate Counsel, 41, 106, 117

American Institute of Certified Public Accountants' Personal Financial Specialists, 44

American Society of Appraisers, 105

Ameritas, 103

Annual gift tax exclusion, 70–71, 112, 121

Annuity trusts, charitable remainder, 60

Antiques, 12

Applicable exclusion, 67–68

Appraisals, 84, 107, 116, 125

Art collections, 66

Assets:
 defined, 3
 liabilities *vs.*, 12–13
 list of, 5, 11, 32, 47, 77
 in living trusts, 56
 valuation of, 84

Attorney, *see* Estate attorney

Attorney-client relationship, 42

Automobile insurance, 77

Automobiles, 12, 66

Baby boomer generation, 2, 75, 126

Bank accounts:
 as asset, 66
 for children, 83
 family limited partnerships, 106
 opening, 88

Bank loans, 12

Bankruptcy, legal claims and, 54

Basis, stepped-up, 66–67

Beneficiary:
 change of, 39, 111
 charity as, 99–100
 children as, 91, 97–98
 contact information, 32
 death of, 39
 defined, 3, 11, 32, 120
 for IRA, 90–91
 naming, 93–94
 pets as, 35–36, 122
 secondary, 96
 spouse as, 91
 as trustee, 54

Bequests:
 unlimited marital deduction and, 8
 unusual, 35–37

Bleak House (Dickens), 7–8

Bonds, 12, 66

Brokerage accounts, 66